GOING TO
THE MATCH

The Passion for Football

DUNCAN HAMILTON

HODDER &
STOUGHTON

First published in Great Britain in 2018 by Hodder & Stoughton
An Hachette UK company

1

Copyright © Duncan Hamilton 2018

The right of Duncan Hamilton to be identified as the Author of the Work has been
asserted by him in accordance with the Copyright, Designs and Patents Act 1988.

A CIP catalogue record for this title is available from the British Library

Hardback ISBN 9781473661783
Trade Paperback ISBN 9781473661790
eBook ISBN 9781473661813

Typeset in Baskerville by Hewer Text UK Ltd, Edinburgh
Printed and bound in Great Britain by Clays Ltd, Elcograf S.p.A.

Hodder & Stoughton policy is to use papers that are natural, renewable
and recyclable products and made from wood grown in sustainable
forests. The logging and manufacturing processes are expected to
conform to the environmental regulations of the country of origin.

Hodder & Stoughton Ltd
Carmelite House
50 Victoria Embankment
London EC4Y 0DZ

www.hodder.co.uk

GOING TO THE MATCH

To football fans everywhere; but especially to those who support clubs who seldom win anything.

Contents

CONTENTS

Prologue
A KIND OF
GENTLE MADNESS

21 June: Salford

On the afternoon of the summer solstice, beneath a flat, grey-white sky that he could have painted in a dozen sweeping brushstrokes, I am going to meet L. S. Lowry.

Elsewhere, especially in the far south, the temperature has shot into the nineties, making it the hottest day for forty years. Not, however, beside this long bend of the River Irwell, the water so still and so black that it looks 20 fathoms deep. There's a cuff of wind here and even the odd spit of rain. This seems perfectly appropriate. It's as though Mother Nature, curtseying deferentially to Lowry, is making sure the weather reflects his landscapes, almost always captured in such a beautiful gloom.

Factory chimneys were to Lowry what daffodils were to Wordsworth. So were back-to-back houses and tiled roofs, sombre curls of smoke and matchstick men and women, scraggy dogs on spindly legs and hulking buildings. He painted them for us in a wintery palette. Earth brown. Lamp black. Greys that were the colour of slag heaps. A light touch of flake-white, like snow, as highlights.

The Salford in which Lowry grew up, eventually making a reputation as well as a living from it, would be unrecognisable to him now. There are swanky bars and restaurants and high-rise flats with balconies that look across the distant spread of Manchester. There is an arched, elegant footbridge, the wire supporting it as delicate as the strings of a cello. And there is the upward curve of the building – all glinting steel and polished glass – that bears his name and hangs his art. With its aerofoil canopy above the entrance, the place is almost, but not quite, the Guggenheim of the North.

I stand in front of it and gather in the plain lines and the sharp points of the architecture; then I imagine Lowry staring at them too. I see his broad back, hunched a little. I see his chubby fingers combing through the frost-coloured stubble of his hair. I see, most of all, the large but slightly deflated balloon of his face, the pink flesh sagging around the jowls. From eyes that are as small and as black-bright as buttons comes an expression of incomprehension. For he can't believe that the canvases he created in a scruffy back room of a scruffy stone house are now reverently lit and labelled in a gallery as grandly gorgeous as this.

I think Lowry deserves nothing less.

I never thought, as some still do, that the simplicity of his marks were crude or ugly. Or that the compositions were deliberately unpretentious because he lacked the skill to make them otherwise. I instinctively took to Lowry, the Constable of the cobblestones. In painting the ordinary and giving the mundane its due, he ennobled it somehow. He caught scenes to which I required no introduction either. I was born on the Northumberland coast, the village then downtrodden and in some disrepair. It was cramped and sullen and failing. Lowry's North West was my North East – even though 150-odd miles and two and a half generations separated one from the other. I saw the same unprosperous people in hats or caps and mufflers, most enduring life rather than enjoying it. I saw the same homes, the same chimneys, the same consequences of the coal fire – dust and dirty air. I also saw how manual labour could be markedly different – the mines (my world) and the factories of Cottonopolis (his) – without being lenient on those obliged to do it. The workers in them were worn equally to the rim.

One Lowry work above all others was hypnotic. I repeatedly went back to it. Each time I found something new in it; something which before had given my eyes the slip. The tall slither of a distant chimney, almost indistinct in the smog. A man carrying a cane. A boy not much older than me. A tiny, blank window.

The painting was *Going to the Match*.

I came across it, aged around ten, in a book celebrating British landscape art, which was half hidden in the reference section of the local library. I have forgotten the title, but the painting was spread across two glossy pages and the book itself was square and flat, like a paving stone, and weighed as much as one too. To read it, I first had to carry it to a wooden table, which was a mighty feat of strength for my puny arms. Beneath a downcast Lancastrian sky, I saw Lowry's trademark figures lean into the wind on their way into Bolton Wanderers' Burnden Park. The rise of a stand behind one of the goals reminded me then, as now, of a ship about to sail out of dock. It was transfixing. I was already obsessed by football. I was always kicking a ball about the back garden. Or collecting stickers, as if each was a piece of treasure, and affixing them preciously into albums. Or buying the weekly magazines and cutting out their full colour posters, pressing each of them on to my bedroom wall with bronze drawing pins. I also read every newspaper that came into the house, starting them from the back page. But – and this is the thing – I hadn't yet been to a proper game: a game where I was reliably informed that the heavy, slow click of the turnstiles sounded like the mechanism of a Town Hall clock . . . a game in which the goals had nets . . . a game where the pitch was saturated in early season colour . . . a game in which the crowd noise constantly assaulted your ears. I had been to Newcastle United's St James' Park when no one was in it. The steps of the terraces were like a long wide ladder leading straight to the clouds. And, later, I regularly crossed Nottingham's Trent Bridge, where Nottingham Forest and Notts County, the world's oldest league club, faced one another on opposite banks of the river. But I began to imagine what three o'clock on a Saturday afternoon would really look like – and be like – primarily from *Going to the Match*. Lowry took me there, as though by the hand, before I actually experienced it for myself.

The painting had a rushing energy about it and a sense not only of occasion but also of expectation. Conveyed within it, too, I found the conviction that nothing else was more important on that day – and perhaps not for another week – than the ninety minutes to come. I gazed at *Going to the Match* so intently that I could almost hear the tramp of 10,000 or more feet towards the gates and also the restless stir of those already banked inside, the kick-off looming. And because Lowry was clever with perspective – he paints the view as though standing on a slightly raised platform, looking down on it – I felt as if I could step inside the frame and follow the lone figure,

cunningly positioned in the central foreground, who was walking
away from me.

I didn't know then that Lowry, born at the fag end of Queen
Victoria's reign, had once gone regularly to Burnden Park and to
Manchester City's Maine Road. The two grounds were almost equi-
distant from his boyhood home in Pendlebury. His father coached the
Sunday School team, St Clement's. Old maps show the church and
the nearby fields where the games must have been played. Lowry,
diffident and fond of his own company, preferred to be a spectator
rather than a participant until the side, short of a goalkeeper, appealed
to his conscience. Lowry, the loner, found the solitariness of goalkeeping to his liking. He had a talent for it too. He flung himself across his
muddy line and around the box, gradually becoming caked in filth
and repeatedly making fine saves, as though being between the posts
was a birthright. The match was won. The emergency goalkeeper had
even kept a clean sheet, his agility and the elasticity of his reach
surprising his friends. One of them, who had persuaded Lowry to
play, called him 'the hero of the match'. With what was described as
a 'beatific' glow, Lowry walked home in his kit, most of the pitch still
clinging to it and also to his bare knees. His mother evidently believed
that cleanliness truly is next to Godliness. She saw her son arrive home
like a street urchin and immediately had what was called a 'fit of the
vapours'. The ensuing row was said to have been 'frightful'. She was
appalled that 'any son of hers could have walked through the streets
in such a state'. Lowry's career as a goalkeeper ended after that one
game, his mother issuing a lifetime ban for the sake of respectability.
His father, it seems, had no say in the matter. From then on, resisting
his friends' pleas to join in, Lowry's record of never conceding a goal
remained superbly intact. We can only think about the goalkeeper he
might have been . . .

Lowry could be an exasperating conundrum of a man, often claiming a lame and lukewarm interest in the game when, in fact, he
possessed a savant's memory for the recall of matches, of teams, of
results. Nat Lofthouse was the Bolton centre forward who scored an
FA Cup Final goal with a heaving charge, shoving the goalkeeper over
the line when the ball was still in his grasp. He once told me that
Lowry could be seen occasionally at Burnden Park in the very early

1960s, wearing the dark trilby and the long dark coat that made him look like one of the characters in his own paintings. Lofthouse remembered a conversation in which Lowry, as though these things had only just happened, began to animatedly recreate the Manchester City teams that won the Cup in 1904 – City coincidentally beating Bolton at Crystal Palace – and then again thirty years later. He spoke of their 'outside forward', the match-winning and thickly moustachioed Billy Meredith, who was famous for the achievement of scoring the only goal and infamous for being banned amid a bribery scandal not long afterwards. He spoke, as though recalling his own goalkeeping exploits, of City's Frank Swift, who calamitously let a shot squirm through his ungloved fingers and beneath his body on a greasy Wembley surface against Portsmouth in 1934. He spoke of Fred Tilson, who scored twice in the last seventeen minutes, and also of Matt Busby, responsible for instigating City's late comeback as much with the presence of his personality as his passing. And then, suggesting he still saw himself as part of the goalkeeping brotherhood, Lowry spoke again with sympathy for Swift, who fainted at the end out of sheer relief, knowing he was off the hook; his mistake was mercifully irrelevant. Lofthouse could not bring back the monologue verbatim, so he could offer no direct quotations, but he was conscious, as Lowry talked, that something appeared in his face that had not been there before. It was a conspicuous joy. Those games and the players who had shaped them clearly counted as landmarks in his past, their legacy cherishable.

I like the story because it confirmed the conclusion I reached as *Going to the Match* became more familiar to me. It could not possibly have been painted by someone who wasn't wholly smitten with football . . . who didn't see himself among the men hurrying into Burnden Park . . . who hadn't before felt the frisson of afternoons just like it . . . and who didn't have an overwhelming desire to share it. Lowry was a fan; no doubt about that. He imbues *Going to the Match* with love, compassion and understanding for the emotional charge of the game and especially for those who watch it. That quality is evident in every lick of paint.

It's about locking down a memory too, I think: something he didn't want to forget, which is the way a place looked. You could say that artists routinely do this, and also that Lowry in particular was always making an historical record of what he thought would perish if he didn't paint it. I still believe that *Going to the Match* is about much more than the piquancy of that. It's about personal pleasure. Lowry is giving us a glimpse of himself. He is also giving us a glimpse – as Lofthouse could testify – of what football meant to him, and also how it could carry him away. Football was his own passion apart from art, but he could only articulate the fact through art itself.

Going to the Match was painted in 1953. Lowry entered it into a competition called Football and Fine Arts, which was run by the FA to celebrate its ninetieth anniversary. Rather sniffily, the anonymous art critic of *The Times* announced that in his opinion 'no single picture' among the 1,710 the FA received was 'of outstanding merit'. For him it explained why the first prize was split four ways (Lowry took his share of the booty, which was £250). For me it reaffirms the fact that classics aren't always recognised as such from the off, but acquire status slowly, their worth and value determined through the accumulation of many decades. The newspaper's picture editor clearly had a more discerning eye than its art expert. The painting he sent to the sub-editors to illustrate the column was *Going to the Match*.

Lowry declared that he'd 'never been so surprised in my life' after the painting's success. If still alive, he'd have gone into comatose shock when, in 1999, The Professional Footballers' Association displayed a canny appreciation of art and a cannier nose for investment by paying £1.9m to acquire it. What seemed a colossal amount then is absolutely piddling now. In today's football market, £1.9m wouldn't get you a lock of Lionel Messi's hair. In today's art world, where Lowry is in demand, it wouldn't buy a small corner of that painting.

I don't know how many times I have seen *Going to the Match* in a gallery. At least a dozen, I suppose. It never disappoints. Today, apart from a guide-cum-guard sitting on a plastic bucket chair, I am entirely alone with the painting. It's as near as I can get to a private viewing in a public place.

That library book on British landscape art was quite sumptuous for its day, but even then I knew it would be no substitute for the real thing. Nor, though I own one, are the multiple prints you can buy, framed or not, from the downstairs shop. I lean forward and almost press my eyes right against the canvas, picking out the small intricacies of Lowry's brushwork. Not only in the figures, of course, but also in the chimneys and in the belches of smoke from them, the patchwork slats of the wooden stands, the firm tramlines that give depth to the foreground, the roofs and the low front garden walls and also the flag flying like a medieval pennant high above the ground. The stand-out cadmium red of that flag, billowing against the pale sky, was painted with a dry brush and drags your gaze upwards, balancing the composition. I start to count the chimneys (six), the church steeples (two, I think) the dogs (three) and even, for a while, the figures. (I get as far as 103 before losing the thread.) After a while the guide-cum-guard begins to get suspicious, as if I am about to overstep the bounds of propriety and gallery etiquette. She is unsure whether I am just over-enthusiastic or some sort of crank intent on causing havoc. I think she expects me to suddenly pull the painting off the wall and make a dash for it, the gallery alarm clanging behind me. I step back and take a seat in front of the painting, nodding politely to acknowledge her tolerance.

I want to share with her, but don't, the reason that *Going to the Match* endures and why everyone should make the pilgrimage to see it. It's because of what the painting evokes. Anyone who has ever gone to a ground can see themselves reflected in it. Recognition comes instantly from the fact that you're so familiar with the story Lowry tells. The words he chose are important too. Lowry was never a literary man, which probably accounts for the plainness of the painting's title. For a football fan, however, the phrase 'going to the match' is redolent of so much and consequently as evocative as any sentence in the English language. For the boy that's still in me, it captures the ritual pleasures of match day, every one different but also essentially the same: a shilling bus ride; the first glimpse of the ground; the shuffling queue and the banter traded in it; the dash to the front of the perimeter wall; familiar faces around you (for football fans are determinedly territorial); a programme with the *Football League Review* stapled inside it; half-time Bovril so hot you can barely drink it; a transistor radio with a barley-twist cord and earpiece to catch the scores on *Sports Report* and the upbeat da-de-da tune of the brass band that preceded them; and then buying, less than an hour later, the Saturday tea-time miracle, a 'football special' that was blue or green or buff or pink and arrived still inky off the presses.

As for the adult me . . . well, he remembers working for a newspaper exactly like that, and the ticket privileges it brought. Roaring afternoons and nights at Old Trafford and at Anfield. At the Camp Nou and at the Bernabéu. At ageing Olympic stadiums, such as Tokyo's, and at the old Wembley, beneath the towers. And, of course, at places long-since gone, preserved only in photographs or on film or from whatever token relic someone salvaged, such as a rectangle of turf or a favourite seat in the stand. These are the Lost Grounds, their foundation stones lain in the early age of liniment, dubbin and ankle-length boots with steel toe-caps. The wrecking ball and the bulldozer wiped dozens upon dozens of them off the map, but not from the memory: Roker Park at Sunderland and Ayresome Park at Middlesbrough; the Victoria Ground at Stoke and Derby's Baseball Ground, where you were so close to the touchline that you felt physically part of the game. Gone also is Coventry's Highfield Road, once considered to be the acme of modernity, and even Lowry's Burnden Park, the demise of it adding to the poignancy of his painting. These landscapes were levelled and something else built on them after the spit and polish of reinvention got underway, which was the arrival and super-growth of the Premier League

A golden anniversary looms for me. It's almost half a century since I saw my first match as a fan. Being one persuaded me that becoming a sports reporter, thus receiving a wage for what I'd gladly have paid to see, seemed not only a natural progression but also a cushy substitute for actually having to work for a living. Also, I had no skills, other than touch-typing, which would have made me employable in anything but Kipling's Black Art. The trade, it should be pointed out, has traditionally attracted misfits such as me with nowhere else to go. Somehow I muddled through, constantly astonished when I didn't find myself in a dole queue. Eventually I stopped covering football, believing I'd had my fill of it. I could not watch any more. I had the feeling that something was over. For a while afterwards I went through a cagey withdrawal period, becoming apathetic towards the game, which made me agnostic about its importance. Eventually I divorced myself almost entirely from matches and results, the carousel of transfers and the comings and goings, and particularly the utterances, of managers. I put it all behind me, never intending to go back.

But I sorely underestimated the pull of football and also the place it held in my life. With hindsight I know why this happened. Making the game my business, turning it into a plain job of everyday work, leached the deepest pleasures out of it. I no longer saw football the way a supporter did.

It is difficult to fasten down exactly when and how the romance was rekindled, but major things can start in minor moments. I dwell on a contributory factor, which even now seems foolishly inconsequential but proved crucial nonetheless. This was the sight of the moderately undulating pitch on which I used to watch our village team play and also where I played myself as a boy. A memory can be exhausted by reflection. You can summon it too often so that, finally, almost nothing of it comes back. Or the passage of time uncomfortably reduces you and it to strangers; you feel as though what you're recalling belonged to someone else.

But as I stood there our knockabout games came back as clearly as watching them spool past me on a screen, the picture in glorious colour. When this happened, unexpectedly and after a long absence, it was bleak midwinter. The surface was already more mud than grass, a churned and lonely-looking patch of earth. But the sight of it, and also of the bleached white goals, took me back to the beginning of everything, those first stirrings of interest in football. The goals, though one of them listed a little, had a strange and very moving beauty about them that can only be experienced rather than explained. In boyhood, when coats and jumpers were usually heaped up as posts, a real goal with a bar validated the fantasy that you were not performing on a recreational park but instead at some grand stadium in front of 100,000 people, the crowd figure always issued for big matches at Wembley. I always maintain that a true fan, irrespective of age, can't spot the whites of a goal – even one glimpsed only from a passing train – without wanting to get a ball and take a shot at it. The sight is conducive to dreaming. I loved that village pitch, which was an escape from formal education, and it reminded me of why I loved football too. Each of our games had lasted for hours, the score only guessed at and darkness alone signalling the final whistle.

You know you've lost your heart to football when you swoon over the sound the ball makes ripping against a net, thumping against the woodwork or twanging off the outside of a boot . . . or when the sight of a long pass spinning in easeful flight seems something supremely sublime to you . . . or when an unexpected shot rises dramatically from distance, travelling like a fired shell . . . or when a goalmouth melée, in which no one knows exactly what is going on, counts as the highest possible pulse-racing drama . . . or when you spy a set of floodlights miles away and are drawn to them . . . or especially when you begin hoarding piles of old programmes and ticket stubs because throwing them out would be like burning a diary or tossing out the family photos. All this is a kind of gentle madness, which among fans counts as a virtue. It gradually took hold of me again. I couldn't resist.

Entwined with everyday life like no other sport has ever been or ever will be, football has become, as near as damn it, everyone's game. Almost all of us have colours to wear, a team to shout for, a result to seek out. Following every nuance of your team becomes passionately necessary, your mood rising dramatically and falling precipitously with each pendulum swing of its fortunes. The football fan will know exactly what I mean. But, though the game matters so much to us, we can't always explain *why* – either to the few who are still immune to its charms or even to ourselves sometimes.

I am going to try.

Every long journey is always a quest. My own into the new season to come, which starts in seven weeks, is about that *why*. I have decided to travel as a fan, paying for my own ticket and my own programme, so I will be an ordinary, anonymous spectator like everyone else. I am starting here, with Lowry in Salford, not just because of my small history with the painting, but also because it seems perfectly logical. We easily identify differences between present and past, but don't necessarily recognise – or we choose to overlook – the similarities. Over the next nine months *Going to the Match* will remind me of a significant one.

I have been looking hard at both the finished, gilt-framed canvas and the rough, preparatory pencil drawings that he did. These hang alongside it. With a thick line, Lowry has marked the admission price: 1s/9d. We know the players didn't earn much more than those who came to watch them then: the maximum wage was £15 and the British transfer record had broken £30,000 only three years earlier. But even as a heritage piece, *Going to the Match* still speaks to me and still seems fresh too, as though the oil has yet to dry properly on it. That's because the spectators Lowry depicts – and who were his motivation for painting the scene in the first place – are exactly like us in so many ways.

The men and women of his Burnden Park were as avid about football then as we are now. They cared as much. They fed their heart with fantasies and were easily pleased and easily disappointed. They also handed over their money, as we do, and demanded of the players what Diaghilev demanded of his dancers. 'Amaze me,' he'd say.

Someone today could take a decent stab at producing a contemporary picture at another ground, but it would be derivative of *Going to the Match* and reveal nothing much but the obvious changes in fashion and architecture. Lowry's hope for his painting was modest. He wanted us to look at it and know, without recourse to further research or anecdotal evidence, what it was like to go to a game in the early and mid 20th century. He achieved much more than that. In *Going to the Match* he told us what it had always been like – and, essentially, always will be.

After half an hour, during which I've paced about and stared at it from every available angle, I take a last, lingering look and then I thank the guide-cum-guard. She seems slightly relieved when I say my polite goodbyes to her. But I am not, of course, saying farewell to Mr Lowry and his painting.

They are coming with me – in spirit at least.

1

HOME IS THE OLDEST PLACE YOU WILL EVER KNOW

13 August: Newcastle United v Tottenham Hotspur, Premier League, St James' Park

Every match has a moment in it that reminds me of an earlier one, often played a long while ago. I see a goal, a save, a sliding tackle, an arching, cross-field pass or a satin-slick move that is reminiscent of another, buried and forgotten until then. Or, just occasionally, something slighter or even more ordinarily mundane ignites dimly the same small spark of recognition. The way a particular player runs or pivots or even the posture he temporarily holds, hands pressed on hips, as he waits for the ball. A goalkeeper, through habit or superstition, abstractly knocking his boots against the base of his post to get rid of imaginary mud from his studs or needlessly tugging on the back of the net to test the strength of it. The walk, taken from a railway station to a ground, through streets that aren't familiar but seem so. The ragged outline of a town or city that somehow reminds me of somewhere else. Time shifts, the sudden memory disturbing it, and what comes back is a feeling, a place or an image. More than three hours before the kick-off at St James' Park, where Newcastle United return to the Premier League against Tottenham, the first of those memories is already ghosting in.

The morning is still rising, the sun low above the North Sea. It is one of those flawless, ravishing days that the very start of a season always seems to bring like a blessing. For the past week August has masqueraded as mid-November. We've endured a long blow of wind and miserably cold rain. Today, as if summer is only starting rather than rounding its curve, the light is so strong that I have to shield my eyes to look at the sky, shining cloudlessly, and also at the wave-less sea, which is full of tugs and oily tankers and the odd sailing boat, each full canvas like a splatter of white paint. On the beach, far below me, nothing but a frothy ripple of tide is washing on to the sand. Everything is as sharp as an etching: the horseshoe bend of the bay; the dark spire of St George's Church; the dark worn skeleton of Tynemouth Abbey on its rocky outcrop and the bleached stone of St Mary's Lighthouse, like a rising finger, and also the cathedral-like dome of the Spanish City. On this spot almost all of England is well behind me. I am on the coast road, taking a dog-leg route to the match. It's an impractical and labyrinthine detour. It's also a deliberately sentimental one.

The 1970–71 season began not much more than a month after England surrendered the World Cup in Mexico. I was on holiday, our annual return to my birthplace. We'd left only because the mine my father worked in had become exhausted of coal. We returned every year like refugees desperate to see home again. I was eleven years old then, tiny and chronically shy. Newcastle were about to face Wolverhampton Wanderers and, for reasons I cannot remotely fathom now, my father, my maternal grandfather and I left for the game from this same stretch of the coast. We walked along the sea front for a while, looking at the horizon, and then we caught a rickety, over-crowded bus that moved slowly and blew billowing exhaust. The bottom deck was full of women, including my aunt – ostensibly there as a Saturday shopper, clutching her long-handled bag. The top deck, where I bagged a front seat, was choked with working men in black and white scarves. Nearly all of them puffed on cigarettes, another fag lit as soon as the previous one became an ashy stub. Outside the bus there was barely a fist of cloud to be seen. Inside it the air stank of Woodbines and Capstan Full Strength and was clogged with grey-blue smoke that gathered thickly all around me.

We all strip down and simplify the past because we only ever see it as a slide-show instead of a continuously running film; for that's the way the mind works. But I remember we arrived preposterously early in Newcastle because of my father's irrational hatred of being late, a trait I inherited from him. I remember that I was smuggled into the murky corner of a pub – perhaps The Strawberry, closest to the ground. I remember that we shuffled in a queue and paid on the gate.

I remember the old gold glow of Wolves' shirts, which I can see in flashes, and the panelled ball, which was a pale daffodil yellow. I know my father dressed for the occasion: tweedy jacket, white shirt and a narrow tie. His shoes were polished better than our best silver. I know my grandfather wore his cloth cap, for he almost never took it off except in bed. I also know – because I've checked contemporaneous reports of the match – that Newcastle ran out winners 3–2. Afterwards, waiting for the terraces to empty, the three of us bowled down the slight bluff on which St James' Park stands. We were reunited with my aunt beneath Grey's Monument, the ribbed Doric column that I regard as finer even than Nelson's. I went back with her, discovering this had been her sole purpose for travelling with us in the first place. She handed me a still-hot copy of *The Pink*, and I read and re-read it, checking the scores and scorers from elsewhere until the newspaper's headlines inked my fingers. My father and my grandfather stayed on, the beer in the Bigg Market awaiting them.

All this happened so long ago. That day is some far off country, visited once and to which you can never return. My grandfather died three years later. My father died in the 1990s. Now my aunt has inoperable cancer, diagnosed during a month that seemed certain then to be her last. She even said her goodbyes weakly to me in her semi-conscious sleep. She is six years older than the Queen and has never lived anywhere except the village in which she was born. She is bed-ridden, and reluctantly on my part – but not on hers – we have discussed what she doesn't want at her funeral. I know what she expects of me, but I can't conceive of making the arrangements or clearing her house or being the executor of her will. She has accepted her death phlegmatically; she is waiting for it. I have not accepted it at all. She has always been here, invulnerable; ergo, she always will be. I regard her as my 'second mother'. She, a spinster through choice, regards me as her son. Her looming death has made me think hard about my own life. About the past. About roots. About belonging. About what – and where – home is. And, bizarrely incongruous as this sounds, each of those has made me think about football too, and specifically the way in which it has tethered me to the city I left as a young child. She is responsible for that.

My aunt found herself in a household of inveterate football buffs, which was split between the rivalry of Newcastle (my father and the rest of us) and Sunderland (my grandfather), but she initially possessed only a flickering interest in either of them. The discussions about the game, always a vital part of the experience of watching, meant she was educated in the history of it involuntarily, purely from catching the drift of conversations in which she got held as an innocent living room hostage. When she realised my absorption in the game was not only genuine but also incurable, she set about pandering to it. We had moved to Nottingham by then, my father swapping one glum pit for another. For the next half century – even when the internet made this unnecessary – the letterbox rattled each Tuesday with a thick roll of newsprint. She cut out and posted to me every story about Newcastle that appeared in the local newspapers: the *Evening Chronicle*, the *Journal* and the *Sunday Sun*. Until the Web killed it off, along with every other Saturday night sports paper, she sent *The Pink* as well, wholly intact. Sometimes I would find a short note written in blue Biro on the blank border beside a story. She'd point out that a player had scored his first goal for a while or otherwise she'd highlight a quotation or a fact, peculiar or especially interesting to her. During Newcastle's all too infrequent years of lousy form, she'd often write that someone ought to give the team 'a really good shake', implying she might be the only one capable of doing so. When I was old enough to travel alone, I would head to Newcastle to watch a match and stay with her. Eventually, because of me, she found an interest in football too, lavishing her affections on a different club than mine. Hers was Blyth Spartans. The strange infatuation began, I think, during the early and mid-1970s when the amateurs in candy green and white flourished in the FA Cup, knocking out professionals several divisions above them. Every Sunday morning she searched first for Blyth's score and read their match report. She still does.

In the village post office, where my parcel was expensively dispatched, my aunt became such a familiar figure that her absence was conspicuous. Everyone there knew not only the day but also the hour she was due, exactly what she was sending and why, and also how long she had been doing it. Occasionally, along with the football cuttings, she'd include news stories about Newcastle as it changed and spruced itself up. In weekly instalments I got to piece them together like the world's biggest jigsaw. Once you leave the place you are from, you can never belong to it in the same way again. But the cuttings made certain that I clung on to a lot of it. Home is the oldest place you will ever know, and because of my aunt Newcastle felt – and still feels – emphatically mine.

There is a song, which I heard first at St James' Park, called 'Comin' Home Newcastle'. It's a Geordie love poem about the imminent return of the native. Exiled from Newcastle in London, entirely through circumstance, the protagonist longs to go back, likening his parting to a stretch in gaol. He promises to walk the streets 'al day, al neet' just for a bottle of the River Tyne. The verse that made me well up – and still does – is the eighth:

> I'm Comin' Home, Newcastle
> If you never win the Cup again
> A'll brave the dark at St James' Park
> In the Gallowgate End in the rain
> I'm Comin' Home . . .

I am that melancholic man, and the pull of the place occurs in sly ways, often catching me unawares. Finding a photograph – especially of the Tyne Bridge or St Mary's Lighthouse – unexpectedly in a newspaper. Hearing the accent and a line of dialect, a language of its own. Standing on a railway station platform when a Newcastle-bound train is announced. No matter where I live – or for how long – I am a tad out of joint, never feeling as though I quite fit in. I consider myself as a trespasser, an outsider; someone without passport status. Only in Newcastle do I feel *at home*.

Part of the reason is that those of us fortunate to have been born close to the sea are always plotting a route back there. We miss the sight of it. We miss the salt in it. But another part, which is the main one, is Newcastle's great and indomitable sense of self. It is geographically separate, and can seem remote and rather alien to those solidly planted in the South – especially people who are insular enough to believe the North starts on the motorway turn off to Leicester and that a lot of the land beyond is so primitively wild that modern cartographers, like their medieval predecessors, should scrawl 'Here Be Dragons' across the map. Difficult though this is to believe, I meet people even now who suppose Newcastle is shabbily anachronistic, the air full of dirt, and that coal gets tipped into the bath when the pet whippet isn't being washed in it. This was a myth even when I was growing up, the region known then for mining and ship-building and football. Just the football is left, which explains why the sort of hope that can kill you is focused on St James' Park. The filthy industries were missed, grievously at first like an amputated limb, but only the loss of the game would be inconsolably mourned. Football is bone and blood and breath here. I refuse to accept as pure coincidence that one of the symbols of Newcastle, The Angel of the North, was sunk into the soil beside another – the football pitch. She stands, her iron wings outstretched, behind a net-less goal, the bar sagging a little. She looks like a goalkeeper, about to stride down from her grassy hillock for a penalty shoot-out.

In Newcastle a baby still sleeps, largely metaphorically but sometimes literally, with a ball in the cot and almost everyone, however tangentially and to whatever degree, follows the team because what it does or doesn't do seeps into so much of everyday life. Results are responsible for the mood and the character of the place, detectable in the cold air. If you don't understand this, you won't understand Newcastle at all. In 2016, only a week or so after their last, ignominious relegation, I meandered around a city hurt and diminished by it. Everything was as sombre as a state funeral. I half-expected to glance up and find the tops of the Georgian buildings trimmed, as a mark of sad respect, in black velvet.

How seriously Newcastle cares about football is reflected in how much the disappointments the game regularly inflicts on it are tolerated and forgiven. It's a form of masochism. Newcastle last dazzled us consistently in the early and mid-1950s when the FA Cup sat in St James' Park, gleaming like a family heirloom. It being there was taken for granted, ownership considered a proprietorial right. The Cup occasionally went out on 'temporary loan', but was always expected back. That achievement now carries the dust of the ages. Newcastle's recent history reads like a misery memoir, so perpetually wretched as to require publication in multiple volumes. In *The Boys of Summer*, a book about his addiction to the Brooklyn Dodgers, Roger Kahn writes that: 'We may glory in a team triumphant but you fall in love with a team in defeat'. We know a good deal about that in Newcastle. Following them has meant becoming expert in wishful thinking, romantic hopefulness and the comfort of what ifs and what might have beens. It is commitment to a conceit of sorts. The team haven't been Champions of England for almost one hundred years. They haven't won a major trophy for nearly fifty. They haven't reached the Wembley final of a cup – any cup – for almost twenty. The wilderness is without apparent end. Honestly, I don't expect Newcastle to win a scrap of anything in my lifetime.

None of the fanatically supported clubs on Merseyside, Manchester or in North London would be so understanding or as faithfully stoical as Newcastle's supporters have been about all of this.

The proof is that 50,000-plus of them will be here today.

No rickety bus for me. I catch the Metro instead and then climb the shallow, forty tiled steps towards St James Park', the ground suddenly breaking into view. I come across a programme seller leaning against his stall, a lugubriously weary look on his pudgy face. A couple of thin, sallow-faced teenagers sit on Jackie Milburn's statue, their heels kicking the plinth, and a bloated middle-aged man takes a photograph of them with his mobile phone. He is evidence that no one of a certain age and a certain girth ought to wear replica kit. The material is stretched so tightly across his corpulent belly that Newcastle's stripes are horribly distorted, like something you'd see in a fairground mirror.

What is striking on the way in, and what is more striking now, is how solemn, almost maudlin, the atmosphere is. It's like no opening game I can remember. I go into the club shop and find few customers in the narrow aisles. I walk around the back of the high stands, the shadows there cold and oppressive. I hear no chanting and no banter. I see no bunting either. The weeks between the end of one season and the beginning of another are passed usually in a state of expectant bliss. You possess the optimism of the inveterate gambler, who in those few seconds when a chucked dice is still in mid-air or the roulette wheel is still spinning, persuades himself that anything is possible. The season's first day also usually has a glow about it, like the anticipation of Christmas morning. Newcastle, returning as Champions of the Championship, should be buoyantly brash about this umpteenth new dawn – even though the Premier League's fixture computer could have been kinder. To hand them Tottenham, title runners-up to Chelsea last May, is not a benevolent gesture.

But Newcastle is subdued, hushed even. This isn't because of the torture Tottenham's marquee players, principally Harry Kane and Dele Alli, are capable of inflicting on them. The cause is closer to home. The fearful symmetry of former seasons is seen in the messy preparations for this one. St James' Park offers a perpetual drama of intricate plot, disproving the theory that it is always better to be talked about than not. Newcastle are being talked about now after barely causing a tremor in the transfer market since promotion. Only £30m, the equivalent of a pocketful of loose change, has been spent on strengthening the squad. And no signing – among them Jacob Murphy from Norwich, Javier Manquillo from Atlético Madrid via Sunderland and Florian Lejeune from Eibar – is inspiring a chorus of 'The Blaydon Races'. Worse, the owner, Mike Ashley, chose the build-up to this match to illustrate that, even after a dysfunctional decade in charge, he still has no big plan. Few, it seems, are better at stirring up apathy on Tyneside than him.

With his short hair shaped in a Caesar cut, his prominent blade of a nose, his bull neck and his wide fleshy face, Ashley looks in profile like a plump Roman emperor. The image hardens whenever, from his lofty seat in the stands, he folds his arms and looks hopelessly exasperated or rather bored, his expression blank and staring. You expect him to turn a thumb downwards in regal disapproval, never quite appreciating that he shares responsibility for the standard of the entertainment. The most recent Rich List, compiled by *The Sunday Times*, calculated Ashley's worth at £2.16bn, making him the fifty-fourth-wealthiest person in the country. There is something satirically tragi-comic about listening to him explain why he can't find enough sixpences to fund properly the fourteenth best supported side in Europe. His money, Ashley says, is in 'Sports Direct shares', which he compared to 'wallpaper'. The metaphor is clumsy. The picture you immediately see is Ashley's living room walls decorated in million-pound notes.

Where the media is concerned, Ashley usually keeps himself in one of those hard to reach places. His previous substantial, set-piece interview was given to Sky Sports more than two years ago. He took advantage of the same soapbox to share his latest thoughts with us this week. If not exactly conducted with wide-eyed worship from the prayer mat, the fairly short Q and A could not be confused with a hard interrogation. Questions were lobbed at him respectfully. An aura of calm enabled Ashley to get into his stride. But even with everything going for him, he still managed to muck it up. In attempting to come across as an ordinary, blokey billionaire, doing the best that possibly could be done, Ashley sounded more than ever like someone who, even after all these years, has little understanding of – and absolutely no empathy with – his own club. He struck me as a little over-rehearsed too. The phrases he used seemed prefabricated and welded together on the spot, but the whole they made was too shaky to become a solid defence of his stewardship. Ashley did lay claim to just enough mistakes – mostly about sacking managers – to sound contrite. He still reminded me of a businessman who is in completely the wrong trade. Ashley is not the first to discover that playing the part of a grandstanding owner and the hands-on demands of ownership are not the same. He's not the first either to be naive and wrong-headed in assuming that his retail success would transfer easily to football. And he's also not the first, after realising it wouldn't, thus making his experience in other board rooms almost irrelevant, to find himself floundering. In his early days Ashley wore a Newcastle shirt to matches, and he sat beside and also drank with the fans in an ostentatious attempt to show brotherly solidarity. It was doomed to fail, as gesture politics always will, because the practical decisions he made in Newcastle's name soon contradicted the flashy claims of commitment. Bobby Robson, the archetypical Football Man, once asked 'What is a club in any case?' and then nailed the definition of it in eighty-one words, imagining his beloved Newcastle as he did so. 'Not the buildings or the directors or the people who are paid to represent it,' said Robson. 'It's not the television contracts, get-out clauses, marketing department or executive boxes. It's the noise, the passion, the feeling of belonging, the pride in your city. It's a small boy clambering up the stadium steps for the first time, gripping his father's hand, gasping at the hallowed stretch of turf beneath him and, without being able to do a thing about it, falling in love.' Someone still needs to explain to Ashley what Robson meant. He doesn't get it – not really. He owns the flesh and the body of Newcastle – the bricks, the steel, the mortar and the glass – but not the soul; and he never will because he seems unable to recognise what it is, or what it is worth to those who do.

If the season's first, bright sight of that 'hallowed stretch of turf' doesn't move you viscerally, then you shouldn't be here. Your ticket belongs to someone else. I look across it, thinking there is always something unusually beautiful about a ground as it begins to fill slowly, the noise rising around you. The Newcastle fans, soon raucously singing in the Gallowgate End, arrive and unfurl huge banners beneath me. Each is indicative of how long it has been since the club were a potent force. One of them depicts Hughie Gallacher, scorer of thirty-six goals when Newcastle won the Championship in 1927. Another is of Bob Moncur, captain when their last trophy, the Inter-Cities Fairs Cup, came here as the 1960s were about to swing to a conclusion. A third is of Malcolm 'Supermac' Macdonald, a boyhood hero of mine, whose thumping left foot took them to an FA Cup Final, albeit a frightful one better forgotten. I watch his banner ripple in the lightest of breezes and I realise, despondently, that present-day Newcastle wouldn't be ambitious enough to sign a luxury product such as Macdonald; he'd be too expensive for Mike Ashley. In 1971, aged twenty-one, Macdonald cost £180,000, a sum equivalent to almost £30m today. The club's transfer record – £15m for Michael Owen – has stood since 2005. Contained in that statistic is the reason Newcastle will limp along, avoiding relegation the best to be hoped for, unless Ashley becomes more like Midas and less like Scrooge.

As Newcastle look so horribly mismatched against Spurs, I'd settle for something joylessly goal-less today: an ugly point to get us going, leaving only another thirty-nine to make completely sure of sidestepping the drop. But I look at Harry Kane – marvelling again that his long, sharp features resemble an Easter Island sculpture – and also at Dele Alli and Christian Eriksen, both lithe and lively, and all I see is defeat; 2–0 would be respectable.

In less than a minute, Rafa Benítez, carrying a few more pounds than last season around his waistcoated stomach and beneath his chin, leaves his high-backed seat in the dugout and begins signalling from the technical area, a semaphore of distress. He jabs the warm air with an index finger, points towards the Leazes End, which Tottenham defend, and then cups a hand beside his mouth. The instructions he hollers seem more for appearances' sake than for practical purpose, the words whipped away and lost in the cacophony around him. It must feel to him like screaming beneath a waterfall.

The early tempo is sluggish, the passing slack. Every move is cautious and creaks a little, as though requiring a squirt of oil to lubricate it. The shooting is wayward too. With a yard and a half of space, Dwight Gayle snatches at one chance from the angle of the box, throwing his left boot at it hopefully. The effort balloons off his shin and is going over the bar before the lack of power in it sends the ball into a late, veering plummet towards the corner flag. I think again of Macdonald, who in his prime would have barrelled in from the same position and blasted at the target, a left-footed shot hard enough to tear the pegs out of the bottom of the net.

Soon Newcastle are having to make do and mend, grafting hard when two unfortunate circumstances force adjustments from Benítez. With the game in its infancy, Paul Dummett tweaks a hamstring in an innocuous challenge. It's no more than a muscular stretch for the ball, but he knows what damage has been done, instantly holding up a hand towards the bench and asking to be rescued. Then Florian Lejeune's debut ends prematurely. Kane, searching for his hundredth-goal, has looked off the pace, as though the season's start has come at least a week and a half too soon for him. He's made the usual sort of striker's runs, but either the passes from Alli or Eriksen have been struck too quickly, fizzing out harmlessly, or Kane has been a shade too slow to get to them. Afterwards he reacts rather like a mime artist – head thrown back, arms thrown skywards – who wants to convey his displeasure with himself broadly and extravagantly, so everyone is aware of it.

When Kane, after tracking back, loses possession near the halfway line, he tries to reclaim the ball with a scissor tackle on Lejeune, cut down from the ankle. The tackle is about bad timing rather than maliciousness, proving again how maladroit most forwards tend to be when asked to defend. It shows Kane's rustiness. The mistake gets him a booking, a scant price nonetheless compared to the high one Lejeune pays in comparison. In an awkward, twisting fall, he tears a ligament.

Jonjo Shelvey, handed the Newcastle captaincy today, dominated in the Championship last season because he had the room to do it. So many goals came from one of his long passes. He strolled back, often nearer his own box than the halfway line, and took in the view the way a painter leisurely absorbs a landscape before deciding which angle to frame. Not now. Tottenham, attempting to capitalise on Newcastle's reorganisation, press too far up the pitch for that to happen, squeezing both the space and the seconds available to him. Shelvey is rushed and frustrated, the sweat sticking to the bald, hard-boiled egg of his head. He's restricted to swift flicks and glancing nudges, mostly in crab-like movements of compromise, because anything more adventurous is beaten down or intercepted. When he does spy a gap, Shelvey can't plonk the ball into it. His radar is awry. So is his range. With Shelvey curiously detached, Newcastle can only ever respond to what Tottenham do rather than dominate them. You still expect more from Tottenham than Kane and his support staff are giving. It is consoling Newcastle, for whom the fixture hasn't been as intimidating so far as it originally seemed.

At half time – after much ado about nothing – the noteworthy stuff doesn't fill half a page of a pocket notebook: Eriksen bending a shot past the post from 20 yards . . . the Gallowgate End booing Moussa Sissoko, his punishment for being an ex-Newcastle player . . . the odd hash of a hacked clearance from goalkeeper, Rob Elliot . . . Gayle on a couple of occasions bereft of a finishing touch.

Relief is the overriding emotion from inside St James' Park. Newcastle, toiling hard, are holding their own at least.

Only a month ago, idly surfing the internet, I came across a YouTube clip of one of Newcastle's matches that became simultaneously famous and infamous. Like so much film of that period, I thought it had been wiped, lost or misplaced, never to be seen again. It was the

1974 FA Cup quarter-final against Nottingham Forest, the old First Division meeting the old Second. In the second half Newcastle, who were supposed to win in a gentle canter, were down to ten men and losing abjectly 3–1. Embarrassment awaited them when more than 500 home supporters among a crowd of 52,000 poured across the scrubby, bare pitch, a ragtag army of discontent. Their lame excuse was anguish and frustration. The referee had no option but to take the teams off until the outnumbered police, some of them with Alsatians, were able to herd the trouble-makers back on to the terraces, chiefly into the Leazes End which Forest had been protecting without too much difficulty. A total of twenty-three people were taken to hospital that afternoon: three of them had fractured skulls. There was a ten-minute delay, and the display of fan aggression jarred Forest psychologically, throwing them out of kilter afterwards. The team became more conscious about its safety than the result. Newcastle drew level and then won improbably, 4–3, in the dying fall of the match. When the invasion began, my father was watching from the back of the Gallowgate End. Disgusted with the sight in front of him, he shook his head and walked out, never caring then or later that he'd missed Newcastle's comeback. I was wedged into the Gallowgate End too. I was at the front, near the left-hand corner flag. The following afternoon my father and I sat together to watch the recorded highlights on *Star Soccer*. I was startled to catch myself briefly on the screen. Terry Hibbitt was about to swing in the corner that led to Newcastle's opening goal. I could have reached out my hand and almost tugged him down by the ankle.

I called up the film, stopping and starting and finally freezing it in a search for my fifteen-year-old self, which I did and did not want to find. Eventually there I was – a flop of my overlong blonde hair, trendy in the 1970s, almost covering my right eye like a pirate's patch. I was wearing a parka, also trendy, which was like a second skin, seldom off my shoulders then. Seeing myself as I used to be felt peculiar, as though a quick glimpse in a mirror had revealed someone I only half-recognised and barely knew. My ticket today, which was bought randomly, has coincidentally given me a seat high above that same spot. I gaze down at the corner flag, thinking of the clip and unable to conceive how much time has passed.

I am still thinking about it when, almost immediately after half time, the axis of the game abruptly turns.

It happens like this.

The ball is played up to Dele Alli mid-way in Newcastle's half. There is a swivel and then a nothing kind of kerfuffle with his tackler, the ball coming on to Alli's hand. He is on his bum, still holding the ball, when Jonjo Shelvey comes behind him, stretches out a tattooed arm and knocks it away, petulantly and unnecessarily. Shelvey could trot off, allowing the free kick to be belted up-field, but instead he takes two more short strides alongside Alli and plants a third deliberately on to his ankle, stamping down on it with the studs of his banana-yellow boot. The act is vicious, vindictive, pointless and egregious. The referee, Andre Marriner, has previously waved twenty-five red cards in his Premiership career. The twenty-sixth is a foregone conclusion, requiring no second thoughts. Marriner is less than 5 yards from Shelvey. His view of the crime is unobstructed. We all know about Shelvey's foul temper. He's flammable material and nothing much – even a few spiky words – is sufficient to set him ablaze. The stamp, as though caught in the clutch of madness, is probably retribution for some piffling earlier exchange that no one noticed. Shelvey still reacts to his sending off with a mock incredulity and open-palmed innocence. As he walks towards the dressing room, there is even an ever-so slight shake of the head, as though he is the wronged man, not guilty at all of besmirching the captain's armband with his idiocy. In the privacy of the dressing room, Newcastle will search for those brain cells of Shelvey's that refused to come out for the second half.

Of course, without him, Tottenham take over. And, of course, the opening goal is Alli's. It comes just after the hour. Passes around Newcastle's box are exchanged with the speed of a card sharp shuffling a pack. The defence swivels this way and that, never getting the measure of the attack. Eriksen is 20 yards out when he gets the ball and sees what Newcastle don't, which is Alli moving across Eriksen's peripheral vision. The run carries him 18 yards and between two defenders. The floated pass, which Eriksen strikes with some swerve and fade, anticipates where Alli will be when the ball starts to drop.

Rob Elliot hesitates. Alli steers his shot in on the volley from close range, his left leg outstretched.

Newcastle have spent so long in the apparent security of their own half that venturing out of it is a wrench, like leaving home for the first time. No sooner do they scurry forward than Tottenham force them to scurry back again. There is more nippy passing. There is more disarray in the defence. And there is another through ball from Eriksen, who is doing to Newcastle what Shelvey did to all-comers in the Championship. The ball is shorter and flatter than before, but the goal – this time from the left back, Ben Davies – is scored on almost the same yard of turf. After Harry Kane nearly adds a third, his shot smacking against the base of a post with such a thud that you could hear it on the Scotswood Road, Tottenham begin to indulge in Walking Football, that variation of the game designed for the over-fifties. Newcastle can't take the ball off them. By now the sun has dropped so low that the cross hatching of steel supports in the clear, truss-cantilever roof that overhangs the Milburn Stand and the Leazes End is shadowing the pitch like a drape of black lace.

There's still time for Eriksen, constantly superb, to demonstrate with a party piece the difference between a top team and a lowly one. He is 10 yards inside his own half and pushed against the touchline. Facing his own goal, he accepts a chipped pass. Nineteen out of twenty players would hold the ball in a jockeying sort of way and wait for someone to support them. Not him. Eriksen, sensing when his marker is bearing down on him, improvises audaciously. With his right foot, he flicks the ball up and over his own head as well as the defender's, and then he turns and dashes off alone. His head is up. His eyes are always on the spinning ball. He gets there first, cushioning the drop of it on his left thigh before creating at speed something out of nothing. In less than five, fabulous seconds Eriksen has gone on to the attack. The defender looks an idiot.

In the closing seconds, I fix for a while on Rafa Benítez, who continually takes off his spectacles and presses his forefinger and thumb on to the bridge of his nose, as though his eyes are sore from seeing too much already. Or perhaps, as a Champions League winner, he's merely asking himself: Why am I here? Benítez, at fifty-seven, has a prize-winning past in England, Spain, and in Italy too. This job will only offer a mid- to low-table finish unless the owner's ambitions change. Benítez is a much better man than his boss, and he will go on to better things. But at full time, which has not come soon enough for Newcastle, the Gallowgate End is still behind him and his team: 'We love you,' it sings – a declaration that is touching and also part of the problem.

In love there is always someone who kisses and someone who offers the cheek. The love the supporters demonstrate – against reason, against promise and against hope – is not nearly reciprocated enough.

But how dearly Ashley relies on it.

13 August 2017: Newcastle v Tottenham
Newcastle United 0 Tottenham Hotspur 2

Newcastle United: Elliot, Manquillo, Lejeune (Mbemba 34), Clark, Dummett (Lascelles 8), Ritchie, Hayden, Shelvey, Atsu, Pérez, Gayle (Merino 77).
Subs not used: Darlow, Murphy, Aarons, Mitrović

Tottenham: Lloris, Walker-Peters, Alderweireld, Vertonghen, Davies, Dembele (Winks 90), Dier, Sissoko (Son Heung 58), Alli (Wanyama 83), Eriksen, Kane.
Subs not used: Vorm, Wimmer, Carter-Vickers, Janssen

SCORERS
Tottenham: Alli 61, Davies 70

BOOKED
Newcastle: Ritchie
Tottenham: Davies, Kane

SENT OFF
Newcastle: Shelvey

Referee: A. Marriner
Attendance: 52,077

2

DON'T THINK YOU'RE SPECIAL . . . WE LOSE EVERY WEEK

28 August: Guiseley Town v Hartlepool United, National League, Nethermoor Park

The boy, dressed in Hartlepool's broad blue and white stripes, is about nine years old, an age so impressionable that the heroes we adopt on the pitch stay with us for life, preserved forever as we first saw them. He is standing close to his father on the cracked path. He looks puzzled; you can almost see the thought bubble, containing nothing but a question mark, floating above his head. He pauses, gathering in the sights around him, before asking in a small voice that is edged with incredulity and also disdain: 'Is *this* the ground?'

There is certainly no Vanbrugh elegance or architectural sweep about Nethermoor Park, which has been Guiseley's home since the club's formation in 1909. The ground is flanked on one side by a row of terraced houses, rendered in a particularly depressing grey, and on the other by the oval of a cricket pitch, the front of the pavilion resembling a back garden conservatory, built circa 1980. Behind the far goal is the drop of an industrial estate. At the end where the boy, still fearing his father has taken a wrong turn, looks ever more perplexed, there's a children's playground, a bowls club and, directly across the two-lane Otley Road, a modern structure proclaiming itself to be 'Yorkshire's Biggest Skin Clinic'(facial vein removal and anti-wrinkle injections are a speciality there, apparently). You could wander past Nethermoor and never notice it. The small wooden sign proclaiming this plot of land as Guiseley's is planted on the corner of the road and easily missed; and the shallow-pitched roofs of the four stands – only two of which have seating – are low and unprepossessing. It doesn't take much welly to send the ball over the top and into someone's flower-bed or vegetable patch.

Guiseley is obscure enough that its name is regularly mispronounced, and I doubt anyone unfamiliar with the foot of Wharfedale could take a blank map and accurately place an X on the spot it occupies. It is just about a town, the population a sliver or two above 20,000, but I always think of it as a large, growing village and I always think of the club as a kind of Steeple Sinderby Wanderers, the creation of author J. L. Carr. In Carr's book, *How Steeple Sinderby Wanderers won the FA Cup* – described by the writer D. J. Taylor as 'nothing less than an exercise in wish-fulfilment' and also as 'one of the greatest football novels ever written' – the amateurs win the FA Cup, a fantasy of immense proportion. In both reaching the National League, one stride from the Football League, and by somehow staying in it for the past two seasons, Guiseley have become Steeple Sinderby-like. Their feat is almost, if not quite, as implausible when you assess the rank of the opposition, the teams for whom recent exile from League Two is a shaming purgatory: Leyton Orient, Torquay, Tranmere Rovers, Chester, Macclesfield, Wrexham and now Hartlepool.

As the red kite flies – the bird is nearly as common a sight here as the crow is anywhere else – only 3 miles separate my front door from Nethermoor's narrow turnstiles. I first came one Christmas when the brass of The Salvation Army belted out every carol you have ever heard of. On a dismal afternoon, full of the sort of fine drizzle that slowly soaks you, I saw a dismal game; so bad I thought it had been staged for the sole purpose of allowing us to trot out afterwards that whiskery joke about the band being the only ones who could play. I was last here on the last day of last season. For the second time in twelve months Guiseley stared into the doom face of relegation. The mathematics were not complicated. York were one place and one point below them. Whatever they did, at home to Forest Green Rovers, Guiseley had to equal against Solihull Moors. The crowd spent half of the match watching Guiseley and the other half stuck on mobile phones, checking the latest score from York. Guiseley fell behind. York shot ahead twice, pegged back on each occasion. So in the ninety-first minute York were safe, and Guiseley were down. And then one of those booted long balls, desperate and unimaginative, dropped towards Solihull's box on a lowish arc. The goalkeeper, choosing ambition over common sense, hurried towards it. He miscalculated the lot – height, distance, trajectory – and arrived a millisecond after a glancing, backward header took the ball past his leap and then his flailing arms. I was standing near his right hand post. I watched the muddy ball bounce once and then fill the empty net. The great Geoffrey Green, parodying Shakespeare, once wrote: 'If a rose is a rose is a rose, then a goal is a goal is a goal,' a line both brilliant and unarguable. Guiseley's goal was hardly a gift to posterity. It was conceived in despair and then delivered to them only because of a crass, messy mistake. No one cared. In Guiseley it was received the way that Maradona's slalom run in the 1986 World Cup quarter finals against England was received in Argentina. After Guiseley's match had finished, the one at York dragged on for ten minutes, which seemed as long as ten days. The players stayed on the pitch. The crowd stayed on the terraces. When the result eventually came, you couldn't hear more than the opening few words of the tannoy announcement confirming Guiseley's safety. There was pandemonium and a pitch invasion. I wish now I had taken a diehard sceptic with me that day; someone who doubted football's capacity to absorb anyone so completely that, for a short while at least, nothing else is remotely important, the outside world and all your troubles in it entirely abandoned and forgotten.

I have adopted Guiseley as my 'second team'. I buy the *Wharfedale Observer*, where the news about them is crammed alongside staple parochial stuff: the parish council meetings, the amateur societies and the luncheon clubs, the church fairs and the community coffee mornings. On Saturdays I follow the National League as scrupulously as the Premier League. On Sundays I read the match reports in the *Non-League Paper*. I like the plain cosiness of Nethermoor, always hospitable. You half expect to find the pitch slopes, the music to be exclusively of the 1970s and the scores from elsewhere chalked on a board and carried around the ground. Some Premier League dressing rooms are larger than its car park. The programmes are sold on a fold out, Formica-topped table, the type you take camping or caravanning.

The programmes themselves contain advertising for local businesses – the fish and chip shop, the funeral parlour – rather than High Street conglomerates. In the bar, where a pint is relatively cheap and the cakes are home-made, you'll find posters tacked to the walls promoting their fund-raising events: sponsored bike-rides, speakers' evenings, pie suppers. There's also always a half time raffle in which you can win a bottle of whisky or a restaurant meal for two, the coloured tickets torn out from those thick books of thin paper.

There's frequently a to-and-fro debate about what constitutes the beating heart of football and where you can find it. Well, for me it's in Guiseley and other places just like it. They exist, frequently against the odds, without fuss, frills or flummery only because enough people pull together to make it so. Guiseley owe a debt to their match-day volunteers. Without them, the club wouldn't exist.

Kick-off is still an hour away, so I sit quietly for a while on one of the wooden benches that ring the boundary of the cricket club. It's a rare thing: an August Bank Holiday with not even the vague threat of rain. The sun is hot enough to burn the skin. Guiseley are nicknamed The Lions, and the costume for the team mascot arrives in a big plastic box, the head with its dark red mane sitting on the top, like a pig's laid across a medieval banqueting platter. Whoever wears the costume today is going to bake inside it.

Usually you can go anywhere at Nethermoor Park, swapping the view behind one goal for the other at half time. But for today's match the supporters are segregated, which means the boy who was so unimpressed with his first sight of the ground has to trail with his father to the opposite corner of it. The away fans will occupy one of the stands there and also the end where the electronic scoreboard – Guiseley's bow to modernity – is already flashing up garish advertising. The planes from Leeds-Bradford airport, less than 5 miles away regularly roar above it.

I stand as near as I can to the Guiseley dugout, which is a curve of Perspex and a row of white plastic bucket seats. The edge of the technical area is so close to the touchline that only a foot separates the edge of one from the other. Opposite is a row of tall trees, still nicely plump in their summer foliage, and the well-mown pitch looks a tight, shut-in space. It seems preposterous for Hartlepool to be here at all. This is their first year outside the Football League since becoming founding members of the Third Division North in the aftermath of the Great War. More poignant still is another detail: a decade ago, almost to the exact week, the fixture list also sent them to West Yorkshire and to defeat against Leeds United at Elland Road in League One. Guiseley then sat five tiers below them, unobtrusively facing the likes of Ossett Town, Ilkeston and Leek in the Unibond Premier League. The decline and fall of one club, and the unlikely slow and steady ascent of another, has brought them together like an incompatible couple pushed into a marriage of convinience. Hartlepool can't afford to be haughty about hobnobbing with them now. Without a win in their opening six matches, and lying second-to-bottom of the table, the convulsions of the previous season continue to impact on this one, the after-shocks still to settle. Hartlepool have almost an entirely new squad – a dozen players went and eleven were signed to replace them – as well as a new boss. At the start of the summer Craig Harrison, once a full back with Middlesbrough and Crystal Palace, found himself rebuilding a side and also managing the dizzy but daft expectation that instant, easy success was guaranteed.

Guiseley have at least won a match. It came in a bit of a thriller against Torquay. There was such a confusing shemozzle over their winner – following a prolonged scramble in the 6-yard box – that the goal was originally credited to someone who wasn't even on the field. Purely because of those points, filched at the absolute death, Guiseley are two places higher than Hartlepool, but have already leaked a ruinous thirteen goals, which is why the gap between them is just a squeak. After a West Yorkshire derby at Halifax only forty-eight hours ago, which was lost limply, their manager Adam Lockwood shut the dressing room door, conducting a post mortem that lasted nearly an hour. The training ground would be the more obvious place to pick through another bad defeat, but both Lockwood and his team (unlike Hartlepool's) are part-time because the club's economy demands it; Guiseley can't afford to be anything else. This has meant, during this month's rush of midweek matches, that Lockwood has only once been able to gather everyone together for practice. It shows, of course.

Guiseley also lost Jake Cassidy as a consequence. His eight goals were sufficient to get him lured away two months ago, the dangled bait of a full-time contract too tempting to refuse. Off Cassidy went, signing for Harrison at Hartlepool.

Lockwood's team nonetheless contains three notable figures. The first is midfielder John Rooney, unmistakably brother of Wayne. The shape of his face is identical. So is the frame of his mouth, the sticky-out ears, the slightly deep-set eyes. He arrived at Guiseley towards the end of last season via diverse stops, among them Macclesfield, Chester and New York Red Bulls. The second is Alex Purver, released by Leeds at twenty-one years old. He's another midfielder with a wiry frame, long lank hair and a scraggly black beard. The third is Kayode Odejayi, a striker who is always asked to describe only one goal in his whole career. You'll find the clip of it on YouTube. It comprises a long diagonal cross, a flashing leap and a close-in header – enough to beat Chelsea at Oakwell and take Barnsley into the FA Cup semi-finals in 2008.

Lockwood is a former player at the club, approaching his first anniversary in charge of it. His appointment was made when Guiseley were in straits so dire that you wouldn't have risked a shilling on their survival. He's done miraculous things since, but you wouldn't necessarily wager that shilling on them now either. Guiseley will be damn lucky to cling on again.

I guess there is a crowd of about 2,000. Half of them have come down the A1 from Hartlepool. One of their fans has draped the Flag of St George near the corner flag. The phrase 'NEVER SAY DIE' is stitched across it. Others bang the flat of their hands hard against the tin advertising boards around the perimeter of the pitch, making a sound like the discordant percussion of punk rock.

Those who go to football always travel hopefully. We *hope* this game – or the next – will be the rousing classic that everyone who wasn't actually there will pretend, years or decades later, to have seen live, succumbing to a combination of envy, wishful thinking and outright denial. A game to equal Luton against Bristol Rovers in the Third Division South; Joe Payne claimed ten of the dozen goals the home team scored that day, each markedly different from the other. A game such as Portsmouth's 7–4 win over Reading in the Premier League, which was celebrated deliriously, as though no one could believe what had been achieved. Or a game like the one that guaranteed immortality in the blue half of Manchester for Sergio Agüero and gave City the title, which became theirs with almost the last kick in almost the last minute of the 2011–12 season, a contrivance no fiction writer – no, not even J. L. Carr – would dare invent for Steeple Sinderby Wanderers. We don't feel any differently just because this is a National League game staged in a town usually used as a route to somewhere else and played between two teams jammed at the foot of the table.

But the players look jittery, even a little scared. Two managers have already been sacked in panic in the National League this season, and the chopping block and the axe could await this afternoon's loser too. We soon realise, as clearances are walloped high and long through the warm, windless air, that we won't be charmed with Brazilian flair. The merit in this match will come from what is offered attritionally rather than artistically. It's going to be like watching Wimbledon in the mid-1980s, the ball almost perpetually in flight. There's a lot of scruffy passing, a few over-hit crosses and only a solitary chance – albeit a superb one. Cutting abruptly in from the left, Alex Purver feathers in a cross, floating it into the space over and behind the defence. His target is Frank Mulhern, who muscles in front of his marker to meet the ball, but then steers it up rather than down. His diving header zooms against the bar, almost making the metal twang.

The rest is as pretty as trench warfare. You long for someone to pull the ball down, plant his foot on it and take a perceptive glance or two before deciding where the pass should go. Walking here I met a Hartlepool season ticket holder whom age had given wrinkles, folds and bags, and also cheeks covered in a criss-cross of minute red veins. He was old enough to have been a young man when the 1960s began to pulse and Hartlepool gambled on two managerial unknowns called Brian Clough and Peter Taylor. Clough, already the arch-publicist, learned to drive the team coach, which created a back page photograph, and he and Taylor sploshed paint on the main stand at the Victoria Ground, which got more column inches for a club sometimes overlooked even in the classified results. The man, addicted to Hartlepool since boyhood, was aware already that the National League would test his patience, but not his loyalty. 'I may not see them in the Football League again,' he said, without joking. He added that in their last game, against Fylde, there was 'no decent shot on goal at all'. Had I not known this, I wouldn't have understood the sarcasm loaded into a throaty roar, which comes after forty slow minutes. The ball, mishit from outside the box, hops past the post. It is a timorous peck at goal, but the Hartlepool supporters acclaim the effort from Devante Rodney as though it had been struck into the net's top corner at the sort of speed that makes the atmosphere pop.

Nothing clicks for Guiseley either. Adam Lockwood is not a shouty, look-at-me manager. He's been watching the game in a scholarly, studious manner. His hands are pressed against cheeks. His eyes half-close and his gaze is sometimes tilted downward, as though he doesn't really want to look as Guiseley lumber about disjointedly and shape-lessly in front of him. Kayode Odejayi is 6 feet 3 inches, but appears taller and is warming the bench, so Guiseley can't succeed in aerial squabbles up front and don't win any at the back either because Jake Cassidy, only a smidgen shorter than the Nigerian, is dominant over the defence that knows his tricks well but can't master them. You look at Cassidy and then at Odejayi and imagine them as a partnership that could have saved Guiseley from the grief you suspect is about to close in around them.

One moment is emblematic of Guiseley's woes. It's a piece of circus slapstick, which only long, tiring rehearsals could possibly synchronise again. When the ball shoots out of play, leaving Lockwood to retrieve it, he tries to get a move ticking with a quick throw-in. He tosses the ball too strongly, sending the thing a foot above the head of the player who is coming towards him to claim it at full pelt, his arms wide open. The manager's body sags. The player turns immediately and runs back, chasing the bouncing ball like a dog chasing a stick. There is a groan and then a sigh from the crowd – partly through anguish and partly through resignation; for Guiseley, it seems, can get nothing right, not even the basics of the basics. Mercifully for them the first half, which has paradoxically dragged without ever seeming to start properly, is over shortly afterwards.

Lockwood has more talking to do.

A week or so ago the Guiseley chairman James Ferguson went for a haircut in Otley, a market town that is only a handful of miles down the road. The conversation drifted onto football and the hairdresser, not knowing him, said she often cut the hair of Burnley's chairman, who lived nearby. Ferguson said he was a club chairman too. 'Which one?' she asked. So he told her. 'I didn't realise there was a team in Guiseley,' she replied, nonchalantly but candidly. Her answer shook Ferguson profoundly. He'd assumed that Guiseley had, if nothing else, established a defining presence on the pitch – even among those who, like his hairdresser, aren't sufficiently steeped in the game to necessarily recognise Giroud from Azpilicueta or Mkhitaryan from De Bruyne if one of them wandered in off the street for a quick trim. He immediately called a staff meeting to share his story and also to discuss Guiseley's profile.

Ferguson is thirty-seven. His day job is commercial director of TateOil, an independent fuel supplier. Since becoming chairman as recently as last May, he's put in 'about forty hours a week' for Guiseley. The 'about' in that sentence suggests the estimate is somewhat conservative. He's a Kipling-sort of a fellow, always forcing sixty seconds of absolute effort out of every minute run. He came to football comparatively late. He was eleven years old when he and his mother swapped Ballymena in Northern Ireland for Burnley, arriving with not much more than a few suitcases between them. Since 'there wasn't a lot to do in Burnley,' he got pulled towards Turf Moor, where a sympathetic gateman allowed him in without paying. Ferguson is a Bobby Robson boy: one of those who saw the grassy pitch and fell instantly, irrevocably in love with it. The arrangement with the gateman lasted until he grew too big to get through the turnstile without holding his breath. To fund his football addiction, he blagged a job collecting glasses in a bar, where the blindest of eyes was turned to the fact he was under age. Ferguson knows what it is to be a fan. Not only to care about a team, but also to lose sleep about it. He's already given an open-house invitation to Guiseley's supporters, offering them the chance to moan face-to-face to him. While Ferguson is a current of entrepreneurial energy, he can also sound quaintly philanthropic, as if he's living completely in the wrong era, when discussing his responsibilities, assumed like a duty of care. He's sincere in wanting the club to be more profitable and successful when other generations inherit it. He knows football is a business, but he also knows that almost all the customers are family, a point which has seemingly escaped the Mike Ashleys of the football planet. Guiseley's owners – there are three of them, each local businessmen – poached Ferguson from Silsden, of the North West Counties League. He'd come, he told them, but didn't want to be part of some 'raggedy-arsed Rovers set up'. He's since become convinced that Guiseley can eventually be a Football League club – despite the sight of Leeds United looming over them as near neighbours.

Leeds will break back into the Premiership eventually, but won't be Guiseley's only obstacle in reaching the Promised Land. The distance between the National and Football League looks as though it could be cleared with a decent jump, but building a bridge between them that will actually hold demands complicated construction. The National League is the Fifth Division, a term that won't be formalised until the Football League is prepared to share the cash bounty it receives, which is probably never. Get televised live on BT Sport, the National League's broadcaster, and Guiseley will get £7,000 for a home game and £3,000 for an away one. In the Football League, even the lowliest clubs banks £1m – simply for being there. As it becomes prohibitively expensive to invest higher up, so more businessmen take a punt lower down. Ebbsfleet United are backed by a Kuwaiti consortium, not exactly counting the ha'pennies. Fylde have something that is more like a stadium than a ground, and supermarkets, bars, cafes and a petrol station are dotted in or around it. Even Billericay, of the Bostik League Premier Division, have a budget of £22,000 to spend weekly on wages. Money matters, and Guiseley don't have much of it. The average salary in the National League is £900 to £1,000 per week. Guiseley have to be selective and cautious. Sometimes a player, nudging towards his thirties, can be persuaded to Nethermoor Park because becoming part-time enables him to train or educate himself for a career beyond football. But – and it's a considerable one – there aren't enough of them worth investing in.

Adam Lockwood is already chasing Ferguson for another player. One may not be enough, however.

I have begun to think of today as one of those chess matches, which ought to be declared a draw as soon as the opening moves are made. Stalemate seems the only possibility. But then Guiseley, still dozing after their half time cup of Yorkshire tea, fall behind in the forty-ninth minute. The build-up is routine – an ordinary bits and pieces attack down the right. It leads to a pushed-over cross that looks benign. It certainly produces no red flag in Guiseley's defence. The trouble starts when a shot, tame and standard, is blocked. Guiseley are caught ball-watching, as though standing outside what is happening to them. The rebound breaks to Jonathan Franks, unmarked and in sufficient space to dig an allotment. Bang. His shot flies hip-high into the net from 10 yards. Franks goes dancing off towards the corner flag, his arms outstretched; perhaps, like the rest of us, he can't believe there's been a breakthrough. Craig Harrison fist-pumps the air furiously. Adam Lockwood briefly covers his face with both hands. Hartlepool's supporters, swaying now, celebrate as though promotion itself, and not just three points, is only forty minutes away. Guiseley's fans concoct a chant laced with black humour. 'Don't think you're special,' they sing. 'We lose every week'.

Years ago I cut out an article in the *Guardian* by the writer and broadcaster Mark Lawson. The topic was whether swearing had lost its power to shock. When the *Observer*'s drama critic, Kenneth Tynan, slipped out the first broadcasted 'fuck' on the BBC, as far back as 1965, the House of Commons was appalled: 133 backbenchers signed four separate motions about it and the BBC apologised very publicly. There are few apologies nowadays; expletives are seldom deleted. Barely anyone seems to mind their language anywhere; and certainly not at a game. Lawson tailed his piece with a family anecdote, which is the part I remember so well. He had taken his son, aged just ten, to watch Arsenal against Leeds. Some 'supporters' around them began verbally bashing Oleh Luzhny, a right back who had won the Double in 2002 under Arsène Wenger. He was continually called a 'useless, Russian cunt'. At half time the son asked his father: 'You know what they were shouting about Luzhny?' Lawson braced himself to deliver a tenderly paternal and 'liberal lecture' about that 'grossly offensive term' when his son, unfazed, merely said: 'He isn't Russian. He's Ukrainian'. Lawson's story came back to me abruptly. Here, a boy has just responded to another terrace chant with the baffled enquiry, 'Dad? What does wanker mean?'

You are always on top of the match at Guiseley and sometimes almost in it, so close does the play come. Before the game started, the match officials walked past trailing the reek of liniment behind them, the stink pungent enough for chemical warfare, and one of them also warned the other two about a dip in the pitch where 'I once fell on my arse'. When it began, you could hear the thump and crash of every boot as it made a pass, a shot, a tackle. You were aware, too, of almost every spit and fart and curse – especially the curse. There is no crowd noise to drown it out. Fans in the National League are only slightly more polite and complimentary than fans in the Football League – Hartlepool's tunelessly sing about the 'shithole' of Nethermoor – but the dialogue on the pitch isn't fit for the pews of a church either. And, as the spike of tension climbs, the language becomes more choice. It is as though the Shorter Oxford English Dictionary has been whittled down simply to 'fuck' and every derivative of it. The players of Guiseley and Hartlepool, like players everywhere else, use the words naturally and liberally. It is normalised vulgarity. 'What the fuck was that? . . . 'Play the fucking ball' . . . 'That was fucking offside, linesman' (notice how no one ever says Referee's Assistant; the term is too much of a high falutin' mouthful). 'Fuck' and 'fucking' are always being rolled out for emphasis but don't grievously offend and have no intrinsic meaning because constant, boring repetition strips them of such a thing. So it is like being part of another era when Alex Purver talks to the linesman about a lunging challenge that has gone unpunished. 'Did you really not believe that was a foul?' he says. Purver is making an enquiry, rather than issuing a disguised rebuke, and he delivers it politely, like a Corinthian-Casual asking for his tea to be poured into a china cup. 'No foul,' replies the linesman tersely, and the two of them almost shake hands on it.

Purver is one of the few Guiseley players who looks capable of reviving them. He weaves. He darts around. He tries to demonstrate some skill. But the ball is constantly whacked rather than caressed and there are huge, box-to-box booted clearances, as though no one exists below them in midfield. The pattern of the game is repeated endlessly, the same approach inevitably leading to the same result. At one point a red kite, looking for a late afternoon snack, appears in the middle distance in the opening between the trees, every tilt and tip of its wings visible. The bird is about to fly our way and hover over the periphery of the pitch when the ball is once more booted upwards. The kite wheels in retreat, judging no doubt that it is safer to stay away. A stray clearance could have taken it down like buckshot.

Guiseley allow dogs into Nethermoor. The unofficial mascot here – much more impressive than the costumed one – is a four-year-old Great Dane called Mowgli, who is fond of putting his huge front paws on to the pitch-side rail and standing on his hind legs. His owner dresses him in one of those lion's manes that you can buy online. Mowgli suddenly lollops past me, his tongue lolling out pink and glistening. His large eyes avoid the field, possibly because Guiseley already look so weary, disillusioned and beaten all ends up. Even when a goal seems probable, something extraordinary thwarts them.

Not long after Harrison's arrival, the *Hartlepool Mail* published an article that not only marked the fiftieth anniversary of Brian Clough's departure from Hartlepool to Derby, but also highlighted parallels between the two bosses and the situation each of them had inherited. These were not entirely strained or spurious, but efforts to compare Clough to anyone who hasn't won – and certainly won't win – two European Cups always run the high risk of ridicule from the opening paragraph. I reckoned, however, that Harrison had already done something for which Clough would have given him one of those famous, approving thumbs ups. He bought the best goalkeeper Hartlepool could afford. In the autumn of 1978 Clough paid £250,000 for Peter Shilton, a decision derided as insanely profligate until Shilton 'won' Nottingham Forest the Championship in the spring of the following year. In a goalless game, which made the title theirs on a dusty pitch at Coventry, Shilton made one twisting, diving, falling save after another, making certain with such virtuosity that those who still had doubts about his fee shed them afterwards.

Harrison went out and claimed Scott Loach. Broad-shouldered and 6 feet 3 inches. tall, Loach has a past that includes 130 consecutive League appearances for Watford and a slot in two England squads, chosen by Fabio Capello, alongside the luminous company of Gerrard, Terry and Rooney. A downward slide since has seen him stop off at ten more clubs, often on loan, where there has barely been time to hang up his coat. But Loach is only twenty-nine, still a tender age for a goalkeeper. Even if you didn't know any of this, you could work out simply through observation that he's a cut above the rest. Loach fills the goal with a presence that is more than just physical bulk. He looks formidable even when doing nothing but pacing his line. With a quarter of an hour left, he shows what had once made him such a rising star. Loach saves at his near post, parrying a forceful shot into the air, which is the most anyone could have done with it. The ball hangs in front of Kayode Odejayi, a belated substitute. The goal gapes open and Odejayi thrusts himself towards it, his close range header hard and clean. Guiseley have their equaliser – no question about it. But somehow, as if a trampoline has sprung him to the right spot and then a theatrical wire is suspending him there, Loach gets off the turf, leaps to his left and slaps the ball away with a big, gloved right hand. The shout of 'goal' gets stuck in Guiseley's throats. Odejayi puts his hands behind his head and stares directly into the net, amazed to find the ball isn't in it. Loach's save is almost Shiltonesque.

You can see the energy drain from Guiseley drop by drop now. Galley slaves could not have worked harder than them. They try to be plucky, but you can tell this takes a great effort and you also know that nothing will come from it. Hartlepool begin spinning out time, every stop-start action like the end of a slow bicycle race. The referee turns his hand in the air, as though imitating the whirl of a Catherine wheel. It's a weak gesture to push them along. He adds on eight minutes, but doesn't impress Guiseley. A voice from their bench, unmistakably angry and unmistakably Yorkshire-bred, gives a blast of: 'Tell 'em to get a fuckin' move on, ref'.

He doesn't. Instead, he blows his whistle.

Lockwood goes along the line, giving decent and perfunctory handshakes to Hartlepool's coaches. His half-smile looks pasted on, underlining something desperate and never disguising his sharp unhappiness. He looks like a man who can hear a bell tolling. Ask not for whom . . .

*   *   *

Nethermoor Park empties rapidly. Few want to hang around at the graveside of another defeat. I look across its narrow acres. Guiseley possibly won't be here much longer. The club is planning an escape. Two sites have been identified for possible development. One of these is near the airport. Their goodbye, sad as it will be, could be necessary. Since there is no scope for development – no hotel, gym or offices to give them a regular income – Guiseley must consider moving on. I think of what the land will look like if the stands go, the pitch is dug up, the dressing rooms demolished. I also think of that nine-year-old boy, too young to know now even what he will one day wish for.

He'll be able to say he saw all this before it vanished.

28 August 2017: Guiseley Town v Hartlepool United
Guiseley 0 Hartlepool United 1

Guiseley: Green, East (Hurst 81), Lawlor, Palmer, Lowe, Hatfield, Rooney, Purver, McFadzean (Molyneux 12), Correia (Odejayi 63), Mulhern.
Subs not used: Brown, Atkinson

Hartlepool: Loach, Magnay, Harrison, Watson, Deverdics, Featherstone, Hawkins, Woods, Franks, Cassidy (Simpson 78), Rodney (Donaldson 68).
Subs not used: Richardson, Newton, Munns

SCORER

Hartlepool: Franks 49

BOOKED

Guiseley: Odejayi
Hartlepool: Rodney, Franks, Featherstone

Referee: A. Young
Attendance: 1,723

3

A TAN SUIT AND A WAD OF TICKETS

12 September: Chelsea v Qarabag, Champions League Group C, Stamford Bridge

The whole, beautifully powerful movement, starting from the collection and control of the ball and ending with the sight of it belting against the net, lasted just ten seconds. The impact it made on the senses nonetheless summoned immediately that familiar, worn tale about George Best in which, after witnessing a goal of sublime improbability, the novice reporter is told by his worldlier colleague to ignore the time it was scored and instead log down the date. The punchline is so neat that the story itself, like so many about the complicated life of dear George, sounds apocryphal the more you hear it. It happens to be true, but you have to trust the gospel word of those who were actually there in the mid-1960s because no film exists of Best, master of the art of the impossible, slaloming in from the corner flag at Old Trafford and then scoring from an angle so acute that the feat defied belief because it also defied the fundamental laws of geometry.

Davide Zappacosta is more fortunate than Best. Whenever the urge takes him, which may be often in his sedentary old age, he can again watch his 25-year-old self reducing a crowd to near stupefaction. He'll see what we saw on this wet night under floodlights. The bright, white number 21 ironed on to his blue shirt. The sheen on the ball as Thibaut Courtois gently rolls it to him, the goalkeeper originally looking to his left before going right and picking out Zappacosta. The long, wide corridor along the touchline that beckons him and also the first, light touch he takes towards it. And then his abrupt acceleration of speed, sparking what comes next. In the slight, forward tilt of his body, Zappacosta is like a sprinter bursting away from the blocks. He outpaces two challenges before reaching the halfway line, one of them with a half-skip and a semi-sidestep, and he then deters the threat of two more, the defenders holding back because of his momentum and also because the assumption is made that, promising as it is, this run will go nowhere and come to nothing. Zappacosta has travelled 60 yards. He is almost parallel with the area. He glances up, his gaze no more than a flicker of the lids, before giving the ball a hammering. Every pair of eyes, on the pitch and off, follows it through the air. Qarabag's goalkeeper, Ibrahim Šehić, is closer to the edge of his 6-yard box than to his own line. He's already too far out and his weight is on his front foot. When Šehić finally detects the line, discovering a shade too late that the ball is going to land behind instead of ahead of him, he can't easily back-pedal. The recovering dive he attempts is not one of lithe grace. It is sprawling, despairing, useless. He looks faintly ridiculous, like someone trying to stop his trousers from falling down before anyone notices. The ball beats him for speed, dropping into the far corner with a whoosh as he paws at it. Zappacosta slaps his chest twice and runs to The Shed, arms outstretched and waiting to be embraced, which he is. His head is back. His mouth is wide open. The jugular vein on the right side of his neck is as prominent as a ridge. Šehić, getting off the floor, stares about him as though searching for anyone he can accuse of negligence except himself – Lady Luck, perhaps, or a colleague, now in hiding on the halfway line, who ought to have gone at Zappacosta like a desperado, hauling him to the turf if necessary.

We are never shock-proof against sensational drama. The unexpected, the sudden unforeseen twist, will always make us catch our breath; and that is what Zappacosta, on his Chelsea debut, has done so deliciously – and that is why we will remember both it and him. Chelsea are already in front, the lead fashioned by a fine and a classily attractive goal, coming after only five minutes. Pedro was given the present of 5 square yards of space and he capitalised on it with a flourish, his side-footed shot from the shallow arch of the D rising with a slight curl. This was achieved almost with disdain, as if Pedro was responding to a dare someone had given him on the training ground. What he did, so memorable before, will hardly be worthy of a mention in dispatches now and especially not later. Zappacosta has eclipsed it. The match itself will fade from the memory too, a clear sight of it becoming so patchy amid a fog of other things that eventually we may even have to check the score. What will remain, however, is Zappacosta's goal and our ecstatic reaction to it. For something like this stays with you, season after season.

We don't know whether or not what he achieved was actually meant. The alternative is that Zappacosta spectacularly mis-hit a cross and became an accidental hero. But all of us, caught up in it, don't want to let that suspicion spoil our moment. We want to believe that somehow, more than 20 yards out and from an angle, the Italian gave the Bosnian the eye and fooled him. And we want to believe that the gap was spotted and gone for with the audacity of hope. We do so because we want the goal to remain perfect, unblemished by any fact that jars or doesn't fit or is simply inconvenient to the smooth telling of the story around it. This may be selfish, bred wholly from the desire to say with cocky one-upmanship that 'we were there' rather than at home in front of the television, or that we caught up with the highlights through belated curiosity because everyone else began discussing Zappacosta's goal. And so we do believe, with implacable faith, that what he did was intentional, planned and immaculately executed in the few nano seconds in which he had to think about it. To anyone who claims otherwise – even to Zappacosta himself – we'd respond with: 'Say it ain't so'. For the surge of the run alone, which gave the game a terrific jump, Zappacosta deserved his goal and also the wild approbation it brought him.

You feel the expectation of something grand at Stamford Bridge; something, indeed, that suggests the Premier League winners are about to make a bold statement. Pride demands it. Chelsea's absence from the Champions League last season was chastening for them. It was rather like missing a society wedding, stuck outside looking in on the ceremony, their social standing severely devalued as a consequence. The club's otherwise regular spot on the guest list is taken a little less for granted now, and so is the need to rehabilitate themselves across Europe with something barnstorming, something to get tongues wagging.

On the way into the ground I trailed along the North End Road a pace or two behind three fans in their late teens. Each was as thin as a mop handle. Even the short name on their replica shirts – declaring allegiance to the summer signing Álvaro Morata – was almost too long for their slender backs and their sloping shoulder blades. They spoke to one another about how many times Chelsea would score. Three, said one after much huffing and puffing about it. Four at least, said another more decisively, folding his thumb into the palm of a hand and holding up his spread fingers to reinforce the point. The third was giddier still. 'Could be seven or eight,' he pronounced confidently, as though the gift of prophecy was behind the claim. There was relief among them that Qarabag, rather than either of the other two Group C opponents, Roma and Atlético Madrid, were rolling up first. It was a nice, soft start for Chelsea, a mismatch. The huge inequality in talent between the teams is demonstrated in pounds. The market value of Chelsea's squad is £355m. Qarabag's is barely £20m, give or take the odd Azerbaijani manat.

That Qarabag are here at all – the first team from their country to get this far – is widely described as a fairy tale. The cliché is convenient, a piece of shorthand that everyone instantly understands. The phrase is also useful, saving whoever leans on it from the burden of original thought. On the one hand, however, it is cloying and unimaginative. On the other it automatically lulls you into thinking just of happy endings. And, as the novelist Hilary Mantel has pointed out, the traditional fairy tale almost always contains serial atrocities – among them murder, starvation, cruelty and 'desperate human creatures' – before all becomes lovely. Qarabag are capable of rousing even the hardest heart to tenderness, but to label them as a fairy tale is legitimate only up to a point. For the club's many upheavals go on unabated, and no resolution to them is in sight. Until 1993 Qarabag's home was the Imarat Stadium in Agdam. But the stadium, like the western Azerbaijani city itself, was turned into one of the most blasted strips on the planet. War with Armenia over the disputed region of Nagorno-Karabakh disfigured the terrain so terribly that aerial photographs make this scorched corner of the earth seem almost as bare and as desolately bleak as the Moon. The buildings that still stand are mostly crumbling or completely ruined, bringing to mind how Pompeii must surely have looked after Vesuvius had finished pouring lava over it. Armenia's military holds what little is left of Agdam. The other inhabitants are ghosts. Ever since Qarabag, known as The Horsemen, have been footballing refugees, a peripatetic club suffused with the pain of life. Comparatively recently they have established shallow roots in the capital, Baku – 159 miles to the east of Agdam – because there was nowhere else for them to go. The state bankrolls the team, who have become a point of light in Azerbaijan and are sent abroad to shine it, highlighting their poor country's plight and also a conflict that few are conscious of and fewer still can discuss knowledgeably. Qarabag have become Azerbaijan's way of introducing itself to the rest of the world.

Chelsea won't be charitable even in these fraught circumstances. What Qarabag are going to get – as Davide Zappacosta's goal has already made clear – is the bludgeon rather than a bouquet. Qarabag, insured against failure because of colossally low expectations, are seen as a tasty sacrifice. What's on offer is the chance to swank against them and command the biggest stage again. Qarabag, fretful and dazed, seem initially complicit in this. Their coach Gurban Gurbanov has the laudable objective of playing 'good football', which he says is paramount to him. Those who saw Gurbanov play – he is Azerbaijan's record goal-scorer – are in thrall to a rumbustious striker of indomitable courage. He was a battering ram of a man, prepared to throw himself at a chance even when he risked a kick in the guts, the groin or even in the head. His team is not shaped in his image. He has focused on possession and short passing and trim organisation, earning Qarabag the much too generous sobriquet of 'The Barcelona of the Caucasus'. Nothing so far supports flattery of this obsequious kind. It should not be inhaled.

Gurbanov is tackling the game without illusion, evidently afraid that Chelsea will go on a goal-riot unless he loads up midfield and plonks five defenders on the edge of the box. Qarabag have already battled through three two-legged ties to qualify for this, and their number nine, the South African Dino Ndlovu, claimed four goals, including the most precious one, against Copenhagen, which unexpectedly put them into the group. To see him now is to feel sorry for

him. Ndlovu is alone and lonely up front. He flings himself in perfunctory pursuit of what he cannot possibly catch, which is the odd sprayed
pass. Every forward rush and rapid backtrack, down the middle and
through the channels, reminds you of someone madly and pointlessly
trying to pick up waste paper in a gale.

Chelsea aren't at full strength; seven games over twenty-one days in
three different competitions choke their September, and so 'rotation,
rotation, rotation' is the mantra of Antonio Conte, notably resting
Morata. It is an act of mercy for Qarabag. Morata's understudy,
Michy Batshuayi, drags himself about, seldom profiting from the
space Willian exploits and the openings he inspires. Willian is going
on the mazy sort of runs that are longer than a Henry James sentence;
he is the prince of circumlocution, sometimes indulging in wispy
figures of eight to retain possession. He does it simply because he can;
Qarabag struggle to nail him down.

A month ago I came across a piece Chelsea had published on their
website about Jimmy Greaves, so synonymous in Tottenham white
that his seasons in blue tend to be overlooked and even forgotten, like
a memory lost. The photograph beside the article was a frame of
intense colour. The material of Greaves's shirt, with its pendant collar,
looked thick enough to have been cut from 2 yards of flannelette.
Greaves was juggling an orange ball and you got the impression he
could have been talking to it, the way a master talks to a servant.
Behind him – and this is what made the scene so captivating – was the
panoramic sweep of Stamford Bridge itself. This was the ground as I
had first seen it as long ago as the early 1970s: a curve of space big
enough behind the goals to have built a five-a-side pitch at both ends;
the grey block of flats, twenty storeys high, rising in the middle distance
and above the sharp ribbing of concrete terracing; the brown weath-
ered pitch entirely shorn of grass as though some rapacious insects
had flown down and eaten it. I thought of Greaves as I watched the
ponderous Batshuayi; for on a night like this the stealthy poacher in
him would have darted instinctively around in destructive alliance
with Willian, always anticipating the pass before it was played. I also
thought of the old Stamford Bridge, where the gap between spectator
and touchline, which seemed a country mile, made the pitch look
wider and deeper than anybody else's except Wembley's. How

claustrophobic Qarabag must feel in this much more compact space, hemmed in to the hilt at every turn – the crowd constantly pressing over them and Chelsea constantly pressing towards them.

It has begun to rain. The rain comes on a diagonal wind that sends swishing drifts of it across the pitch. The ball is soon glistening under the lights and Chelsea, especially Willian, send it more quickly than ever over the wetted turf. There's such an easy lightness about their every move that barely a divot is dug up. Chelsea gorge themselves on possession and Qarabag are falling into full retreat, content already to limit the damage. At half time I can't believe I have seen only two goals.

As a contest the match is already done and dusted, but it isn't drained of interest – or of significance either – because of what Qarabag represent. A scalping won't disgrace them because what counts is their mere presence, which is the real achievement. What Qarabag have become proves yet again that football is at last, truly and indisputably, the global game it erroneously claimed to be long before actually achieving that status. When I originally heard that boast being made, the blazers in charge of the game must have owned an atlas based on Ptolemy's *Geography*. Only sixteen nations then competed in the World Cup Finals. 'Soccer' in America was scoffed at as irrelevant. Africa and Asia weren't entirely blanked, but definitely made telephone calls to Fifa that went unreturned, the voice and potential prospects of two continents sidelined by indifference. Now football really is everywhere, and the statistics stack up to underline it. The Premier League is broadcast in so many countries – more than 200 – that listing those who don't get it would hardly fill the flap of a matchbook. Its matches are beamed into 730 million homes. It has an audience of three billion. The Champions League Final, aired even more widely, has become the biggest annual sporting event ever seen. Its audience is over 300 billion; America's Super Bowl doesn't break 120 million. A generation has grown up with football's unchallenged superiority as the norm, but those of us who lived through the 1960s, 1970s and 1980s needed to be convinced of it. When the penny finally dropped for me, I was 12,000 miles from home.

*   *   *

Between the entrance into Fulham Broadway tube station and the turnstiles in Chelsea's West Stand, I read a verbose notice that was attached with rusty fixings on to a fence. It warned the unwary about the perils of buying a ticket from a tout. Anyone doing so would not 'necessarily' gain admission, it claimed. Not 10 feet away stood a man who bulged with a monstrous amount of flesh. He accosted passers-by in a stage whisper: 'Need a ticket?' he asked. He couldn't have been more brazen about it. He was like someone unwrapping a Churchill-sized cigar and then lighting up beneath a No Smoking sign. The man was past sixty. He wore a light tan suit that hung off him like the creased sheets of an unmade bed. He was unshaven too, the grey-black bristles of his beard looking a week old. His hair was combed over, like Bobby Charlton's used to be, but the whispery threads of it accentuated his baldness rather than disguised it. The front of his shirt was dirty. So were his nails. The high toes of his brown boots were badly scuffed, as though he'd been dragged to Stamford Bridge.

I looked at him and what came back to me was a different tout in a different country. The country was China. The match was Beijing Guoan against Sanfrecce Hiroshima of Japan in the Asian Champions League in 2014. I hadn't been aware the game was on until I found myself outside the Workers' Stadium in Beijing. I made the impulsive decision that it couldn't be missed. I had no option but to buy my ticket from a tout, choosing him with some care and considerable trepidation. The first one I approached was a gaunt-cheeked man, dressed in a Barcelona shirt at least a size and a half too big for him. The two of us began, as best as we could without a common language, to negotiate a price, but he appeared a bit too eager to please and had a nervy shiftiness about him, like someone about to steal your watch. The second was pushy – aggressively so. His glassy eyes were rimmed red and bulged a little from their sockets. He had a row of broad-bladed swords tattooed on to a forearm and a small hand-pistol inked on to the side of his neck. I had an idea he was not the sort of busi-nessman who would be offering a money-back guarantee. I mouthed some polite excuse and moved on. I learned later that all match tickets in China are supposed to be bought in advance, which means there are always good pickings for touts, able to exploit the ignorant and the unsuspecting like me. I was a virgin at this. I'd never before haggled surreptitiously on a street corner, and I felt self-conscious about it. In retrospect there was no need to be coy because the old hands traded openly, yelling the prices in an effort to undercut one another.

Eventually I settled on someone harmless-looking: a gut-heavy student-type with puffy fingers, a bad basin cut of black hair and a pair of square, black-framed glasses. He slowly swapped a burning cigarette from his right hand to his left before showing me the contraband, removed from an inside pocket. His wad of tickets was bound by an elastic band. I paid him 35 Yuan, having no idea whether that sum was a bargain or extortion. I peeled off a 100 Yuan note, decorated with Chairman Mao's moon face, and received in return what I guessed was the correct change. 'Good seat. Enjoy game,' he said in a burst of broken English. He smiled, revealing a row of nicotine-stained teeth.

It was a muggy spring evening and the smog, the colour of cold ash, sat like a lid across the city. The last of the day's light was bleeding away and the floodlights were already on, creating a spectral-like glow around the Workers' Stadium, which is in the Chaoyang District, north-east of the Forbidden City and Tiananmen Square. It was rush hour and black exhaust billowed from the commuter traffic, going nowhere along a jammed, eight-lane highway. I could taste petrol and diesel in the fumes. The noise was even worse than the stench of the pollution. As one driver pressed his palm to the horn, and held it there in an angry protest, so another few hundred more did the same, as though replying to him. When it came, the blast of these horns was so loud that you couldn't think and weren't able to hear the sound your shoes made on the pavement. Then there was the drone of the vuvuzelas, which fans of Beijing Guoan blew, the instrument usually a fluorescent emerald to match the club's colours. One supporter had a base drum, its leather strap around his neck, and another banged a pair of cymbals. I hoped I would not be sitting near either of them.

On the main thoroughfare, which was impossibly congested, the hawkers were bawling and gesticulating towards trestle tables heaped with souvenir merchandise, like a pop-up bazaar: shirts, scarves, baseball caps, triangular pennants, enamel badges, silk flags and glossy posters of Cristiano Ronaldo and Lionel Messi, Zlatan Ibrahimović and Gareth Bale. You had to zigzag past these stalls and time and again I waved their owners away, but each was convinced that a firm no, even if accompanied by a vigorous shake of the head, was simply an invitation to barter. In the days when the Iron Curtain divided Europe, and I occasionally watched matches behind it, the use of the army as a deterrent to trouble-makers was a familiar sight. But nothing – not even beside the Berlin Wall – was as conspicuous as the appearance of the Chinese soldiers, who had arrived in battalions in immaculately brushed, light brown uniforms. Their silver buttons gleamed like cat's eyes. There were so many of them that I wondered whether China feared a third Sino-Japanese war would breakout in the second half. More peculiarly still, as kick-off approached, the tannoy blared out a military march, but the soldiers, as if completely deaf to it, stood to rigid attention in regimented rows. Their faces were stone masks; you'd have thought someone had just embalmed them. When the music stopped, the announcer spoke English with an accent that suggested the influence of west coast America. His pronunciation, however, was way off – ludicrously so, in fact. His 'Welcome to the Workers' Stadium', recited over and again, sounded like 'Welcome to the Wankers' Stadium,' which made everything seem more surreal than ever, like one of those crazy dreams that makes no sense when you wake from it.

Beijing Guoan against Sanfrecce Hiroshima was not combat on an eloquent scale. Since nothing short of national pride was at stake, you could argue that nerves were responsible for the scruffiness of it. There were scuffed corners, sliced and misplaced passes and the sort of missed chances that your granny could have put away. The tackling was triple X-rated. One player threatened to remove another's spleen with a high lunge. Another attempted to bulldoze the goalkeeper through the net. Beijing somehow went ahead 2–0 and then became sloppy. The two goals Hiroshima claimed as a consequence, forcing an unlikely draw, were punishments for complacency.

The stark lack of quality on show was much less important to me than what the game represented. The previous weekend I'd been in another Chinese city, which is 300 miles south-east of Beijing. In the evening I'd switched on the television in my hotel room and discovered I could watch, live and uninterrupted, Liverpool and Manchester City in the Premier League. Home thoughts from abroad arrived in an arresting flood. I saw the pictures from Anfield, amazed to find them sharp and brilliant, and a feeling of great misery washed over me. England and I seemed so desperately far apart. I looked at the heave and toss of The Kop, as wonderfully colourful as I think I have ever seen it. I looked at the shorn grass, a soft rich English green. I looked at the sunshine enveloping the ground on a tranquil, gorgeous day and the hard cast of the shadows, densely black enough to appear as solid shapes. I wished I could walk into the widescreen TV and out again on Merseyside. This was the match in which Liverpool began to think the title could be theirs for the first time since 1990. In The Kop fans unfurled a long banner that pleaded: MAKE US DREAM. And, after City were beaten 3–2, Liverpool were dreaming.

Next morning I met a retired doctor, a short and dapper man in his early eighties. He was a Liverpool fan and had seen the match too. We swapped thoughts about it, and then he asked whether I'd ever been to Anfield. When I replied 'many times,' he was ecstatic on both our behalves. Had I told him that I took tea with the Queen every week, I swear he couldn't have been more impressed. He had come to the game late in his life, he said, but soon found himself caught in the spectacle of it. He had supported Liverpool because – in common with many Chinese fans – the vivid 'China Red' of their shirts attracted him. He had become devoted to a city he would never visit and a team he would never see play other than on television. To him England *was* the Premier League; he knew the geography of the country primarily through the clubs, which were scattered dots on the map for him. He also explained something crucial. The football results were 'always available'. He spoke about it in a low, conspiratorial voice, as though discussing this openly was delicate and could bring him trouble. I nodded, fully aware of what he meant. He was tacitly acknowledging how much other information from inside and beyond China is either censored or goes unreported. But, since the football results and the tables are not considered politically sensitive, he was able to follow Liverpool, certain now that his team would be Champions.

Football consumed this intelligent old man in a way that would have been inconceivable only a quarter of a century ago. He was not alone. There was a crowd of 70,000 inside the Workers' Stadium, and I began to study them, rather than follow the ball, as the match wore on. There is no such thing as good or bad if you don't possess the palette to differentiate between them, so the game we'd have derided as dreadful over here was applauded over there. When it was over, I walked within earshot of several groups of fans. I can't give you a translation of their debates, which were animated and sounded anguished. But from gesture and expression I understood well enough that football was no casual pastime in China. It had become central to these people's lives. The game had won them over, and there was already an addiction to it.

'I will not live to see it,' the old man wrote me to afterwards, 'but China will host a World Cup and it will also win a World Cup. One day.' China usually gets what it wants; and what it wants from football is to become a world superpower. There's a masterplan to achieve it, which is welded to political will. So, with a population of 1.4 billion, China intends to seed one pitch for every 10,000 people. Football appears compulsorily on the national curriculum. More than 20,000 'football schools' have been created, and a further 50,000 are promised. The Chinese Super League welcomes the players it attracts from Europe and South America with a ticker-tape parade of banknotes. Chinese businessmen, richer than Croesus, ambitiously buy up or into clubs abroad that are prestigious but somehow ailing slightly. And Sky beams the Chinese Super League into our living rooms.

I left China knowing it had fallen besottedly in love with football.

The coda to this story comes only four months later. I am browsing in the basement of the Strand Bookstore in New York when a dozen college students, all female, walk in and head for the shelves marked 'Soccer'. Each wears a Liverpool shirt. That night Liverpool, who had eventually lost the title to Manchester City, were facing them again in a friendly in the Yankee Stadium. I ask a few of the students what it is about Liverpool that attracts them. One, exactly like my new friend from China, is fashion-conscious, particularly enamoured with that deep shade of Merseyside red. Another has an older brother utterly devoted to The Beatles. A third regards Steven Gerrard as 'kinda cute'. In a different bookshop, on Fifth Avenue, a sales assistant registers my accent, asks whether I am a football fan and then pours out his brimming affection for Arsenal. On West 44th Street, near the Algonquin Hotel, stands a line of London Black Cabs, hired for promotional purposes by the television company that has bought the broadcasting rights to the coming Premier League season. Every cab is adorned with a different club badge. I see them over the next fortnight, selling football in Brooklyn and the Bronx as well as in Manhattan.

I think about that now, and of China, and I see Qarabag in the same light. The Azerbaijani side are pioneers too, another symbol of the game's vast reach, which is spreading, and also of the developing talent emerging because of it. The club was only formed in 1951 and the country only declared independence when the Soviet Union crashed after Gorbachev's Glasnost years. Qarabag still have a way to go, but Stamford Bridge could mark the beginning of something for them instead of the end.

It is still teeming with rain when the second half begins. The downpour forces Antonio Conte to sartorially slum it. He puts on a padded jacket and a baseball cap. Earlier in his technical area, completely unsheltered, he stood as ever in a black suit, a white shirt and a dark tie narrower than a school ruler. He looked like an undertaker with a penchant for designer labels and expensive haircuts: a tailor on Savile Row, a bootmaker on Jermyn Street, a boutique barber in Mayfair. His new clothes look incongruous on him, as though he's borrowed them from someone else's wardrobe. He is able to watch rather than conduct Chelsea now, his arms almost permanently folded tight against his chest. He sees Chelsea go further ahead in fifty-seven minutes. Cesc Fàbregas dinks in an angled cross with the outside of his right boot and César Azpilicueta breaks unmarked from a congested area, scoring with a flicked header. Not long afterwards the substitute Tiémoué Bakayoko – Conte is chopping and changing at will – sees a low shot take a heavy deflection off a defender's leg. Qarabag, spent with exhaustion, have lost shape and will and purpose, the punch of their performance gone. They forage for any consolation but don't find it.

The remaining goals are gathered as casually as windfall apples; Chelsea have their pick and don't take all that they could. Even though Michy Batshuayi is no more convincing now than earlier, he scores one and can claim half of another. What is his alone comes from a drive that isn't cleanly hit. It bobbles slightly and beats Ibrahim Šehić only because the goalkeeper is as out of position for this effort as he was for Davide Zappacosta's. The second is scruffier still. The ball is bundled in almost on the line. The last, decisive touch belongs to Qarabag's Maksim Medvedev, who wouldn't have been forced into it without the pressure Batshuayi applies on him. Qarabag are unfortunate to have found Chelsea in this mood. Near full time Willian, continuing to lead them on a dance, loses possession with a flippant back heel. Within seconds he tenaciously chases it down and wins it back. He could have shrugged and let the ball go. That he didn't is indicative of how much Chelsea want to impress even against inferiors. In the end it is six goals for them, but it could have been anything if Willian had been bloodier on occasions, less concerned about prettifying every move with excessive finesse and nearly always determined to add one more touch or the unnecessary embroidery of an extra pass.

Qarabag, still to launch a worthwhile attack of their own, sag completely in the final quarter of an hour and revive themselves only because gratitude and dependence obliges them to trot off and thank the few hundred supporters, penned behind a corner flag, who have travelled a couple of thousand miles to follow them. They take defeat with good manners.

This summer I stood beside a park as three dozen boys arrived for a football-themed birthday party. Only five of them wore the kit of clubs from England (there was one Chelsea shirt). The others flew the colours of Barcelona, Real Madrid, the Spanish national team, Juventus, both of the Milans and also Bayern Munich. This seems a minor thing, but it said something not only about the way we follow football now, but also the way in which it has changed – and will go on changing. Traditionally you supported the side to which you were either geographically closest or the one your father followed. Present day football isn't like that. It's without borders. Anyone can support whomever they like – and they don't have to physically go to a match to see them regularly either.

A luxury once enjoyed becomes a necessity and then an addiction, and so flirting with the elite will grow on Qarabag until being without it feels diminishing. It will spur them on, and perhaps one day a boy off to a birthday party will want to wear a Qarabag shirt to it. If this sounds far-fetched, imagine a stranger walking up to you in 1970. He tells you that China will not only soon find Liverpool irresistible, but will also develop a passion for English football to almost match our own. You dismiss him and it as ludicrous, so proving to yourself that the future has a habit of turning out in ways we never expect.

12 September 2017: Chelsea v Qarabag
Chelsea 6 Qarabag 0

Chelsea: Courtois, Azpilicueta (Rudiger 75), Christensen, Cahill, Zappacosta, Kante (Bakayoko 63), Fàbregas, Alonso, Willian, Batshuayi, Pedro (Hazard 58).
Subs not used: Caballero, Morata, Moses, Luiz

Qarabag: Šehić, Medvedev, Huseynov, Sadygov (Madatov 70), Rzezniczak, Garayev (Diniyev 70), Henrique (Elyounoussi 77), Michel, Almedia, Guerrier, Ndlovu.
Subs not used: Kanitbolotskiy, Amirgullyer, Ismaylov, Yunuszada

SCORERS

Chelsea: Pedro 5, Zappacosta 30, Azpilicueta 57, Bakayoko 71, Batshuayi 76, Medvedev 82 og

BOOKED

Chelsea: Cahill

Referee: A. Sidiropoulos
Attendance: 41,150

4

THIS SIDE OF PARADISE

23 September: Burnley v Huddersfield Town, Turf Moor, Premier League

It was a late spring morning and the road-sweepers were still in business, tidying up the last remnants of the revelry. The day earlier Huddersfield had returned home from Wembley after beating Reading, their Championship rivals. It was one of those stale, timid and nervy play-off finals that really ought to have skipped the grind of the match and gone straight to the penalty shoot-out, thereby saving everyone the long, sleepy drone of the preliminaries before the exciting bit began. The fear of making even a minor mistake, and the consequences of it, had paralysed the game, which was grim and goalless until the roulette began. No one in Huddersfield cared a jot about that afterwards, but the rest of us had half a thought about how we might get at least two hours of our lives back when the time came to haggle with the Grim Reaper.

Huddersfield became the forty-ninth club to reach the Premier League, an unlikely return to the top tier for the first time in almost half a century. What followed was the obligatory open-topped bus ride, a parade amid a flurry of flags. The bus carried the town's new heroes slowly to St George's Square, where awaiting them was a makeshift stage that faced the Corinthian columns and colonnaded wings of the town's railway station, which is an architectural picture. The poet John Betjeman, admiring the mellow gold stone and the clean lines of these low buildings, declared the whole plot 'so lovely' that he could have 'lived there happily'. On that warm evening it looked as though all of Huddersfield was packed inside St George's Square to serenade the side. The crowd was so broad and so deep that I imagined elsewhere row-upon-row of homes silent and unlit, the roads empty and the pubs with no one in them.

To go there in the aftermath of all that was like arriving far too late at a party. The guests had gone and I had to pick my way through the disarray, only the detritus and the dregs of the night before remaining. Outside the entrance to the station, the statue of Harold Wilson, the local boy who became prime minister, was dressed up in a couple of scraggly blue and white scarves. One was draped across his shoulders. The other was wrapped around his bronze neck. Trapped forever now in brisk mid-step, his face turned appropriately to the left, Wilson looked as though he could be hurrying off to the John Smith's Stadium, afraid of missing an early goal.

A few strips of plastic bunting sagged, like a row of flags at half-mast, between two lamp posts. A newspaper bill, advertising a souvenir supplement of the club's triumph, was ragged, as though the news it contained was already months old. The corners of the paper had curled and the sun had bleached some of the colour out of it. Blue and white confetti clogged the gutters. There were even a few burst balloons, trodden and dirty underfoot.

I trekked up and down the main thoroughfares for a while, gazing at the dull hegemony of chain stores. I was soon aware that, with St George's Square behind me, there was nothing much to distinguish Huddersfield from most places of the same size. Like almost every-where else in the north, the town was clearly a little on its uppers. TO LET signs appeared regularly, making a plea for attention. Some properties were shells, gutted bare behind big front windows. 'It's all pound shops, betting shops and tattoo parlours,' complained an elderly man, a cigarette whittled almost to ash between his fingers and his shirtsleeves rolled to his elbows. He had a large, overfed dog of indeterminate breed on a short leather lead. He and the dog didn't so much walk as waddle, as though every pavement was a 1.6 gradient. By now I had taken a series of wrong turnings, going too far out and getting lost, discovering only the backs of high houses and derelict garaging. In one of those damned fool moments, which was instantly regretted, I stopped him, asked for directions and also slipped in an innocuous question about Huddersfield and the Premier League. I had found what I suppose was the only grumpy soul completely immune to the headiness of the week. He couldn't understand 'what fuss was 'bout,' he said. He didn't want what the town was about to receive. 'Bloody football,' he said, more than once. 'Makes sane people go daft'. The dog lay down wearily and shut his eyes; it had clearly heard the tirade before. You can only make your excuses politely and leave. So I did, watching him flick the butt of his cigarette into the road, light another and then rouse the dog with a tug.

I got back into the heart of the town and came across someone more congenial. He was a supporter in a retro Huddersfield shirt. The round, high collar of it was almost as wide and as white as a vicar's. He was slim and well-tanned, his shiny black hair slicked back. I guessed he was too young by twenty-five years at least to have seen the side that last wore a shirt like his own. He was, however, waiting for his father, who soon arrived in a flat felt cap, the peak so low that the shadow it cast across his eyes looked like a mask. During the late 1960s and the early 1970s, Huddersfield played snakes and ladders in the extreme. The fat of promotion into the old First Division was followed by the famine of three quick relegations into the oblivion of the old Fourth. I remember that team. The manager, Ian Greaves, benignly gruff with hair like compressed wire wool and a face of manifold creases. The star-turn, Frank Worthington, always rakishly flamboyant in appearance and approach, like the footballing Elvis he aspired to be. The centre forward, Alan Gowling, so spindle-limbed that he looked as though a breeze would blow him over the Pennines. The father, a slip of boy then, remembered the town as transformed, initially made to feel 'much prouder' about itself because of Huddersfield's success and left sore and bruised and almost worthless after it ended. 'But that was nothing compared with this,' he says. 'We are somebody now, for however long it lasts'. The father and son had gone to Wembley and got splendidly drunk on the way home. The hangover was worth it – even though, the father admitted, his skull reverberated early next morning as though the Grimethorpe Colliery Band were performing the William Tell Overture inside it. There was, I thought, already a restlessness in them for the new season to start and also, with the celebrations over, a small dread of what it could bring. 'What if we can't hack it, like?' asked the son. The father shook his head. 'We'll do enough,' he said before attaching a few qualifying ifs to the prediction, covering himself against the possibility of ridicule later on. 'If we sign a player or two . . . If we get ourselves organised . . . If the manager doesn't bugger off.'

There was already a photograph of the manager, David Wagner, taped crudely to a wall inside the Wetherspoon's pub, The Lord Wilson. Someone had snipped it out of a newspaper and then displayed it beside half a dozen others, which were action shots of the match. Wagner, immaculate in black, was gripping the play-off trophy. Huddersfield's ribbons tumbled from its tall, wide handles. With his metal-framed spectacles and his beard flecked with grey, Wagner looked bookish as well as distinguished. He could have passed for a professor of something; possibly of philosophy. Below the picture, at a table cluttered with empty pint pots and the wet rings of earlier ones, sat five fans, each in his early twenties. One of them had been to a tattooist. Huddersfield's badge had been inked on to the top of his arse at a discount price. No one believed the recipient when he claimed, time and again, that the gesture was inspired while under the influence of euphoria rather than a gallon of ale. His flesh was still blotched and smarting, apparently. He stood up, offering to drop his ripped jeans to prove it. A friend told him to sit down, earning all our gratitude. I heard them discuss those places, like previously unexplored continents, where the soon-to-be-published fixtures would send Huddersfield. They planned to go together to Stamford Bridge, The Emirates Stadium and back to Wembley, which was temporarily Tottenham's. The idea was to make a long weekend of it. To see some sights. To export some northern hospitality to the capital – if a pub could be found where bitter at £4.20 a pint didn't taste 'like a donkey's piss'. It was going to be an awfully big adventure, costly but worthwhile. None of the men was blinkered. As one of them pointed out, as soberly as he could in the circumstances, Barnsley had once blitzed into the Premier League and then blitzed out of it again even before finding a peg on which to hang their hat. If Huddersfield became the wonders of one season too, those who followed them might as well squeeze out of it whatever was going. The bookmakers had marked Huddersfield for a quick death. The odds, calculated even before their Wembley lap of honour was half-done, made them favourites to go down. 'We could be back at Preston before we know it,' he snapped, being pragmatic rather than pessimistic. He took a massive swallow of beer, as though preferring not to think black thoughts of another Championship Saturday at Deepdale. I sympathised with the safe logic of his thinking – the Premier League could easily turn out to be too brief a treat for him – and I also understood perfectly his need to see the bright lights in case relegation switched them off too soon.

I had decided already which of Huddersfield's games was most important to me. I was going to Burnley, the junction where past and present meet.

If you've never been here, but have seen Burnley's ground in old photographs – published either in a newspaper or in one of those hardback annuals published in the 1950s and 1960s – the landscape will still seem familiar. Whatever alterations have been made to Turf Moor, it and the nearby streets look fundamentally the same. With my back to the Leeds–Liverpool Canal, I walk past a jam of convenience stores and takeaways, a church with attractive finials and a couple of pubs and then a solid block of tall Victorian architecture with small neat pediments and high windows, the plain beauty of it easy to miss from the pavement. Turf Moor lies in a minor dip. Behind it is a rise of trees and also rows of scattered rooftops. It is a lovely autumn Saturday and some of those trees are turning red-orange, the same colour as hot coal. I see them before I get my first glimpse of the long, grey edge of the North Stand and a pair of floodlights, their thinness making them look immensely tall.

Turf Moor adjoins Burnley Cricket Club, and the back of one of the stands has been given a skim of concrete, making it the world's biggest sightscreen for a batsman. I stand on the outfield, taking in the air, which has an Alpine sharpness to it, and I listen to the tannoy from the ground. The music is faint, the announcements inaudible.

What looked likely in the summer to be a mid-to-low table scrap is actually sixth versus seventh. Huddersfield, joint top after two matches, are now below Tottenham on goal difference. Burnley are above Liverpool and also Arsenal. The two teams have lost only one match apiece. David Wagner, unbeaten in August, was named as the manager of that month. He feigned humility and also some surprise at the honour because it would have been undignified to say the four-word sentence that is the most satisfying in the English language. 'I told you so.' In one week, building up to the season, Huddersfield accumulated eight players and Wagner broke the club's record transfer fee six times, including £12m spent on Steve Mounié (currently injured) from Montpellier. He got Huddersfield in trim shape and made them Premier League-ready, but no one noticed even during that flurry of signings, so quietly were his preparations completed. It's a compliment to Burnley that Huddersfield under Wagner are striving to become exactly like them, a side everyone believes is too resourceful to go down.

Few matches nowadays are branded as typically English, which used to be the polite way of saying that there was more grunt than guile in them. The 'English Match' was stereotyped, always broken down as a slog of tough tackling and physical endurance on muddy pitches, containing few chances, a lot of long high balls and little that was lacy or la-di-da. The muddy pitches have been replaced with lawns on which you could play a half decent game of bowls. And red-meat muscularity will only get a team so far unless it is supplemented, rather than completely subjugated, with a lightness of touch and the sort of skill that makes you sit up straighter in amazed admiration of it. What is more, how can games be considered typically 'English' any longer when the teams playing in them are so cosmopolitan, a cross-section of the world?

But watching today immediately drags me back a few decades. The game has hardly got going before there is a crunching coming together, close to the far touchline, between Burnley's Matt Lowton and Huddersfield's Abdelhamid Sabiri. Sabiri tramples on the top of Lowton's foot, a rotten tackle that could have been a red card but is only a yellow. Within a minute, Sabiri is on the floor himself – another lunge, another booking – after Jack Cork sends him sliding, perhaps in retribution. For both Huddersfield and Burnley the game offers the chance to bank early points, which could be worth double much later on. The raw tackling, plus the odd body-check and the occasional stray elbow, are indicative of that, but also of something pugilistic in which the protagonists soak up the pain of every blow and barely show it. This is a toe-to-toe affair. Burnley are doing most of the slugging while Huddersfield, allowing the punches to come on to them, rely on ring-craft to avoid being hit. You realise how well Wagner has done his work. Huddersfield are ordered, organised and unflustered, comfortable in their boss's gegenpress formation.

Burnley, however, should take the lead on twenty-three minutes; Huddersfield are caught flat-footed by the old one-two – passes exchanged between Scott Arfield and Stephen Ward – and then a cross, exquisitely whipped in first time by Ward from the left. At Wembley last May, Christopher Schindler punched in the winning penalty to take Huddersfield into the Premier League, a defender doing a striker's job because he felt it was 'my responsibility'. So far Schindler has been immaculate, reading every attack. This time, as the speed of everything catches him out, he is adrift and struggling. Chris Wood sneaks ahead of him. The chance, from 7 yards, is shouting at him and Wood shapes to reply to it, but in his eagerness he makes an infinitesimal misjudgement. He leaps half a second too early and can't defy gravity to hang there long enough. The ball gets only a glancing touch, skidding off his forehead and beyond the post. Huddersfield are off the hook. Through action and expression, Wood, signed for £15m from Leeds United before the transfer deadline, accepts he is to blame. He gurns his features into a scream of silent anguish.

Near the half hour you would bet on Wood to make amends for his miss. Ward is 5 yards inside the box. Wood is free, peeling away towards the back post. You see the goal: a simple cross, a simple, side-footed finish, the goalkeeper unable to reach the effort but diving for the sake of it. Wood must see all this too. Schindler is a yard and a half behind him. There's no possibility of the German gaining enough ground to cut the ball off – until, of course, he does. He makes a dashing diagonal run and hurls himself at it. Schindler looks like someone performing an airborne kung fu kick in a martial arts movie. He clears the cross over his left shoulder with his right foot. Wood is off the floor too, already in position with his boot raised. He watches the clearance soar off into midfield and looks around him like someone who can't believe a pickpocket has just filched his wallet; he never felt a thing.

Wood's chances aside, this is the sort of incoherent game, full of lumps and bumps, that only the connoisseur of the mundanely old fashioned will enjoy. Nothing more than the palpable grittiness of it sustains the interest. I am lost in it, glad to be here no matter how many goals are rattling in somewhere else.

Occasionally the novelist Arnold Bennett dropped football into his fiction, focusing always on the matches he remembered watching in his birthplace, The Potteries. A passage from *The Matador of the Five Towns* continues to be anthologised because, even though the scene Bennett describes has changed considerably, the absolute essence of what it is like to stand in a crowd and look around you has not. Anyone reading it can't fail to summon some experience of their own. Bennett writes: 'Around the field was a wider border of infinitesimal hats and pale faces, rising in tiers, and beyond this border, fences, hoardings, chimneys, furnaces, gasometers, telegraph poles, houses . . .'

There are no furnaces and no gasometers at Turf Moor, but there are tall brick chimneys in the town and also on the outskirts of it, and the V-shaped gaps at either end of the North Stand give you another view of the roofs and the trees that you see on your way in. The filmiest of mists is drifting across them and so are a few swollen clouds, which are beginning to smother the light a little. Environment will always impact on the atmosphere, and it does so powerfully here. It feels intrinsically northern. I am in the belly of the Bob Lord Stand, sitting on the sort of wooden tip-up seat that I thought was a relic, long gone. The odd slender post obstructs the view, something else I thought long gone. I am not complaining. I picked Burnley v Huddersfield because the match means more than it seems. On paper the fixture belongs to another age, over well before the Premier League was a glint in anyone's rapacious eye and the clubs and Rupert Murdoch became joined in matrimony. It reminds me of the kind of football I never saw, but was told constantly about by my father, my grandfather and, after I got to know them, even some of the players who took part in it, earning a pittance in front of full houses. There were steel toe-capped boots and a laced ball. There were long shorts and jerseys with collars you could fold up. There were rattles and rosettes in the crowd. There were few seats and a mountain range of terracing. And, if you wanted to see the highlights of the match on the screen, you had to buy a threepenny cinema seat and wait for a black and white newsreel, the commentary in an upbeat and plummy Mr Cholmondley-Warner voice, the vowels strangulated.

Outside Turf Moor, nailed to the walls, are photographs on canvas, shaped like enormous cigarette cards. Each celebrates a Burnley player of the past, history commingling with modernity. One of the photographs, a colourised print, shows Jimmy McIlroy, the Northern Ireland inside forward and the organising brain of the Burnley side that became English League Champions in 1960. The stand behind the goal, which Burnley's supporters occupy, is named after McIlroy, the undisputed greatest of the club's greats. I knew someone who had been a youth player at Burnley when McIlroy was in his prime. He told me that to see McIlroy simply walk around the town was to appreciate what being a deity must be like. Out for a stroll, McIlroy would be followed, his worshippers respectfully a step or two behind him. He would be applauded into and out of shops. Women would queue to plant a kiss on his handsome face. Sometimes my friend was designated to be McIlroy's boot-cleaner. He would spend an hour on them, rubbing dubbin into the leather to preserve it and then heaping on the polish with a soft brush, buffing everything up to a silver shine. The white laces would be laundered and then ironed. At the end of the week McIlroy would toss him a shilling as a thank you. 'What you need to know about McIlroy,' he used to say, 'was that he could send a low pass through a ginnel from 50 yards without touching the sidewalls.' Johan Cruyff was adamant that 'you play football with your head . . . if you don't use your head, using your feet won't be sufficient.' McIlroy was like that. He was an erudite player, delivering the right pass at the right time, which frequently only he recognised.

On the way in I had stood beside McIlroy's photograph and thought of my friend's adoration of him. McIlroy's arms were folded and his hair was gorgeously waved, as though held in place by a whole tub of Brylcreem. I've only ever seen a few snatches of film of him. In them he zips about, always pushing the ball smoothly forward and catching up with his own pass almost as soon as the receiver has controlled it, impatient for possession to come back to him. With half time nearly here and no sign of a goal for Burnley, who continue to scuffle along, I think about how fantastic it would be if McIlroy could defy reality, stepping out of that photograph and on to the pitch in those big, heavy boots that my friend has tenderly scrubbed for him. You'd hear the firm thump-thump of his studs on the concrete and then see him on the touchline, an unblemished and debonair 25-year-old again. He'd come on, pull down the ball immediately, look up and arrow it towards Wood, who is starving for the morsel of a half-decent pass.

If only . . .

The second half mirrors the first. There is something in Huddersfield that will not bend; and Burnley, without Jimmy McIlroy or anyone remotely comparable to him, can neither open them up nor summon enough clout to pulverise them. Jonas Lössl, Huddersfield's goal-keeper, has hardly sweated to reach any shot. Every save he's made has been comfortably regulation, the ball always clutched against his stomach or chest after a short sidestep. On the touchline Sean Dyche, Burnley's manager, looks increasingly agitated. He's stripped off his jacket, like someone preparing for a stretch of heavy lifting, and is pacing around in the cold in his white shirtsleeves. Dyche has a growly voice – it sounds like a half-ton of gravel sliding out of a plastic bag – and occasionally you hear it when he shouts over to the far side of the pitch. I remember him as a teenager at Nottingham Forest. His hair, shaved to the skull now, was abundant then, a flame-red ginger. He's assertive and confident as a boss, but I always see him coming down the main corridor at the City Ground, still in his training kit and bouncing a ball on the carpet-tiled floor until he spotted Brian Clough through the double doors ahead of him. Clough was leaning against a wall. Dyche stiffened, cradled the ball tightly in his arms, the way a mother might hold a new baby so as not to drop it, and walked past silently, his head bowed and his eyes shyly lowered. No sign was made. No word was spoken. Clough gave him a stare, which Dyche never saw, that could have cracked ice. He had a dislike of anyone bouncing a ball near his office, and so I waited for the acid one-liner that would cut Dyche down. Clough, as capricious as ever, merely shook his head very, very slowly.

Dyche is shaking his head a lot at the moment too. He is also frown-ing fiercely. Burnley aren't supporting Chris Wood, his nudges and flicks going anodynely into unfilled space behind him, and aren't pushing on generally either. I spend ten minutes watching only Wood, tracking his hikes up and down the pitch, his arms held high as he runs and his head tilted back as though he is trying to look over the top of something. Wood is no quicksilver, but he isn't sluggish and has wide, burly shoulders on a 6 foot 3 inch frame. He puts the miles in, and he puts the effort in too, never getting much in return. He looks a nimbler, cleverer version of West Ham's Andy Carroll. Another comparison nags nebulously at me until, the image finally settling in my mind, I pin down who Wood really reminds me of. I am still preoccupied with Arnold Bennett.

In the film version of Bennett's *The Card*, there is a scene in which the eponymous entrepreneur goes to watch his local team called Bursley. The rain is coming down in tin buckets and he sits in the leaking, creaky wooden stand with a newspaper folded across his head as a makeshift hat. Bursley lose disastrously, their ramshackle ground three quarters empty. The score, 15–0, is chalked on to a board. An extraordinary general meeting is called the following week to put the club out of its misery. The Card, played by Alec Guinness, arrives wearing a hooped scarf longer than an anaconda. He goes from floor to stage, having persuaded the meeting to allow him to say 'a few words'. What Bursley need, judging from their performances, is a completely new team, especially a defence, but what The Card proposes is a centre forward – someone to get them 'winning again', he says. He proposes one name, a player called Callear, whom bigger clubs are trailing because of his size and his scoring record. The chairman mocks the suggestion contemptuously and then patronises him, insisting – and bear in mind the book is set in the early 20th century – that 'steam engines and the King himself' couldn't drag Callear to Bursley. Unbeknown to him, but suspected by us, Callear has all along been on the back row among the audience, waiting for The Card to produce him like a trick pulled unexpectedly out of a magician's top hat. He is bought and paid for too. The scene ends, fading into another that begins with a close-up of the poster advertising the coming of Callear. The sun is out, the terraces are congested and he – broad, strong, unstoppable – is steaming towards goal like a bull with a ball. He scores, and Bursley win 15–0. Swap Burnley for Bursley and Wood becomes Callear, the club record signing on whom so much, if not everything, depends. Wood scored on his debut, against Tottenham, and scored again in his next match, against Crystal Palace. But a third

Premier League goal always looks out of reach here, however grimly and relentlessly he chases it.

Huddersfield, particularly through Tom Ince, pose more danger than Wood can muster alone. In the seventy-second minute, a draw looking inevitable, Burnley are back-pedalling unheroically, caught unawares by the clarity of purpose and precision of an attack that allows Huddersfield to claim the home box as their own territory. Four passes and ten seconds is all it takes to get them the length of the field and land there, a back-heel from Laurent Depoitre cleaving Burnley open. The ball comes to the substitute Rajiv van La Parra. He has two choices. He can go on alone or thread a cross in front of the goal, where someone will surely score. Van La Parra takes a third choice, unforeseen and shameful. He dives. He goes over theatrically, like someone snagged by a trip wire. He tries to convince the referee that Matt Lowton, the closest defender, has slyly upended him. We brand such an act as simulation or as gamesmanship, relying on a pair of fancy but weak euphemisms because we cravenly recoil from the use of the word 'cheating'. Van La Parra has unquestionably cheated, a display of idiocy that is pitiable from every viewpoint. After you stop wondering what possessed him to dive in the first place, you then ponder whether he rehearses his stumbling secretly somewhere – in his back garden or the local park during darkness, perhaps. If so, he needs to work far harder at it. The Dutchman's sprawl was as obvious as a silent comedian's pratfall. The con, blatant and pathetic, makes him look worse than a buffoon. Burnley's defenders – especially Lowton – crowd over him with a sneer, despising what he's done and piling on the guilt and humiliation for it. The referee is no gullible sop. Perfectly positioned to see the whole thing, he produces a yellow card. He waves it with van La Parra still on his slim backside. He deserves to be sent off; for what just happened is an affront to the dignity of the game, and van La Parra ought to publicly apologise for it. The manager ought to run on to the pitch, take the player by the scruff of his collar and frog-march him back to the bench. Not only for his dive – criminal enough – but also for spurning the chance to take or fashion a goal.

The best of goalless games can magnetise a crowd. Think back seventeen years to Holland against Italy in the European Championship semi-finals. Think back thirteen years to Barcelona against Celtic in a Champions League qualifier. And think back only three weeks when Luxembourg improbably took a point in a World Cup qualifier against a French team, the cumulative worth of which was over £500m. Turf Moor today isn't in that category – the match peters out – but for Huddersfield, who have now claimed four clean sheets, a season of wide horizons still seems to lie ahead. The proviso is that David Wagner is always mindful of 1974 and Carlisle, who started so well after promotion – soon cock-a-hoop leaders – but who then sank endlessly into the doldrums and were relegated eight months later. And Burnley? They just need to be more forceful and a little less pusil-lanimous next time.

Dusk is crowding in fast, the narrow streets beginning to be packed with shadows. I walk along them, thinking how much of a contradiction it is that Burnley and Huddersfield belong to the Premier League, which was not conceived for the likes of them. It was originally meant as an Eden for big city clubs who were already relatively rich but wanted to be richer still. Those who had most to gain also had most to say about the benefits of creating it and pushed hardest for them. Greed got disguised as altruism, ambition as good-for-the-game benevolence and selfishness as generosity of spirit. The Premier League promised a trickle-down economy, one of those voodoo fiscal miracles in which some pennies from the pounds generated at the very top – through the caboodle of television, marketing, sponsor-ships and the rest – would waterfall into the pockets of the less well off. The package was sold well, but made sense only if you were prepared to accept as a consequence that some would always be more equal than others.

The 1980s hadn't been good for football, which made the 1990s ripe for revolution. The constitution of the Football League had meant that the solidarity of clubs in the old Second, Third and Fourth Divisions could always block the manoeuvrings of the old First. The First Division clubs got one and a half votes each. The rest got a vote apiece, more than enough for mathematical superiority without recourse to a re-count – even if the odd one among them went rogue.

I always cringe at the story of the First Division's early proposal to print names as well as numbers on the back of shirts. It saw the idea as a sure-fire winner. The most impecunious of the lower league clubs did not. Obliged then to recycle match balls to save cash, they complained that the extra expense would be too much for them. All employed 'laundry ladies' only for a few hours every week to wash and sew kit. The First Division stomped off in high dudgeon and in their strop failed to understand not only why the poor were poor in the first place, but also blamed and resented them for their plight. It was the football equivalent of the French aristocracy being unable to comprehend why the peasants couldn't eat cake – and not much caring either.

And now the Premier League is twenty-five years old. A whole generation has grown up knowing nothing else but it. The clubs on the very bottom rung can afford to stick names on to their shirts these days, but some aren't always financially buoyant and a few aren't necessarily solvent. The gap between them and the wealthy widens another thousand miles every season. Too little of what the Premier League earns is distributed lower down; and even what is seems to be handed over grudgingly, resentfully. Now there are even proposals that the 'Big Six' ought to receive a larger share of the money from overseas broadcast rights. Still, and despite this, the Burnleys and the Huddersfields rise somehow and prosper. The Premier League ought to be grateful for that; paradise would lack an earthy romance without them.

23 September 2017: Burnley v Huddersfield Town
Burnley 0 Huddersfield Town 0

Burnley: Pope, Lowton, Tarkowski, Mee, Ward, Arfield (Gudmundsson 77), Cork, Defour, Brady, Hendrick (Barnes 74), Wood.
Subs not used: Legzdins, Vokes, Westwood, Long, Bardsley

Huddersfield: Lossl, Smith, Zanka, Schindler, Lowe, Hogg, (Pilling 80), Mooy, Kachunga (Hadergjonaj 88), Sabiri (Van La Parra 63), Ince, Depoitre.
Subs not used: Malone, Whitehead, Green, Hefele

BOOKED

Burnley: Arfield, Cork, Tarkowski
Huddersfield: Sabiri, van La Parra

Referee: C. Kavanagh
Attendance: 20,759

WHAT THERE IS TO SAY WE HAVE SAID

5 October: England v Slovenia, World Cup qualifier, Group F, Wembley

A bookmaker on Wembley High Road has decorated the front window of his shop with a life-sized cardboard cut-out of Harry Kane. Kane is, appropriately enough, wearing a blood red shirt, the colour of the bullfighter's cape. It evokes 1966, the date no one can ever forget in England because we're still rattling on about it half a century on, and doing so chiefly as a comfort. In the photograph Kane's mouth is agape, accentuating the drop of that long, flat jaw. He is pointing into the distance, his right index finger aloft for emphasis, as though about to signal a charge. Draped behind him is a poster, the slogan arrogantly presumptuous about the outcome of tonight's penultimate World Cup qualifier. It declares, well before the news is official, that England are: 'Storming to Russia'. If so, someone needs to pick up the cut-out of Kane and drop it in the other direction. The new captain, appointed on a trial basis this week, is marching his country the wrong way. The store-front of the bookmakers' faces south, which means Kane is heading due west, towards the Atlantic, rather than east, towards Moscow, where the Finals begin 252 days from now.

This is a minor thing and only the most pernickety kind of pendant would notice, let alone care, but it seems to sum up how England have navigated through Group F. It's been a strange odyssey for them and us. What ostensibly looks like a stroll to the summit – a total of twenty-points from eight unbeaten matches – has, in fact, often been a laborious trek. There have been anguished missteps, some wrong turns and a few about-turns too. Little of this has been worth watching. Even against slight opposition, some of it stuck on outer edges of the Fifa rankings, England have been merely efficient rather than commanding, their successes essentially eked out and each characterised by grim forbearance instead of the flamboyance we had hoped for. Supporters have survived so far on a diet of the thinnest gruel, which is why expectations for next summer are low enough to be almost subterranean. England, under Gareth Southgate, are 30–1 to win the World Cup. Even those odds flatter their chances, but just possibly going to Russia as inferiors rather than equals – taking the pressure off, for once – will be liberating and cathartic. It's an optimistic leap of judgement to suggest that as a scenario, but in hard times you clutch at whatever mercies are closest to hand.

England exasperate us almost perpetually. For too long we have cheerfully expected the worst from them, which is not necessarily a defeat. The worst is usually a level of performance hovering between listlessly workmanlike and scruffily undistinguished. Seldom does anything stand-out or sharply defined occur – an incandescent goal, a move of thirty-one passes, a save of phenomenal agility – that compels you to remember the game once it has finished; and a few of them fairly recently have stunk so badly that you wondered why you bothered to be there at all. You go back through self-delusion, always thinking that the next match will be the one that finishes 5–4, such as the Stanley Matthews-inspired defeat of Czechoslovakia on a winter's afternoon at White Hart Lane in 1937 . . . or that someone will thump in all five goals, the way Malcolm Macdonald did against Cyprus in 1975 . . . or that there will be another earthquake in Munich, where in 2001 England won 5–1 because of Michael Owen's hat-trick.

You wait for the game, which the law of averages surely must serve up eventually, that will arrive when you least expect it and then stay with you for the rest of your life.

Perhaps tonight England, needing only to win to make results elsewhere irrelevant to them, will dance a reel for us at last. Perhaps Kane will claim himself a basketful of goals like Macdonald or Owen. Perhaps someone else will play the exhibition role that Matthews once did.

*   *   *

The writer Arthur Koestler declared: 'There is nationalism and then there is football nationalism, which is more deeply felt'. You wouldn't think so tonight. The upper tier of the stand directly opposite the tunnel is shut. Below and around me are empty seats as conspicuous as missing teeth in a smile. It isn't much of a congregation to celebrate imminent qualification. The paltry size of the crowd, which I calculate as below 60,000, is both a sign of our lack of belief in England and our loss of patience with them.

Seldom these days do their games generate an exquisite sense of anticipation unless the opposition, such as Brazil or Germany, bring it with them. No one is clawing down the doors to see Slovenia. Their team comprises relatively unknown figures – Rotman, Mevlja, Struna – from relatively unfashionable clubs: Göztepe, Zenit St Petersburg, Palermo. The goalkeeper Jan Oblak, who replaced Thibaut Courtois at Atlético Madrid, is nonetheless outstanding. At twenty-four years old, still in his goalkeeping infancy, he has made the last two Uefa Champions League Squads of the Season. The other pivotal figure is the playmaker Josip Iličić of Atalanta, always a vivid presence in determining the flow, the rhythm and the variety of their attacks. Oblak and Iličić would both get into the England side – especially here and especially now. Five weeks ago Gareth Southgate saw his players take nearly an hour to score against Malta, a country who win about as often as the northern hemisphere witnesses a full eclipse. England are no hot ticket, and the indifference towards them, which always makes forthcoming internationals seem like a chore, is their own fault.

Mind you, this disenchantment is far from a recent thing. Shortly before the 1990 World Cup in Italy, I watched them at the old Wembley against Czechoslovakia. It was early spring and England, then under Bobby Robson, were already unbeaten in fifteen matches, including a win over Brazil. Paul Gascoigne, the virtuoso bobby-dazzler, colourfully dominated and then thoroughly crushed the Czechs, weaving away to create the opening three goals and scoring the fourth himself in the last minute. In hindsight that England side, which won 4–2, had an 'Et in Arcadia' glow about it. Before long Gascoigne, weeping into his shirt, was on the cover even of *The London Review of Books*. The literary magazine *Granta* compared him to Milton's Samson Agonistes. As well as Gascoigne, guaranteeing his place in the Finals only after that illuminating show, there was Shilton, Pearce, Walker, Butcher and Lineker too. Their performances deserved a thank you from the paying customer, but I remember that the ground was a cavernous hole of silence that evening. If you coughed, the echo ran around the stands and came back to you distinctly. One end was completely naked of fans, no one in it except a bunch of wandering stewards in fluorescent jackets. Fewer than 21,500 had come through the gate.

This was more than two months before England surprised even themselves, reaching the semi-finals in Italy, and also more than two years prior to the Premier League's arrival, turning the English game into a flashy business, almost unrecognisable from what had gone before. But if Robson's England couldn't pack them in, you can only ask how Southgate's ever can or will.

Nothing, early on, dispels the dread sense that being here only proves our willingness to inflict suffering on ourselves voluntarily. No one without a ticket will question their decision to stay away.

Under a big harvest moon, England are a knot of nerves. It's as if the players have just come together, meeting on a mass blind date, and are awkward in one another's company. Nobody wants to plunge right in; and nobody – except for Harry Kane and Marcus Rashford – knows what to do or quite where to go. Unforced errors mount up. Passes go astray under minimal duress. The ball slips beneath the studs of Alex Oxlade-Chamberlain. Raheem Sterling dashes in circles, like a cat spinning after its own tail. There is the odd, long-range pop at goal that Jan Oblak swallows up or allows to skate by him. England, shooting from anywhere, are like those artists who chuck paint at a canvas and hope something worthwhile comes of it.

Everything is done so dreadfully slowly too, the midfield moving like somnambulists. England, it seems, always need a second and a half longer than Slovenia are ever willing to give them. In particular Jordan Henderson is agonising over every pass, like a chess player who can't decide where to crucially deploy a bishop. Hesitancy becomes timidity, and England, who ought to be enjoying themselves, seem downcast and somewhat afraid in case a mistake is made and becomes irrecoverable. Slovenia should even have a penalty. Josip Iličić – who else? – latches on to a diagonal pass and scoots unchallenged towards goal. The ball has a little too much on it – Iličić is already obliged to go wide – and Joe Hart answers the false alarm, rashly coming out when instinct ought to have told him to stay back. His lunging slide takes him unstoppably into Iličić, his left hand catching the Sloven's right boot almost on the by-line. Neither the referee nor his assistant notice the foul. The incident instantly becomes an advertisement for the introduction of VAR.

Emboldened by that injustice, Iličić comes close to revenge. When a counter-attack pushes England into a dishevelled retreat, the centre halves well split, he calmly accepts possession not far from the angle of the box. It's now you see in close up the kind of artist Iličić can be. Oxlade-Chamberlain, worth £40m in the transfer market and believed to earn £120,000 per week, would have snatched the opening too eagerly. Sterling would have taken the ball on himself and got lost in a maze of his own making. Iličić pauses. He stops and looks around him rather grandly, like someone about to descend a gilt staircase. He sees Roman Bezjak filling the gap England's stretched defence has helpfully left him. Still Iličić waits. The chip finally drifts in off his instep, the ball like an embossed invitation. The unmarked Bezjak, 7 yards out, has only to side-foot the cross in – and a light caress will be enough to do it. He makes a lummox of himself instead, faffing about and flailing at it, dangling his leg in the right direction but misreading the angle and his approach. As the chance escapes, bouncing beyond the far post, Iličić's head sags abruptly towards his chest.

We suppose this scare will wake England up. We wait for them to start passing the ball around on a silvery thread. Some hope. Apart from Rashford, now the only piece of English life in this dead display, there is no get-up-and-go and no ingenuity either. What we see, instead of flair, is another doleful plod of caution and compromise. Even Kane, scorer of fourteen goals in his last nine matches, hasn't got up his usual head of steam, but continues to puff away in an effort to achieve it. He is trying to lead.

Wembley seems to have a deadening effect on England. It's as if the stadium entombs them. The atmosphere, apart from the percussive, boring belt of a drum, is flat, desperate, grave. You think of the big club grounds that would be more conducive to a tie like this – Anfield or Old Trafford in particular – and find it absurd that England aren't in one of them. The national team ought not to be exclusive to the capital anyway. It should be like a repertory troupe on the road, sent out to perform provincially occasionally rather than penned in a corner of London that can only half-fill the house. When Wembley was being knocked down and rebuilt, England toured out of necessity and found the North and the Midlands grateful to see them. There was a frisson there; the crowds a part of – not apart from – the match. The wins chalked up on their travels were a collaborative effort, the fans galvanising the team and vice-versa. Tonight the mood is so low-key that, as half time approaches, the crowd can only manage a pipsqueak chant of 'Eng-er-land'. It is shouted more out of duty than from enthusiasm.

The loudest cheer of the first half came when one face was flashed up on the wide screens stuck at either end of the stadium. From a prized seat Sir Bobby Charlton, dressed in a navy suit, white shirt and royal blue tie, stared impassively at the game through rimless spectacles. He will be eighty next week. When Charlton goes anywhere, smiling courteously at strangers and signing umpteen autographs on measly scraps of paper, what you witness is not merely his popularity but his veneration. Had he chosen to make a fanfare entrance, promenading from the bottom of Wembley Way, you know that the crowd would have parted for him. He could have walked as though a red carpet, rather than grey concrete, was beneath the two feet that had once mesmerised whoever saw him play. It is a life lesson to study those who are suddenly surprised by Charlton's presence and then approach his slight, always immaculate figure. To see it was to understand what hero-worship is and what it means. You notice, behind the shy defer-ence, the sincerity of affection for him, the gratitude towards him and even the slight bewilderment that he is there, actually human.

It can be difficult to make virtuous people interesting, but Charlton is an exception because so much – good, bad, tragic – has happened to him; and the older he gets, the more Charlton is idolised even by those who are aware of what he did only from the familiar film clips of his career. That flop of loose hair. The speed of the body as it cut across midfield. Those 30-yard shots like the explosion of diamond bombs.

Charlton has been festooned with honours, the latest of them bestowed only days ago. A pitch was named after him at the Football Association's training headquarters at St George's Park at Burton. Gareth Southgate also invited Charlton to speak to his squad. This speech was moving in its modesty and simplicity. He asked them to have 'another go' at winning a World Cup, thus giving him what would be 'one of the greatest memories' of his life, he said. There was a photograph of Charlton stretching out a hand towards Harry Kane, as if anointing him. Charlton was a hero for my father and so he became one to me too. We went on an expedition to Ashington to look at his birthplace, which was only a corner kick from my own. We walked the streets and the communal field where he'd practised as a boy. We went together to watch what we knew would be his last match for Manchester United in the North East – against Newcastle at St James' Park – and saw him lash in a top-corner shot of typically Charltonesque power. I made, and still possess, a scrapbook of those last months up to and including his retirement.

The timing of the ceremony at Burton still jarred a little. England were juxtaposing – yet again – a current World Cup campaign with 1966's. A little remembering is all right, but too much is a disease, and our perpetual looping back to 1966 and all that has gone well beyond homage and become a national haunting. The ghosts of that summer afternoon are summoned too often for our own good. We remain compulsively preoccupied with it, we take refuge in its memory and we allow the dust of that history to swirl around and hang over every England team and every England manager. We have absorbed as much as we possibly can about that late July afternoon of sunshine and showers. What there is to say about it, we have said to tedious exhaustion. The goals . . . the extra time . . . the moustachioed Russian linesman nodding his head . . . Bobby Moore wiping his dirty hands on the Royal Box velvet . . . the after-final banquet . . . Geoff Hurst returning home the next day and quietly washing the car and the dinner dishes, doing the supermarket shop and mowing his lawn. The nostalgia of 1966 has no way to reinvent itself because there are no new stories to tell and no new photographs to show. The books already written would fill 10 yards of shelving. The documentaries, if piled upright in their cans, would be taller than a goalpost. This repetition has worn each anecdote to a thin rag. This familiarity has robbed every sight and sound of any emotional charge. To win the World Cup, especially then and especially against West Germany, was a big exclamation mark in a roaring decade full of them. Those who did it deserve the medals, the gongs, the kudos, the superlatives. But must we continue to harp on about it? Fatigue with 1966 was noticeable during last year's Golden Jubilee celebration of the achievement. That ought to do the work of a semi-colon, creating a decent half pause that ushers in – for a decade – a moratorium about referring to it at length. Then, just maybe, things will seem fresh to us again. Then, just maybe too, we will send a team to a World Cup that isn't burdened by a past none of them saw and which must seem as ancient to young eyes now as the first steam age, Queen Victoria in her mourning weeds and the heyday of Empire.

1966?

It was another time, in another country, far different from our own. The day before I came to Wembley I watched for the first time in twenty years every frame of *Goal!*, the official film of those finals. Not for the football, so well known, but to witness how England has changed socially, culturally and even physically, the landscape rebuilt and reshaped.

Goal! gathered on release some tepid reviews and some raves. Looking at it now, you empathise entirely with the latter and can only think someone artistically insensitive wrote the former. You can buy five football documentaries for £1 these days. Some great machinery cranks them out almost weekly. *Goal!* is the big daddy of them all, imitated but never surpassed; a kind of *Citizen Kane* of football movies. It tells the story of the tournament in the same way Dickens or Tolstoy wrote novels. Characters and scenes are multitudinous and constantly shifting. The only bit *Goal!* omits is how it came to be made. The producer, a silver-haired Chilean called Octavio Senoret, bought the rights from Fifa for £15,000. He shot forty-six hours of film, pared down to the 108-minute movie.

Goal! was stitched together not in a studio in Hollywood, but in Cricklewood when funds to support it were draining away – a benefactor rescued the film – and morale was sagging. It was supposed to have been written by the experimental novelist and poet B. S. Johnson, who reported on matches for the *Observer* and later wrote *The Unfortunates*, his melancholy masterpiece, a 'book in a box'. The novel comprised unbound chapters that, apart from the first and the last, could be read in any order and shuffled like a fortune-teller's deck of cards. It recounts how the narrator (Johnson himself) goes to a game (Nottingham Forest v Manchester United) and finds himself caught in a long Proustian-like remembrance of things past, most of them awfully sad and some of them unspeakably painful: the city he is in; the friend, now dead, who once lived there; the structure of his own life and the place football has had in it. Johnson covered the World Cup Final for *The Times of India*, calling it a 'match that must surely stand with the greatest ever played'. But his relationship with Senoret and his directors sank into acrimony. What Johnson envisaged – ideas that were recondite and quirkily idiosyncratic – and what the makers of the movie wanted were as far apart as the goalmouths on a pitch. The differences were irreconcilable. The script Johnson submitted included scenes of London high rises, among them Centre Point, former bomb sites still populated with purple weeds, the hothouse at Kew Gardens, the shop windows along Carnaby Street and what he called the 'snob junk' of World Cup merchandise, a phrase that reveals an inverted snobbery of its own. The leitmotif Johnson chose, looming like personal obsession, was The Post Office Tower, the sight of which stalked camera shots, the presence of it unexplained. There were to be street and backyard games between father and sons, but where Johnson was going with this – and also what he was getting at – wasn't exactly window-pane clear. You read it and are not at all surprised that Johnson was sacked, however much he loved football (he supported Chelsea) and however much you suspect he saw the game as the enlightened path towards an egalitarian society in which the only noticeable difference between commoner and king was whichever team's colours were worn.

Brian Glanville, then and almost always afterwards of *The Sunday Times*, replaced Johnson. Substitutions had only come to British football during the previous season. Glanville for Johnson was the most

inspired of them. By then the film was at the rough-cut stage, the fragments like preparatory sketches for a Cubist canvas. It needed the
shape and order of a good script to become lucid. Glanville, also an
accomplished novelist, understood instantly what Johnson did not:
that the miles of full colour celluloid heaped in the studio were richly
extraordinary, which meant his commentary needed only to supplement the pictures rather than shout over and dominate them. He also
knew that – especially in film – less can be more. *Goal!* does not brow-
beat with a message, but whispers what it has to say sophisticatedly
and intimately and almost subliminally too. Colour television did not
make its debut in Britain until 1967, initially broadcasting only four
hours per week. Even then fewer than 5 per cent of licence payers
could see it. The new TV sets were exorbitantly expensive and BBC
2, the channel on which the programmes were shown, was transmit-
ted across less than a third of the country. So the rainbow of the
World Cup was only ever glimpsed in black and white at home. *Goal!*
offered a new way of seeing, not only taking the game out of the
monochrome era, but also bringing it up close and personal. You get
to hear the smack of boot on ball. You get to see sods of turf fly. And
when Pelé gets roughed up by tackling that is grievous bodily harm in
disguise, you feel the welts and the bruises of the ugly, unforgivable
belting he has been given. *Goal!* provides a peek of all our yesterdays,
which are so different from all our todays. The team buses travelling
along on empty motorways. The city gents striding across Waterloo
Bridge in bowler hats. The vendors from the *Evening Standard* in short
white coats, as though about to sell ice cream. The men on the terraces
wearing suits and smoking pipes. A forest of chimneys and the slate
rooftops of terraced housing. The Queen only forty years old. The
Union Jack resplendent instead of the flag of St George. And as for
the matches themselves . . .

You linger on grounds that are no longer there, such as Sunderland's
and Middlesbrough's, and others, like Aston Villa's and Everton's,
that have changed so radically since as to be virtually unrecognisable.
Every player wears black boots and every shirt is spotless, clean of
sponsors' logos. Wembley has no perimeter advertising. And outside
the stadium you can see plump trees and the slight slope of green hills,
long since tarmacked or concreted over.

Glanville's script is tight to the bone – precise, pithy and sometimes dryly droll. The Brazilian manager is 'plump and brooding like a Buddha'. The sadness of that image of a limping Pelé, unable to go on, becomes sadder still with the words: 'In this World Cup a king is dead'. And England's disappointingly lame opening match, against Uruguay, is damned as 'the epitome of the modern game – the goalless draw'. The narrator's voice is matched to these *bon mots* the way a pair of handmade shoes sets off a bespoke suit. Nigel Patrick was an actor who frequently played patrician gentlemen or posh, urbane rogues. He'd been in films as diverse as *Spring in Park Lane* and *The Sound Barrier*, *The League of Gentlemen* and *The Trials of Oscar Wilde*. Every cadence of his carries style and has a knowing inflection about it. *Goal!* is so bitterly poignant too. Near the end, waiting for the closing credits to begin, you're already thinking about what happened next, a well of regret beginning to sink deep into you. You dwell on those who are now dead and then on others who, though still alive, can't remember winning the World Cup because dementia has stolen the day from them, a robbery that occurred slowly, the irreplaceable treasures of the mind taken one at a time.

I can't help but think about the What If? What if England hadn't won?

That World Cup became a millstone made of gold, and it came at a price hardly anyone at first knew was being paid. In the early 1950s, when Hungary won 6–3 at Wembley and then 7–1 in Budapest, England felt properly spanked, losing in only two matches not just face but also the snooty air of superiority it had almost always lauded over Johnny Foreigner. The 142-page tactical manual, *Learn to Play the Hungarian Way*, subsequently became football's best seller, chock-a-block with diagrams and photos that were devoured like commandments. The new aristocracy had usurped the old, and England accepted it and adapted.

After 1966, giddy with power again, England became too smug. There was no book explicitly titled 'Learn to Play the English Way', but the game here still thought it had only things to teach and not much to learn. It folded inwards on itself and assumed more world cups would follow if England simply turned up to compete in them. They didn't foresee the brilliance of Brazil, the best of the all-time best, in 1970. They didn't foresee either the dominant grace of the Dutch or the durability of the West Germans, coming back far better than before. England have never caught up.

What 1966 teaches is that even victors are by victories undone.

A man of early middle age is sitting at the end of my row, wrapped in an England scarf so tattered that it could be vintage 1966; inherited from his grandfather or father, I think. He returns from a half-time drink, his lips still wet with beer, and jubilantly predicts that England are about to score 'at least three goals'. His assessment is that Gareth Southgate, marking his first anniversary in charge, will have delivered the 'mother and father' of bollockings. 'He promised to entertain us,' the man says, referring to one of Southgate's pre-match press conferences, 'so he has to do it, doesn't he?' But it soon becomes apparent that whatever Southgate said in the dressing room has failed to penetrate the ears of his listeners. There is a moment, not long after the restart, which typifies the funk England are in.

Ryan Bertrand, the left back, is in possession near the halfway line. He attempts to play the ball to Marcus Rashford, who is square of him and less than 5 yards away. Bertrand, under no pressure, manages to push the pass a mile behind him. It slips dismally out of play, not far from where Southgate is standing. The manager rolls his eyes, searching anywhere for succour.

England's formation is alternating between 4-2-3-1 and a loose 4-4-2, but Southgate could plant the team in rows, like root vegetables, and it still wouldn't solve the chief problem, which is the absence of someone sprite-like and sparky in central midfield. England are bogged down there, lacking the speed of thought and the assured touch and organisation that Paul Gascoigne or Steven Gerrard and Paul Scholes once supplied. It is a puzzle why the intensity of the Premier League does not transfer to international matches. The reason is not fully graspable. You're always left dangling between fact and conjecture. It is fact that of 110 players who started Premier League matches last weekend, only 69 were eligible to play for England. Exclude those who have already retired internationally. Rule out others who have won a cap but were then deemed not up to scratch. Finally, remove the stragglers, unlikely to be considered other than in exceptional circumstances. There isn't much to sift through after that. It is still pure conjecture, however, why those who are qualified and do make it lamentably under-perform. Do the demands of the Premier League wear them down? Does the very sight of the England shirt and badge induce paranoia or paralysis? The players Southgate has on the pitch have won twenty-one major trophies between them. You wouldn't know it unless you knew them. So we sit, eyes glazed with a cold, grey boredom, as England rely again on Marcus Rashford, still prepared to run energetically and regularly come inside from the left, and Harry Kane, who is slogging on.

The performance is so poor that it numbs any attempt at interpretation and pushes our ability to endure it to the outer edge. Alex Oxlade-Chamberlain has become so anonymous that we only remember he is on the pitch at all when Southgate substitutes him. He comes off and gives a water bottle a hefty kick on the touchline. It is a confused apology of sorts from him. Nothing much changes, and midway through the half the fans behind me – bemused, impatient and weary with it all – cease to be pacific and start making paper planes from team sheets, advertising flyers and even by ripping pages out of the £6 glossy programme. There is a contest to see who can fling these furthest on to the pitch. Soon dozens of the origami aircraft are littering the turf. One of them, catching a small thermal, drifts over Southgate's right shoulder and nosedives a yard or two in front of him. He hardly seems to notice.

Only in the last quarter of an hour do England perk up, revealing some commitment. Rashford takes a through ball from Raheem Sterling, leaving him one-on-one against Jan Oblak. The goalkeeper is nearly 6 feet 2 inches tall; he doesn't expect to be chipped, so hunches his shoulders and goes into a crouch, awaiting the drive that will come at him low and at speed. Rashford stabs his toes under the ball and lifts it into the air. Over Oblak it goes, the attempt rising too high and too slowly. Rajko Rotman appears, like a man with broom, to sweep the danger away. Close shave number two follows almost immediately for Slovenia. There is a flurry in the box. Sterling's shot from 12 yards – exactly like the one Rashford ought to have attempted but didn't – bowls along the turf. Oblak, out of position, can't dive to

stop it, but Boštjan Cesar's out-stretched boot deflects the ball away.
Many haven't bothered to hang around for these last rites. When the
fourth official signals there are six minutes of added time, even more
get up and leave, relieved to go. For some reason, inexplicable to me,
I am convinced that England are about to score. On the sideline
Southgate looks like a coach hoping for an epiphany, something overlooked that will save him. On the field another England attack has
broken apart, the fragments scattered. Still I sit here. England have
poached late goals recently; perhaps this is what persuades me to stay.
Slovenia relax. A clean sheet and a point represent success for them.

But then Oblak, taking a shot comfortably from Kyle Walker,
decides to launch a counter-attack and get a move on. In too much of
a rush he hurls the ball to his left flank. The decision is eccentric. The
throw is wayward. Walker, unobtrusive and unimpressive all night,
seizes it and out-paces the attempt to take possession from him. With
two touches and eight rapid steps he goes from mid way in Slovenia's
half to almost parallel with the penalty spot. His low cross has an
inward bend on it. Kane is not a turbo-charged runner, but his football brain compensates for that. He anticipates what the defender
Miha Mevlja does not. Kane comes from behind Mevlja's right shoulder and then swerves in front of him. The sprawling touch he gets, 7
yards out, catches Oblak off balance. The 'keeper grasps for the ball,
but can't grab it. The toe-poke is still rolling into the back of the net
when Kane tears off towards the corner flag to revel in it. Kane tugs
at the front of his shirt, brandishing the three lions on it. He now looks
like his cardboard cut-out in that bookmakers' window – eyes wide,
mouth open, finger raised and pointing.

The win has come in the ninety-fourth minute. Russia awaits
England, who have now reached the last four major tournaments
without losing a match, but also without convincing anyone, much less
themselves, that more than good intentions will go with them to the
finals.

The indifference towards their qualification begins as soon as it is
secured. There'd been incredulity when the crowd was announced as
just over 61,000. Even the idealists among us think the FA are massaging the players' egos with that calculation. But, irrespective of how
many actually turned up, there aren't a lot of them left now; fewer

than 20,000, I'd say. England thank them from the centre circle, raising their hands and applauding fulsomely. Most fans have their back already turned from the pitch and are streaming in threes and fours towards the exit. They barely give the team a return glance. A goodly number don't give them the courtesy of turning around at all. The players are clapping empty seats.

5 October 2017: England v Slovenia
England 1 Slovenia 0

England: Hart, Walker, Cahill, Stones, Bertrand, Dier, Henderson, Oxlade-Chamberlain (Lingard 64), Sterling (Keane 85), Rashford, Kane.
Subs not used: Butland, Pickford, Smalling, Trippier, Maguire, Cresswell, Defoe, Winks

Slovenia: Oblak, Struna, Cesar, Mevlja, Jokić, Krhin, Bezjak (Repas 72), Rotman (Matava 79), Verbič, Iličić, Sporar (Birsa 55).
Subs not used: Belec, Koprivec, Mlinar, Samardžić, Sirok, Viler, Bohar, Kurtić

SCORER
England: Kane 90+4

BOOKED
England: Stones
Slovenia: Krhin, Rotman, Mevlja, Struna, Birsa

Referee: F. Zwayer
Attendance: 61,598

6
THE GOALKEEPER'S FEAR OF THE LONG RANGE FREE KICK

16 October: Leicester City v West Bromwich Albion, King Power Stadium, Sky Sports PL Channel

With prescience bordering on clairvoyance, the cartoonist of *All Sports Weekly* got it absolutely right almost a century ago. In February 1928 he drew a middle-aged man sitting contentedly in his living room armchair. The man is wearing a jazzy pair of slippers and he is holding a lit cigarette, the smoke from which twists upwards like a vine. Beside him, standing on a low table, is a bottle and a glass. In front of him is an enormous flat, wide-screen television. Plugged into the television are an assortment of boxes, a curl and coil of small wires conspicuously connecting them to the set. The man is watching two footballers in striped shirts storm over the half-way line, chasing a ball that is a black blob. The caption beneath the cartoon reads:

TELEVISION: The football supporter of 19–?

We can forgive the fact that the cartoonist – he signs himself 'Waller' – doesn't precisely date when his prediction will come true. We can also forgive the question mark pinned to the tail of it, as though he is hedging his bets. For when this was drawn and published, John Logie Baird was still tinkering with the greyscale images on his primitive 'seeing wireless'. Some critics doubted his judgement. Others questioned his sanity. Nowadays we simply wait for technology to constantly amaze us, and so we are seldom thunderstruck when it does. In 1928, when no one but TV's pioneering engineers could recognise a cathode tube, expectations were lower, narrower and more modest. The movies had just started to talk and the nascent BBC had only recently begun broadcasting live commentary of football on radio, the signal drifting about weakly. It often collapsed into a whisper or cut out altogether at the moment a goal was about to be scored. Television was so weird-fangled as to be science fiction at the absurdist, rather than the merely fantastic, end of the scale. The notion that Logie Baird's magic box might one day exist in a corner of the home – and that we'd amuse ourselves to death watching it – seemed about as plausible as flying to the moon and then discovering that it really was made out of green cheese.

Waller's cartoon is an extraordinary collector's piece for reasons other than the way it startles the eye. At first sight you instinctively check the date on the newspaper's masthead to make certain that what looks so modern is genuinely antique. I own a copy of the edition of *All Sports Weekly* in which it appears. What's most curious, a conundrum that can't be solved, is that nowhere else is the word 'television' mentioned in its twenty-two pages. Nor, after searching through back copies – plus a plethora of other newspapers on and before the same date – can I find an article that even tangentially refers to television and the blockbuster boom that football could conceivably make of it. Waller seems to have reached his conclusion independently, drawing what his lively mind foresaw. A week later, in a widely syndicated column about 'the wireless', an anonymous writer put Waller's draughtsmanship into words: 'Without being too fanciful,' the article declared, 'one may be pardoned for expressing the belief that comparatively soon the rather unsatisfying broadcasts of football matches will be accompanied by "televised" illustrations of the actual play, a kind of simultaneous cinematography that will render the word-picture almost superfluous.' Whether Waller's cartoon inspired the paragraph can only be guessed at, but arguing against that conclusion would stretch coincidence more than a little. *All Sports Weekly* is long forgotten now, but was well read then.

Waller was the man who saw tomorrow, understanding almost before anyone else but Logie Baird exactly where television was taking us. He has now slipped so deeply into obscurity, leaving behind only his prophecy for posterity, that I can't dig up the barest biographical details – not even his Christian name – that could make him partly alive again. But, during this long weekend, which comes to a close tonight, I have thought a lot about him and that cartoon. In the past seventy-two hours I have watched nothing but football. From Brisbane on Australia's Gold Coast to Nice and the French Riviera. From Guangzhou in southern China to Kochi in south-west India. From dowdy Vicarage Road, Watford, to the bowl of the San Siro in fashionable, fashion-conscious Milan. So far the full tally is: four continents; twelve countries; fifty-three matches. Like the jolly viewer Waller created, I have seen them all without the bother of leaving the house, the seat of my pants planted firmly to the seat of my sofa.

The television fan never goes cold or hungry, but this hasn't entirely been a cushy number, more of an endurance test for the eyes and certainly for the backside. My muscles there may have atrophied during this sedentary marathon of live matches. Everything has flashed by in a confusion of colour – goals, saves, appalling misses from 2 yards out, the thwack of ball against woodwork, red and yellow cards, penalties squandered and scored, refereeing decisions that were unarguably right or stupidly wrong and supporters enraged, lachrymose or ecstatic, sometimes simultaneously. Often, when the schedule of one channel collided with two or even three others, I tried to achieve the impossible and follow four matches at once with a flick of the remote control. This meant I occasionally missed nearly as many goals as I saw, as though some imp of mischief was deliberately conspiring against me. Usually the game dissolved into a haze as soon it was over. Asked to explain it, I felt like someone who, having completed a speed-reading course, can still only tell you that *War and Peace* is about Russia.

The best of it has nonetheless stuck with me. Since football can't always conform, with artistic satisfaction, to the rules of traditional drama, which demands the organised structure of a plot that pulls you towards a plausible conclusion, I have sat in sufferance through some numbing matches, reminding me of the review an 18th-century critic once damningly gave to John Bunyan's *A Pilgrim's Progress*: 'No

one ever wished it longer'. TV is forever loudly selling the next
match, proclaiming it as an epic before the one you're watching has
finished. The promise of something extra special went spectacularly unfulfilled when Liverpool faced Manchester United at
Anfield. In attempting to bore Liverpool into submission, United
also bored us, collecting a goalless draw but no laurels for it. Even
five minutes of highlights would have been three and a half minutes
too long. I also watched a few matches with the sound turned off
because the commentary was either so trite or so patronising as to
be torturous. I wanted to remind some commentators of the dictum
Brian Moore laid down: 'Commentating,' he said, 'is no more than
finding the right delicate balance between describing the action,
imparting the information and adding a dash of drama and urgency
that draws it all towards the realms of entertainment.' Only this
week a Russian commentator, angry at a refereeing decision in the
game between Torpedo Vladimir and Tekstilshchik Ivanovo, abandoned his gantry in protest. The station's ratings went up. It is
tougher to commentate on a match than you would imagine. Those
who doubt it should press mute and attempt to talk through the
pictures. See how frequently you embarrass yourself with mis-starts,
mispronunciations and misidentifications as well as fluffs and
general cock-ups. I am nevertheless rooting for a day when TV
offers us the option to watch a game without anything but crowd
noise for company.

Post-match interviews also produced the usual evasions or banal,
mannered answers, allowing you five minutes to nip off and boil the
kettle. But even the highly unqualified layman wouldn't have wanted
to miss the first question put to Wilfried Zaha five minutes after his
goal gave Crystal Palace – bottom of the table and pointless after two
months and seven games – their first success of the season. The striker
was asked: 'How important was that result today?' Zaha replied as
politely and as constructively as he could, but his wide eyes told you he
was thinking exactly what everyone at home thought too. The next
question was probably 'How important is oxygen to your process of
breathing?'

There have fortunately been enough games so compelling that I
hoped the fourth official's added time would be preposterously

generous. I didn't want them to end. In particular a grudge contest in Serie A, between Juventus and Lazio, was still boiling furiously during six extra minutes. What occurred during them became almost a match within the match. It was thick with to and fro attacking. Juventus, 2–1 down, hit a post. Lazio broke away and Gianluigi Buffon bravely put his thirty-nine-year-old body between them and a third, decisive goal. Then Juventus, obliged to repay Buffon's courage, bustled up to the other end damn quickly and won a penalty, which was given only after the referee watched on screen the same tackle the viewer had seen four times from three different angles. The attacker buckled easily, like a wind-blown flower, but it was unquestionably a foul and anyone watching on TV knew this conclusively well before the official did. That fact ought to wipe out whining opposition to VAR, however long the pause needs to be before the right decision is reached. Providing a last twist, which left you as nervously exhausted as the players, Juventus fluffed the kick.

In the Bundesliga Borussia Dortmund, the leaders, surrendered to Leipzig in the Westfalenstadion, their first defeat there for nearly two years. In La Liga Barcelona came from behind to draw at Atlético Madrid after a far post header from Luis Suárez. He slipped his markers as nonchalantly as a stage escapologist slips out of handcuffs when your gaze is elsewhere. And back in Serie A, locked in the private war of the derby della Madonnina, Inter and Milan slugged away at one another from the first until the very last minute, sharing four goals, until Inter's captain, Mauro Icardi, thumped in a fifth, a winning penalty.

To do nothing but watch one game after another is a shut in and sealed off existence. It is also addictive, like some mild narcotic, and a respite holiday from the outside world. You lull yourself into the cosy thought that surely nothing important can be happening anywhere else. Not war. Not conflict. Not politics. For a short while, you can pretend either none of these exist or are of only minimal concern. What matters is only whether the ball was over the line. Or whether that trip was inside or outside the box. Or whether Feyenoord can beat PEC Zwolle or Aston Villa will do enough to hold Wolves at Molineux. This is completely irrational, like firmly holding two contradictory thoughts at once, but also a comforting kind of escape.

Now, since it is about to end, I am waiting for the bump back into reality. The last game, a Monday night Midlands derby, is Leicester City against West Bromwich Albion at the King Power Stadium.

The one thing TV instantly teaches you is that a manager is almost always more important than a player in regaling the story of a game as it happens. In the years when *Match of the Day* or *The Big Match* were a monoculture, your weekly fix of football, you'd see only the occasional close up of the dugout. At Leeds, Don Revie, always frowning, would be clothed in a shaggy-collared sheepskin coat. At Tottenham, Bill Nicholson would sit stone-faced and dark suited; he resembled a senior bank executive combing out bad debts. At Arsenal, Bertie Mee, also in a suit, was good at impersonating a smooth block of wood. Mee behaved imperturbably, as though displaying emotion would be an abuse of protocol. Generally he suppressed his own feelings on the sidelines so well that a raised left eyebrow counted as today's equivalent of the angry clenched fist.

   It is a moot point whether TV has encouraged managers to jump around in the lighted stage that is the technical area, or whether society has simply changed so much that putting on a passionate show is not just natural but also obligatory to demonstrate you care. TV needs managers who have an actorly magnificence about them. Live football has more continuity breaks, and so the touchline is the obvious place to go when the action slows down or stops altogether. Nor is the match alone ever sufficient for them. In TV the reaction always requires capturing because it is integral, rather than just supplementary, in powering the narrative. The camera searches out the human factor, and this is frequently the manager's expression. At the end of that game at Juventus, the coach, Massimiliano Allegri was framed in misery and incomprehension. Allegri pursed his lips and half closed his eyes before burying his hands into his trouser pockets. He then thrust his head sharply forward, as though he was butting it against an imaginary brick wall. The gesture articulated his anguish so well that the commentator had no need to talk over it. TV had got what it wanted; not only a picture that renders words unnecessary, but one that also punched you in the heart. You felt sorry for Allegri, reacting as though the whole ground was caving in around his ears.

Wherever he goes, José Mourinho is the money-shot for TV directors. Even his merest facial twitch can be interpreted as a miniature drama. Mourinho also seems to possess some in-built radar that goes off whenever the camera is about to demand something from him. Seldom does he fail to provide it. The game at Anfield, for instance, wasn't a minute old before the director swung from a wide shot of the pitch to a close-up of his face. There he stood – stock still, scowling slightly and smouldering a bit. It's as if everything Mourinho does, even blowing his nose, is for posterity. A few yards away Jürgen Klopp was once more giving the impression that he wears his central nervous system externally. His arms were flaying everywhere. He was like a puppet with too many strings. Klopp is always good news for the camera because he moves so much, but only Mourinho can be the captivating focus of attention when doing absolutely nothing.

When I began watching football, and then when I started to write about it too, players had to impress managers or perish rather than the other way around. Managers earned more than anyone they picked too. The power, as well as the money, has since switched on the shop floor, but as Sky begin their build-up to Leicester–West Brom, the faces as big as billboards in the studio don't belong to Jonny Evans and Kasper Schmeichel or even to Jamie Vardy. As a backdrop, Sky hang portraits of the two bosses, Craig Shakespeare and Tony Pulis, their photographs facing one another in a duel that suggests one of them will be kissing the dust after it is over.

With just one win and two draws, Leicester City are third from bottom. West Bromwich Albion are only four points and six places better off. 'Is this a battle for survival?' asks the toothy presenter, flanked by the analysts Jamie Carragher and Peter Schmeichel. They agree it could be. 'Tonight is so vital,' says Carragher, referring to Leicester explicitly and to Shakespeare implicitly. Schmeichel agrees; though you suspect family ties are forcing him to pack his words in wads of cotton wool.

It is a blowy night in Leicester, the ground catching the draught from Hurricane Ophelia, currently swirling about the Atlantic. The players' shirts ripple like flags. The ball, pumped high, wobbles through the air, making the path of it difficult to read. You know from the start what kind of match this is going to be. West Brom, operating 4-3-3, are anyway the sort of side under Pulis that digs a defensive ditch and then stakes a barbed wire fence in front of it. There is fibre in them but no froth about them; few pine for a season ticket at the Hawthorns because Pulis is the *eminence grise* of attrition. On scant resources he's made West Brom redoubtable and difficult to beat, but they are to entertainment what dirty weather is to a summer's day.

Their regular goalkeeper, Ben Foster, is injured, which offers another excuse for ultra-caution here. Foster's replacement, Boaz Myhill, hasn't played in the Premier League for eighteen months. From the outset Leicester are allowed to spoon up most of the possession – more than sixty per cent of it – and turn to Vardy and Riyad Mahrez, fit again, to make the most of it. Shakespeare has left out the two other figures, Shinji Okazaki and Demarai Gray, capable of getting through minute gaps with a turn or a trick of footwork. Myhill must be grateful for that. Nothing much is asked of him.

Vardy can't get over a header at the back post, instead leaning back and looping it a yard over the bar. And his partner, Kelechi Iheanacho, the replacement for Okazaki, doesn't come close to a skimming cross that Vardy puts across goal. The 21-year-old Iheanacho, bought for £25m from Manchester City in the last window, is still goalless for his new club. Only when half time is ten minutes away does Myhill have to prove his prolonged absence hasn't been detrimental. A long throw scrapes off the head of a defender, dropping towards Danny Simpson. From just inside the box, he meets the bouncing ball with the confidence and conviction that Iheanacho has still to show. The shot is hit raspingly on the run. Myhill urgently throws his hands at it, parrying the ball away.

Not a lot else has gone on, so the camera hasn't skimped on showing us Shakespeare and Pulis even though neither has the handsome looks or the magnetism of José Mourinho. The absence of artifice in both actually makes management seem unappealing graft rather than glamorous. This is a backhanded compliment because so many of their contemporaries, even away from the Premier League, deliberately strike that look-at-me pose, a concocted grandeur. You soon get tired of that and of them. With his wide, fleshy face and his sagging double chin, Shakespeare in a tracksuit resembles someone clocking in for a long, oily shift of labour. Similarly attired, as though about to get his hands mucky too, Pulis in his baseball cap seems a completely different species from Antonio Conte in those slickly cut suits or Pep Guardiola, wearing one of his wardrobe of V-necked cashmere sweaters. There is a difference in behaviour too. In particular Guardiola, whenever seen stroking his chin ruminatively, looks more like an art connoisseur contemplating an old master than a manager assessing the state of a game. Shakespeare and Pulis make more of a scene. Their frantic pointing and waving remind you of castaways signalling distress to ships that can't see them.

Half time arrives. 'Have you enjoyed that?' Jamie Carragher is asked. His palms are pressed into the tactics table. He hesitates before answering, as though discretion and the feelings of others stop him from saying what he really thinks. 'I haven't, personally,' he replies at last.

In *Play All: A Bingewatcher's Notebook*, the polymath critic Clive James examines the cultural phenomenon of the Box Set and our devotion to it. He writes: 'The number of shows, if not their quality, can only go on increasing and the way we talk about them can only become more compulsively attentive . . .' Exactly the same can be said of football. The first Premier League deal in 1992 cost Sky £304m. The most recent in 2015, split between Sky and BT, cost £5.1b. The next may not make that amount look measly, but Netflix, Amazon, Google and even Facebook are said to want in too. Up will go transfer fees – again. Up will go players' wages. Up will go the cost of a match ticket and also of watching from the armchair. Also sure to increase are the number of matches screened live. In 1992–3, the Premier League's debut season, sixty games were shown. Now it is 168. In 2019 it will be over 200. Add to those the Champions League and the FA Cup ties, the international qualifiers and friendlies and also the league and cup games from across Europe. Add in, too, those competitions – the

EFL Trophy and Carabao Cup – that are given life almost solely to fill in the few blank evenings during which you'd otherwise have nothing to watch but re-runs of classics from twenty years ago. Just when it seems impossible to fit any more live games into a schedule, the TV companies carry on doing it. I wait for the day (for it will surely come) when those of us exiled by geography from our own team will buy a TV ticket and watch every match whenever it is played – even at three o'clock on a Saturday.

I am never blasé about football on TV. I am from the generation that innocently thought the convulsions of the 1960s were the norm because we knew nothing of the austerity and social starchiness preceding them. There were only three channels and you even had to get up from your chair to change them. A fair rump of the Football League had originally been militantly opposed to showing even Saturday night highlights, fearing crowds would dwindle. So a live match was a big event and something longed for impatiently. We got the FA Cup and the European Cup Finals. We got the odd World Cup qualifier. It made the end of season Home International Championships, defunct now, one of the season's peaks.

You got so few live games between World Cup Finals that you became an ecstatic witness to those you did see, remembering every delectable detail. I can summon now, as I always will, that whipped, edge-of-the-box drive from Jeff Astle that finished in the top corner and won the Cup for West Brom in 1968. I can summon from that same year George Best's zag around Benfica's goalkeeper and the sure push that came afterwards, his celebrations beginning even before the ball had settled against the net. And I can summon Gary Sprake in 1970. I see him drop slowly – his body falling like a sack of flour off the back of a lorry – to smother a meek shot from Peter Houseman that snaked somehow through his hands and slipped beneath his chest; Wembley's ruin of a pitch was no excuse for that. These TV memories, which made up childhood, are inseparable from the black and white set on which I watched them. It was a wooden block with a convex, postage stamp screen and the gold coloured grille of a radio beneath. My parents bought it in the mid-1950s, a wedding present to themselves. That TV used to take a minute or two to warm up, the picture emerging gradually and mistily, as though you were about to watch a match through a mantle of mist. At times the players were lost in the greyness of it and the ball was hard to find. Sometimes I had to sit on the floor, only a foot away, to follow both of them.

Football on TV then was an inadequate substitute for actually being at the match. Now there is ultra-high definition, the screen on which to watch it large enough to turn even the smallest living room into a cinema. A tuft of grass can be as tiny as a mote of dust, but you can still see it clearly from 12 feet away. Even 'Waller' of *All Sports Weekly* wouldn't believe the clarity and the colourfulness of the picture. While watching a game on TV will never replicate actually being there, the size of your TV and the sparkle of the screen give you the pretence. The facsimile offered improves all the time, but TV knows it can't make the experience the same and so concentrates instead on giving you something different.

Having so recently studied *Goal!*, it gradually dawned on me this weekend how the methods in that film transferred to TV as soon as live matches became a feature of every season. The intently focused close-ups and the arty angles are only part of it. Three sequences in particular resonate. The first, which is ninety-three seconds long, follows Rattín, the Argentinian captain, after his sending-off against England in the quarter finals. Every pace of his ponderous and discon-solate walk from the halfway line to the tunnel is tracked. Occasionally he turns to look back at the match that is going on without him. Rattín is caught tugging at the fabric of the corner flag, the way someone might distractedly pull at the leaf of a flower on a country stroll. He then turns his back on the pitch altogether. The second and third scenes, split by the Final itself, show the Wembley groundsman dressed in a brown trilby, worn at a natty slant, a tweed jacket and slacks. This tall, thin man is seen climbing the steps towards the stadium and opening it with a jangling bunch of keys. It is 7.30a.m. He sits on the red leather bench that Alf Ramsey will occupy later that afternoon. He then begins to assemble the goals, jig-sawing the crossbar to the post and heaving out the net like a fisherman ready to go to sea. Typed place cards are laid on the seats in the Royal Box. England's red jerseys are hung on wire coat hangers and placed on pegs in the dressing room. The game is long over when we see the groundsman again. He locks up the gate he'd opened earlier. He descends those same concrete steps, each of them strewn with the litter of discarded posters, programmes, that morning's newspapers. His trilby is still on that natty slant. *Goal!* milked the sub-plots within the main story, revealing each like a Matryoshka doll. It appreciated that the depth of our investment in the film would depend on the portrayal of characters, minor and major alike. The groundsman, a part of something so much bigger than himself, reminded us that the World Cup wasn't only about Hurst and Charlton and Moore.

TV learnt from that, making whenever possible serious drama out of popular entertainment. Sky and BT take you, as *Goal!* did with pioneering bravado, inside the dressing rooms, along the strobe-lighted tunnel and on to the pitch. So whatever agonies await Craig Shakespeare and Tony Pulis, we'll see them microscopically. TV never allows a manager to keep his misery entirely private.

The second half is only fifteen seconds old when Jamie Vardy forces a mistake, his harrying presence enough to provoke an under-hit back pass out of panic in that tight corridor between the edge of the box and the touchline. Vardy sets off after the loose ball. So does Boaz Myhill. The two of them smack into one another like men colliding in a swing door. The collision is so confused, and also so close to the box, that you can't tell who is to blame or whether it will precipitate a penalty or a free kick. We wait for technology to tell us.

The BBC were the first to import the slow motion machine from the United States. The contraption alarmed some of the audience it was supposed to impress. The BBC's switchboard took calls from viewers who thought the game was pre-recorded, dismissing as bogus the corporation's claim to be televising it live purely on the basis of those instant replays, which seemed to them like hocus-pocus. 'There were people checking their morning paper to make sure the match hadn't been played the night before,' said a producer. We have since become so used to super slow-motion that the prototype of it, when studied again, seems as antiquated as the house telephone is to the mobile. The eighteen cameras used at a game not only search out a million little things, but then break each down one half breath at a time. The armchair fan can absorb immediately what the supporter in the stand either won't see, being too far away from it, or doesn't register at all because so much else is distracting the eye. Earlier this season an off-the-ball elbow from Newcastle's Aleksandar Mitrović escaped the referee's attention. In England's game against Slovakia, Dele Alli flashed his middle finger towards the referee in pique. This also went unnoticed. Punishment was meted out to both Mitrović and Alli retrospectively, the TV pictures used in judgement. Their offences were stupid. Stupider still, however, was an assumption that no one would pick up on them either then or later. The camera sees everything and usually provides enough evidence to extrapolate a motive for the action too. But, even after repeated viewings of Myhill's and Vardy's coming together, you can't tell whether the goalkeeper solved the problem of the striker by deliberately taking him out – or whether the striker leapt at the goalkeeper in the hope of winning a penalty. Myhill is booked. Within five minutes he is clutching his right leg, hurt in that crash. He is hopping like a peg-pirate, an image accentuated by his black beard.

Leicester ought to go in front. From 9 yards out, knowing Myhill can't nimbly get across his line, Riyad Mahrez has only to hit the target with his favoured left foot. The shot is a howler. It goes high over the bar and higher still into the crowd banked behind it. Craig Shakespeare looks as if he might cry.

He will know that one of the reasons for suffering lies in comparisons. It is the curse of future Leicester teams to always be compared to one that only eighteen months ago won the Premier League, the most outrageously implausible, you'll-never-believe-it-in-a-lifetime feat since the Lilliputians briefly got the upper hand over Gulliver. I always think first of those supporters who saw the 5,000–1 odds against their club and dived for their wallet. What a reward for wishful thinking. The tale of that success is all told out, the superlatives are all spent, but the commemorative paraphernalia – souvenir mugs, flags, badges and T-shirts – is still so recent as to retain that freshly minted look. You usually have to wait for hot news to cool down before you can analyse it properly. Leicester's title season is like that. Behind it there seems to be such a uniquely jumbled conjunction of hows and whys. Sorting through them to reach a definitive understanding of the achievement may take a while yet, which is another factor about it that both fascinates and astonishes us. Without the guts there can be none of the glory, so you can't even trust statistics alone to explain everything, the way a mathematician would, because numbers are bloodless things, lacking empathy with qualities, such as heart, that defy accurate measurement. It is only 497 days since Leicester were handed the Premier League trophy and just 255 since Claudio Ranieri, the Fifa Coach of the Year, was sacked because of relegation jitters. Shakespeare stepped in, winning seven of his first ten games. He has now only won one of his last ten. He won't, it seems, win this one either.

West Brom have relied on breakaways, but rarely to the point of causing trouble. When Leicester have the chance to initiate one of their own Kelechi Iheanacho makes a pig's ear of it, not only losing the ball through a lack of control but also giving away a foul with a lumpen lunge. The free kick is nearly 30 yards out. Kasper Schmeichel takes charge, waving his four-strong wall into one spot and then dragging them fastidiously this way and that, the adjustments measured in inches. He's like a wedding photographer framing a group shot outside the church door. Nacer Chadli hovers over the kick before wrapping his right foot around the ball, delightfully lifting it up and over the wall and throwing in some bend. The line of his effort starts just outside Schmeichel's left-hand post. Then the pronounced curl on the shot takes over, the wind pushing it along. Schmeichel anticipates the shot will go to his right and takes a half-step that way. He can't recover from his mistake. He watches the ball drift past him and land with a soft swoosh. An exceptional goalkeeper has been embarrassed. He gestures to his defenders, passing two fingers in front of his face to suggest he'd been unsighted. If so, it is his own fault: the wall is where he put it.

More than forty years ago the title of Wim Wenders's film, *The Goalkeeper's Fear of the Penalty*, adapted from the Peter Handke novel, slipped into common football usage. No longer. As a general rule, goalkeepers don't fear penalties anymore; a shoot-out especially is the chance for them to become the shining hero. It is the type of goal Chadli has just scored that gives them night sweats. The modern ball and modern techniques mean the long-range free kick is the thing to worry about. The drift, the twist, the speed and the up and over can leave goalkeepers feeling as nauseous as Schmeichel must feel now. You don't even have to be Cristiano Ronaldo to crack a dead ball from distance and score; Chadli has proved it.

A spectacular goal is gravy for TV. One replay of this one is following another, each focusing on a ravishing detail unnoticed before: the sweep of Chadli's foot through the right side of the ball; Leicester's wall cracking apart as each player in it jumps; the stir of the shot through the air and the polished sheen of it, caught under the lights; the defenders swivelling their heads as they track it worriedly, as though already knowing the worst; the net stretched as the ball strikes it; Schmeichel flat-footed and stranded, a spectator like all those around him and all those of us watching in pubs and clubs or at home. You always remembered a goal predominantly from where you stood or sat in a ground. Since most games weren't televised, this was about the only perspective you ever got of it. Now you can see what happens as though you've got twelve pairs of eyes and have used them to stand in twelve different places. You don't have one memory of a goal but a dozen, and your mind can switch between them. This is TV at its best, breaking the moment down into component parts and allowing you to live it, vicariously. Eventually a camera finds Shakespeare, who is so doleful-looking. Behind him is the bench, where Shinji Okazaki and Demarai Gray sit like wallflowers waiting for someone to ask them to dance.

With a lead to hold, as well as a limping goalkeeper to protect, West Brom recoil, as though into a tighter shell still, and let Leicester come at them, searching for a way in. Jonny Evans is everywhere; you'd think there were three of him, so frequently does he tidy up anything loose or even vaguely threatening. Shakespeare grows more disheartened, desperately in need of a goal to buck him up. Vardy tries, making runs; Mahrez weaves away; the substitutes Islam Slimani, the Algerian striker, and the defender Ben Chilwell, ginger up the odd move. It's when Leicester look worn almost to the wick that the four of them contrive an equaliser. Vardy's part is simply being there. In the eightieth minute West Brom are so preoccupied with him that Slimani is given space, steering a header from Chilwell's far post cross into Mahrez's path. He shoots across Myhill from almost the same spot where he botched his earlier chance.

As a boy Shakespeare supported West Brom, his local team. He played for them, worked in their backroom and was briefly their care-taker manager. To have lost to them would have been damaging, possibly beyond repair. The draw – the last ten minutes has been ener-getic but uneventful shadow boxing – is nonetheless only a palliative cure for the malady of his team. Again, the camera moves in on him, the intrusion legitimate. What you see is a semi-disguised grimace, as though some icy little thought about the future has just floated across his mind.

I look at him and wonder about the contents of the poor chap's scrapbook. A good, solid career recorded in page upon page of awful puns and bad jokes about the Bard. I assume the next banner head-line in it will be about the sweet sorrow of parting. He will go, and someone else will replace him. For what football offers is soap opera, self-perpetuating because the cast is forever changing in exits and entrances.

It is the box set that never runs out of episodes. TV makes sure of that.

16 October 2017: Leicester City v West Bromwich Albion
Leicester City 1 West Bromwich Albion 1

Leicester City: Schmeichel, Simpson (Chilwell 74), Maguire, Morgan, Fuchs, Mahrez, Ndidi, Iborra (King 90), Albrighton, Iheanacho (Slimani 74), Vardy.
Subs not used: Hamer, Amartey, Gray, Okazaki

West Bromwich Albion: Myhill, Dawson, Hegazi, Evans, Gibbs, Livermore, Krychowiak, Barry, Chadli (McAuley 84), Rondon, Rodriguez.
Subs not used: Palmer, Yacob, Nyom, Phillips

SCORERS
Leicester City: Mahrez 80
West Bromwich Albion: Chadli 63

BOOKED

Leicester City: Iheanacho, Albrighton
West Bromwich Albion: Hegazi, Myhill

Referee: M. Dean
Attendance: 30,203

7

JEALOUSY, SELFISHNESS, HYPOCRISY

12 November: Manchester City v Bristol City, Women's Super League 1, Academy Stadium

The family of four who arrive at the start of the second half, convinced the match is kicking off at three o'clock, have already missed half a dozen reasons why Manchester City are shooting to the top of the table and a lot more about the power structure of the Women's Super League. By now Bristol City are bashed in and beleaguered-looking. The Academy Stadium is lapping it up.

The early winter sun is low and blazing. The light is so harsh and so dazzling that one goalmouth, which City attacked first, gets completely washed away in it. You can't look towards that end of the field without lifting a hand to shade your eyes and narrowing your gaze to a slit. Even that doesn't remedy the problem entirely. The pale ball regularly gets lost, especially against the iridescent blue of the sky, and so sometimes do the players, who flit in and out of the heavy shadow that the opposite stand casts. Someone can disappear into it and then reappear quite suddenly, popping up as though in a game of hide and seek. The cold is gusting through the ground too, a slight wind chilling in from the east. Only several layers and a woolly cap are enough protection against a mild case of hypothermia.

The father has come prepared for this, wrapped up as if on a polar trek, but not for horribly mistiming his arrival. He is all of a fluster. He steals a quick, surreptitious look at the scoreboard, tucked near the corner flag, and then another when staring down the line of the thickly banked crowd. A huge paper ticket flaps in his hands. It resembles one of those white £5 notes you sometimes see in old films. He and his wife compose themselves, trying but failing not to seem too sheepishly embarrassed as the steward checks their seat numbers. The father hopes no one is looking at him and he tries to hide, his chin down on his chest. Their children – one girl, one boy – say nothing but appear exasperated and let down. The boy, who is about eleven years old, gives his father one of those disapproving stares that suggest no explanation he receives afterwards – however convolutedly plausible – will ever be satisfactory for him. This is a promise broken, and he is going to ask awkward questions about it; for it is the sort of glaring, but avoidable, error that can't be covered up, only compensated for in some other way later on. His sister, a year or two younger, becomes transfixed by the match, finally ignoring her parents' discomfort. She grips the metal rail and stands on tiptoes to peer at the pitch as Izzy Christiansen, the City midfielder, comes close to the touchline and surges past her.

I can't be entirely sure, but I'll wager a goodly sum that this is her and her brother's first game. When, momentarily, she turns away you see the expression of someone mesmerised and even a bit overwhelmed. The colour, the commotion and the whirl of action is clearly new to her senses. As politely and as inscrutably as the doorman at the Ritz, the steward offers advice and then directions to the father, pointing him towards some distant seats. Off the family go to squeeze themselves along a row, no doubt offering profound apologies for the disruption and their unpunctuality. The girl lags behind the others a little, only because she doesn't want to miss a thing more, her head permanently turned sideways as she follows another attack and another fortunate escape for Bristol City, showing already marked signs of fatigue and resignation. The fact she is late seems no longer important to her. What matters is simply being there, absorbed in the moment and awed by it. I watch her walking away, knowing that women's football has instantly recruited another convert.

She is not alone. The Academy Stadium, capacity 7,000, is relatively new (it opened at the end of 2014) and sleekly modern, predominantly made up of hard straight lines. There are Football League and especially National League clubs, trapped in a collection of careworn old buildings that require costly upkeep, who will look at it enviously. The Etihad is only a spit away. You pass it, the back of the stands covered by wide, high photographs of ex-players, former managers and every historical scrap worth recording in word and date and picture. The shallow curve of the place then looms behind as you cross a cream-coloured concrete bridge straddling non-stop traffic on Ashton New Road and Alan Turing Way. At the end of it sits the Academy, the atmosphere inside hard to pin down until you adjust to it. You are handed free blue flags and stiff cardboard clappers. A full gamut of ages accepts them: parents, grandparents, babies, tots, infants and also teens early, mid and late. I stand near the programme stall as twins, no older than six, I guess, arrive directly from someone's birthday celebrations, matching pink bows crowning their hair and glitter still adorning their blushed cheeks. Another girl, slightly older, clutches a ruby balloon on a string, the colour hardly appropriate. A third, about thirteen years old, brings her football, cradling it beneath an arm. It is dark blue and stamped with City's crest. I see this small parade slip by, finally puzzling out what the day reminds me of – and also what I feel about it. I am the stranger who has been invited to someone else's family party, knowing no one and a bit unsure about how to behave. The mood, however, is so congenial and friendly that it doesn't matter. It is, I suppose, like going back to a much earlier era when football was less tribal, crowds were better behaved and more respectful and going to the match was a grand day out. I like it very much.

Manchester City are putting on a stylish show. Last season's FA Cup winners and League runners-up have a rarefied air about them, which statistics back up. Their first six domestic games – two of them in the Continental Tyres Cup – have produced twenty-three goals. Their first three European ties have produced eleven. Only seventy-two hours ago City came back nicely all-conquering from Norway, having flattened LSK Kvinner, routed 5–0. Their team has so many luminaries in it – from the England captain Steph Houghton to Jill Scott, from Izzy Christiansen to Jennifer Beattie – that most opposition, both at home and abroad, are blinded by them. Nick Cushing, their coach, has called his side 'the standard bearers' and only their main rivals, Chelsea, could possibly baulk at such an explicit declaration of superiority. The strength of their bench today shows what a dominant force City have become beneath an enormous corporate brand: seven substitutes have 106 full caps between them.

This is the first winter of the WSL, but the title race really has only two participants. The other eight teams can't hire enough quality talent to shake up, never mind consistently challenge, the overwhelming favourites. Even though the season is still at an embryonic stage, City and Chelsea are beginning to separate themselves from the rest, a small gap likely to become a big and irrecoverable one over the next few months. And City now have the advantage. The game here has barely started when news floats in from Adams Park, where Chelsea have conceded a last minute own goal to draw 2–2 with third-placed Reading. These first dropped points mean City can cut clear of them. There is no 'if' or 'but' or 'maybe' about this; only the when.

It is part-timers against pros, and Bristol know it as early as the eighth minute. If they have an inferiority complex, it is entirely understandable. Scott sublimely dinks a slightly angled through-ball to match Christiansen's slightly angled run. The timing of both is perfection. One half of the defence is dozing. The other half is stationary, admiring in particular not only Scott's perception – she is two thoughts ahead of them – but also the crisply accurate pass, struck on the half-volley. The speed of it gives Christiansen a yard and a half on those who are supposed to be marking her. Into the box she pelts and down she goes. The back-tracking Julie Biesmans has mistimed her tackle, despairingly. The penalty, given unhesitatingly, provokes the mildest of token protests, no one's heart quite in it. Christiansen then does what she'd threatened to do before Biesmans's leg had stopped her. She tucks the ball assuredly into the bottom corner, scoring from the spot for a fifth time this season. The Bristol players exchange anxious glances. This is going to be a slog of a game for them. Preserving their dignity is likely to become more important than pricking out a point. Even forcing a draw seems an unrealistic ambition for them already.

Before the game sprinklers had sloshed water about like billy-oh and faint traces of it, still to dry, glisten like glass. The water freshens up the surface, a boon for the smart, along-the-floor passing of Scott and Christiansen and Houghton, who exudes command. Her travels around the pitch are like tours of inspection. She is said to earn almost

£70,000 per year, making her the country's high earner in WSL. If so, she is worth it. Soon Manchester City – Houghton urging them on – bend and fold the match whichever way it pleases them. Their superiority is everywhere and in everything, which becomes more apparent as the minutes pile up. You sit back, just grateful to be able to enjoy it.

The most lucid sides always boil down the fundamentals – the repeat procedure of pass and control – into something that soon appears mechanically predictable and even mundanely routine. This is done so automatically and so naturally that it doesn't look like a talent at all. But the far more accomplished – those teams that win trophies – also add the odd pinch of the unexpected too, something the opposition don't see coming. The punch hits them even when their guard is up. In the thirty-eighth minute, after continually intense pressure, Jennifer Beattie gets the ball 3 yards inside her own half and has so much space and so much time too that plotting her next move can be done with languor. She looks up, sees Claire Emslie hugging the left-hand touchline and finds her with a pinging pass. Bristol don't seem bothered at first. Their defence is in decent order and Emslie has a shadow with her. Within five seconds and with only eight touches she punishes such complacency and you're aware again of the difference in class in this tale of two Cities. Emslie swapped one for the other during the summer. So her former side have no excuse for their negligence in failing to go over and support the unfortunate full back, Loren Dykes, who can't shut down Emslie alone. The winger is a blue flash, feigning an attack on the outside before slicing sharply the other way. Dykes is lost and still turning when Emslie reaches the box and sweeps in a low right-foot shot that dips inside the far post.

Whoever is running the scoreboard either becomes confused or suddenly feels a stab of pity. What flashes up isn't 2–0 but 1–1. It stays unchanged for a minute or two, inspiring some mockery because so far Bristol are prisoners without parole in their own half. Some hacked clearances have produced the odd, brief raid down the flanks, but the box is to them what distant lands were to the 12th-century cartographer – only a rumour, something to be guessed at. To keep herself occupied Ellie Roebuck, City's goalkeeper, has been walking around her area and sometimes mid-way into her own half simply to feel closer to the action. She's been further away from it than some of us. Roebuck has also been slapping the palm of one glove into another, as though trying to keep herself awake and interested. It is just as well.

Whenever the ball has come to Beattie, she has been able to count its panels and admire the maker's logo. No one has put her under pressure. When someone does – Lauren Hemp chasing down a throw in – Beattie flaps uncharacteristically, losing possession to her diminutive challenger. Hemp sprints off, exposing also the central defender's sluggishness, and is left one-on-one against Roebuck, who comes to meet her and the ball. Her decisiveness forces a decision out of Hemp before she is ready to make one. The shot is hasty and under-hit because of it; Roebuck blocks with a stuck-out leg.

Her save means that, when the family of four finally arrive, City are still rolling along, untroubled and with their clean sheet intact.

The crowd is about 1,200, but I speculate how big it would have been a century ago, just before English football deliberately destroyed what had been built because of spiteful jealousy, sanctimoniousness, selfishness of the very heinous kind, rank hypocrisy and misogyny. All of that was disguised behind a whopping lie too.

Earlier this year there was a cord-pulling ceremony in Preston, unveiling a blue plaque at the munitions factory that was once Dick, Kerr & Co. During the Great War, the women who worked in that dangerous environment – a mistake or a waver in concentration could lead to maiming, disfigurement or being blown to ashes – also pulled on their boots, wore striped shirts and woollen hats and changed the perception of the game. In what can be described as an early version of Help for Heroes, the Dick, Kerr Ladies team raised funds for servicemen and their dependants. If Manchester City and Bristol City had faced one another between 1917 and 1921, a ground the size of the Academy would have been too small to stage it. Dick, Kerr Ladies began with a gate of 10,000. At their zenith more than 12,000 were shut out at Goodison Park because 53,000 more were already jammed on to the terraces. The prosperity lasted fewer than four years, scandalously snuffed out as abruptly as a candle because its flame had simply got too hot for the Football Association.

Like almost everything else then – remember, not all women could even vote – the FA was an antediluvian organisation run like a gentleman's club. The triumvirate in charge of it were the president, Arthur Fitzgerald Kinnaird, the 11th Lord Kinnaird; the chairman Charles Clegg; and the secretary Frederick Wall. Kinnaird was the son of a banker turned MP and then aristocrat, a silver-spoon toff schooled at Eton and Cambridge and a distinguished footballer, playing in nine FA Cup finals and winning three of them. Clegg, later knighted, was an FA sort of chap from the waxed tips of his moustache to the soles of his shined shoes; he served them for more than fifty years. Wall was tailored from the same bolt of fine cloth as Clegg; he was knighted too.

There is a theory that the FA wrecked women's football because of political motives, its council spooked by those teams who switched sympathetically from helping servicemen to helping striking miners when the country struggled in the aftermath of war to build homes and create work. The evidence doesn't fully support the ton-weight of that argument and also over-complicates what is a more straightforward matter: the unfortunate collision of male prejudice and circumstance. Clegg and Wall were contemporaries, each censorious mid-Victorians born when a glimpse of a woman's stocking truly was shocking and a naked knee counted as almost pornographic. Wall dismissed 'some girls' clubs' as 'circus affairs'. Clegg was teetotal, non-smoking and devotedly religious. The social habits of Dick, Kerr Ladies' Lily Parr, a firecracker goal-scorer, were not to his taste. Still a teenager, Parr liked a sup of brown ale and smoked fags by the packet.

The FA, it was said, 'bowed down' to Clegg, described as 'football's king (and) very nearly a dictator'. When women's football began to be troublesome for the FA, Kinnaird would have been a reasonable, mediating voice, tempering Clegg and Wall's antagonism towards it. Kinnaird was the liberals' liberal, his social conscience embracing women's rights and equality. His philanthropist mother had been the forming force of the YWCA. But over-work, his own ill-health and his wife's (both would shortly die) sapped his influence at the FA, turning his presidency into a titular affair. He stopped attending meetings, including the crucial one. Clegg and Wall were left to their own mean devices.

The FA had seen women's football as a tolerable fad, a stopgap until the troops came home and the status quo was restored. The raging popularity of it afterwards was a threat to them. Killing it took only 103 words, and the FA were crafty about choosing them. Knowing that banning the game was beyond their powers, Clegg and Wall disabled it instead, blocking affiliated clubs – which was nearly everyone – from allowing women's teams to play on their pitches. The justification for this was a misdirection of thick smoke and huge mirrors. The game was 'unsuitable for females', the FA said. The money from their games was not necessarily funnelled to charitable causes, it insisted. To support the first claim the FA produced a doctor, Mary Scharlieb. She was then seventy-six, her breakthrough into medicine well behind her. Scharlieb had once defied convention to prove that combining motherhood and doctoring was not impossible. Her own history and experience unfortunately didn't soften Scharlieb towards the Dick, Kerr Ladies and their ilk. Football, she announced, was 'too much for a woman's physical frame', a diagnosis made without actually seeing a match. The FA, being thin on facts, produced no lavish proof of financial corruption either, gambling correctly that no one who mattered – i.e. men – would investigate the hole in the story. The accusation was simply left to hang there, like a cloud of noxious gas.

The women's game was down, and there was no shortage of people willing to kick it, shouting their contempt and insults as the boot went in. When one team in Leeds asked to play on a rugby pitch, the refusal also accused them of making 'a ridiculous exhibition of themselves'. One regional FA tried banning a woman for merely supporting her husband's team 'too keenly'. Even relatively minor, insignificant branches of the clergy got involved. In an outrageous display of pomposity, the Dean of Durham declared: 'Women never show to their best advantage when they aspire to become imitators of men'.

The FA's allegations, which Clegg and Wall concocted, were the opposite of the truth, but the game nonetheless collapsed beneath them. So while it celebrates a team, the plaque to Dick, Kerr Ladies also reminds us of what was lost – and the perfidy of the FA in losing it.

Between the lines of the inscription lies only sadness.

*   *   *

The Football Association's formal reconciliation with women's football took half a century – justice arriving on the slowest of boats – and almost another half-century has gone by since. The pulse of the game was always beating, though often so weakly as to be barely felt, but it has begun to quicken during this decade. There was the launch of the Super League, eventually split into two. There was the performance of England, who, despite being ranked outside the top four, fought stirringly to reach the semi-finals of the World Cup in Canada, a nation flag-waving for them at home even at ungodly hours of the morning. The publicity generated begat a higher profile, which in turn begat the 'fancy trimmings' needed to sustain the game and then improve and polish it: a hike in attendances, greater sponsorship and advertising revenue, better TV deals, a Cup Final at Wembley and a certain degree of name-recognition for the players. And yet the Super League, then and now, is a fragile thing, which makes the structures below it more delicate still. At the start of this year Sunderland switched from being fully pro to part-time. Next, Notts County collapsed, the £500,000 cost of running them impossible to maintain. Sandwiched between those two events, the FA produced its 'Gameplan for Growth', publishing an accompanying brochure in which at first glance the words looked subservient to the plush design. Sure enough, the punchy alliteration of the title bounced off the tongue, but the content included some depressing marketing-speak. It was as though whoever signed off on it had a tin ear for the musical lilt of language. The ambition, between the document's launch and 2020, is about doubling participation, doubling fan numbers and 'consistent success on the world stage'. How this noble aspiration would actually lead to solid achievement wasn't convincingly explained. That's because the reader was tripping over phrases such as 'the talent pathway', whatever that may be. In my mind's eye I immediately saw a flat concrete strip rather than a luminous Yellow Brick Road. *Gameplan for Growth* fired out statistics the way a nail gun fires out nails. Among them were: average crowd figures (1,128), the peak TV audience for League games (63,000), the total of affiliated girls' teams (3,504), the numbers who took part in football weeks (130,000). I can quote more of these, but won't, because each only emphasises the same point. For what women's football basically needs to continually top its own success is more investment from the men's game, which is hardly rubbing the farthings together to stay warm and in all other respects – especially in wages and transfer fees – likes to go indulgently mad with its money.

When *Gameplan for Growth* appeared, the FA's chairman Greg Clarke accepted that 'clearly, over the years, the FA let down women's football'. The admission showed that Clarke understood the wanton waste of that and also regretted his distant predecessors' pre-meditated plot to shove the game down a sinkhole where no one would find it again. What followed, however, did not suggest the current management had the expertise to run the shop competently either. Quite the reverse, actually. In the autumn Clarke and three other FA executives appeared in front of the Parliamentary Digital, Culture, Media and Sport select committee. The committee heard evidence about allegations of discrimination and racism by the Chelsea and international striker Eni Aluko. Her claim – vindicated – was that the England manager Mark Sampson had made racially charged comments to her. In the *Daily Telegraph*, Paul Hayward, as he so often does, put it best. The hearing was a 'four-hour manure typhoon' for the FA, he wrote. During it Clarke referred to institutional racism as 'fluff'. Some fluff. The original response to Aluko's complaint, the botched and inadequate investigation into it and Clarke's buffoonery in front of the select committee cast the FA into a glass darkly. The more you see what the FA does, the less confidence you have in it to do anything successfully at all.

By then it had already made a profound announcement about the next women's season before the current one was barely underway. The top tier would become the exclusive preserve of full time clubs and be expanded from ten to fourteen teams. Since there are only five professional sides in the division – Arsenal, Chelsea, Everton, Liverpool and Manchester City – the clock was ticking for everyone else who wanted to travel first class. There was a six-week deadline for the present Super League sides to pitch for a new licence. It would be granted only after certain criteria had been fulfilled, including the creation of an academy. This seemed peremptory, an authoritarian and risky *fait accompli* in which finance, not points, would determine who played at what level. From the off it was difficult not to think that the FA really wanted more big names – coaxing Manchester United into the fray at last, perhaps – and fewer smaller ones. Whatever the

L S Lowry set out to capture the 'atmosphere' of Bolton Wanderers' Burnden Park. He succeeded magnificently.

A canopy of shadow like black lace. Tottenham launch another attack against Newcastle on the opening weekend of the season at St James' Park.

Mowgli the Great Dane, the unofficial mascot of Guiseley, commands a prime view of the game at Nethermoor Park.

Davide Zappacosta soaks up the acclaim of Chelsea's supporters after his fabulously freakish goal in the Champions League qualifier against Qarabag at a floodlit Stamford Bridge.

It always seemed that Jimmy Greaves, master goal-poacher, had absolute command of the ball. He does here on Chelsea's dust-dry pitch.

No one is fooled. Rajiv van La Parra's swan-dive in the Burnley box wins him nothing but a yellow card – and the bitter criticism of the defenders around him.

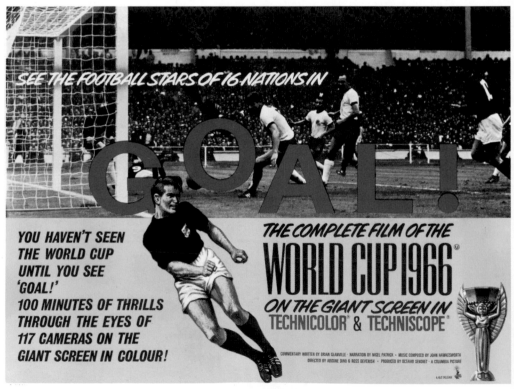

SEE THE FOOTBALL STARS OF 16 NATIONS IN

GOAL!

YOU HAVEN'T SEEN
THE WORLD CUP
UNTIL YOU SEE
'GOAL!'
100 MINUTES OF THRILLS
THROUGH THE EYES OF
117 CAMERAS ON THE
GIANT SCREEN IN COLOUR!

THE COMPLETE FILM OF THE
WORLD CUP 1966
ON THE GIANT SCREEN IN
TECHNICOLOR® & TECHNISCOPE®

COMMENTARY WRITTEN BY BRIAN GLANVILLE · NARRATION BY NIGEL PATRICK · MUSIC COMPOSED BY JOHN HAWKESWORTH
DIRECTED BY ABIDINE DINO & ROSS DEVENISH · PRODUCED BY OCTAVIO SENORET · A COLUMBIA PICTURE

The Citizen Kane of football documentaries. A cinema poster advertises Goal!, the story of the 1966 World Cup.

Not for the first time – nor the last – Harry Kane rescues England with a late, late goal to beat Slovenia at Wembley and secure a place in the World Cup finals.

Jamie Vardy, right, of Leicester City and Boaz Myhill of West Bromwich Albion collide in the Midlands derby, leaving the slow-motion replay to determine which of them fouled the other.

The Dick, Kerr Ladies Team, formed during the First World War, who played in front of packed, astonished grounds and established themselves indisputably as pioneers of women's football in Britain.

Steph Houghton, Manchester City's captain, adroitly stops another Bristol City attack in the WSL.

The legendary knight says farewell. Sir Stanley Matthews, aged 50, plays his final match before retirement at Stoke City's Victoria Ground.

The most beautiful statue commemorating a footballer in this country.
Sir Stanley Matthews' tribute in brilliant bronze beside the bet365 Stadium at Stoke.

The orange flash. The genius that is Mo Salah nonchalantly tucks in his second goal for Liverpool against Stoke.

TELEVISION!
The football spectator of 19——?

The man who saw tomorrow. The cartoonist Waller, of All Sports Weekly, accurately portrays the football fan of the future. The cartoon was drawn in 1928.

intentions, the consequences were potentially dire for some part-timers. Yeovil, needing £350,000 to meet the criteria, began crowd-funding. Sunderland, still struggling, started cobbling together a merger. Lower down, Watford, of Super League 2, prepared to become amateur and depart the pro and semi-pro scene altogether.

Even after this latest episode of turbulence ends, the major questions about the women's game will remain unchanged because only the drip of time – another decade or so at least – will answer them definitively. Can the FA deliver? Will the women's game consistently produce enough talent and do so fast enough to satisfy demand? We can only hope so, but no one is able to plan securely for the long term when a relatively short football career earns them only £20,000 per year. They have to prepare for the day when the cheering stops, which pushes them while still playing into supplementary employment, further education or both. Demanding that everyone go full time, and then demanding it be done in a few eye-blinks, suggests someone got only three quarters of the way down the line of an idea and thought he/she had gone far enough. There is another problem. Manchester City coach more than 100 girls, some of whom will become part of a future team. At present, the club can also absorb the loss of two premier performers, Toni Duggan to Barcelona and Lucy Bronze to Lyon, because it possesses the resources to replace them. However much shuffling occurs for the 2018-19 season, the well-off will hold the monopoly. It will be good for them, but bad for the game. If most of the above sounds a little depressing, we have to realise one thing. Despite how far women's football has come, this is still only the beginning of the beginning for it.

Here, with the sun still full, I see Houghton, Christiansen, Scott and Emslie appear for the second half and think of them as pioneers in much the same way that Lily Parr and the Dick, Kerr Ladies used to be.

Surely, the FA can't muck things up for them too.

You can only guess at the bruising Bristol City would get if Steph Houghton and her team were not recuperating from their journey to Norway and preparing for the return leg here in another four days.

The timing of the fixture has saved them from the sort of goal avalanche that could possibly have buried their entire season. Manchester City are doing just enough, pushing the ball about attractively, constructively and entertainingly without drawing too many hard breaths.

From the start of her career, I have always followed and admired Jill Scott, her game made up of perceptive intelligence welded to tough endeavour. There is an iron reliability about her too. Being slender and almost 6 feet tall, she isn't hard to spot. Some of her best work still goes on almost unobtrusively – a short pass, the willingness to go back and collect the ball, a dash off it to distract a defender. She reminds me of someone from my schooldays, a better footballer than most of the boys (me included). She had balance and footwork and also knew how to take care of herself. Had it been possible then, she would have got into our team either up front or, more profitably, as a creative midfielder. In our park kick-abouts she could skin anyone, a twisting run wafting her on the outside or inside of a tackler as easily as a breeze. Were she a teenager today, she'd be a coveted signing for someone; but the FA's ban on women's football had only just ended – this was the early 1970s – and the game was still busy sorting itself out. She was good at completely the wrong time.

It is difficult enough to judge one generation beside another and absolutely impossible to do so accurately when the distance between them is a hundred years. How good were the Dick, Kerr Ladies? We don't know because we can't tell from the film evidence. In those days cameras were stationary, so you usually saw only segments of matches, the angle changing whenever the man in charge of it picked up his tripod and lens and plonked it down somewhere different. The camera was also hand-cranked. What it recorded was crazily sped up or slowed down depending on the physical fitness of the cameraman. Lily Parr poached forty-three goals in her debut season. Her sledge-hammer shot is said to have broken a bar and also the wrist bones of a goalkeeper (male) who boasted he could save any penalty she took against him.

I can't believe, however, that even Parr ever scored a better goal than City's third, which comes in the fifty-ninth minute. It is a bonny belter, a collector's item, from Abbie McManus, her first in WSL.

When a clearance drops into space and bobbles up, she gets to it ahead of a defender. Her drive from 16 yards rises unstoppably. The ball is past Sophie Baggaley before she can stretch so much as a finger towards it.

Bristol are exhausted, their energy used up simply on making sure there is no slide into total acquiescence, which would turn an emphatic defeat into a disastrous one. A fourth goal arrives near the end, another piece of individualism. It comes from Jennifer Beattie, able to wander out of defence and loiter around the edge of the area. Bristol, for whom the wings are a weakness, fail to cut out a cross and can't rob Beattie of the ball after it lands unexpectedly on her right foot. She sidesteps opposite number, Danique Kerkdijk, creating her own invitation to shoot and then accepting it. The effort bumps against the inside of Baggaley's left post before going in.

After losing the FA Cup Final in 1971, Bill Shankly addressed the half of Liverpool who had bit down hard on their Wembley disappointment and waited on the streets for the team's homecoming. Any plot of land was speaker's corner for Shankly, the orator that Ayrshire made. He demanded silence when he spoke with that raspy voice, and rapture afterwards. He knew which words to emphasise, each stress and inflection carefully measured for maximum impact. Even by his standards, the speech he gave without notes surpassed the occasion, never forgotten by those who heard it. Wearing the red tie he seldom took off, Shankly stuck one hand into the trouser pocket of his smoke-grey suit and pointed at the masses with the other. He felt the grief of his adopted people but assuaged it with two sentences that everyone knew leapt out of his heart. 'I have drummed it into our players time and again that they are privileged to play for you,' said Shankly. 'And if they didn't believe me, they believe me now.'

The modern player, especially in the Premier League, ought to watch and soak up the sentiment in it. It is no bother to go to a crowd after scoring a goal, kissing the badge on the shirt or performing a show-off celebration. This, after all, is done to milk acclaim, not to give it back, some players having a loftier view of themselves than of the fans who contribute to their salary. This is noticeable as players come and go before and after matches. The 'star' arrives pretending to talk on his mobile or has a pair of earphones clamped to his head and stares into the far distance to avoid signing a photograph or an autograph book. I remember a boy who stood for half an hour for an international's signature. The international finally appeared, heading like a shot arrow for the team bus. The boy, holding out a magazine poster that he had bull-clipped to a stiff board, took a half-step towards him and asked politely for a signature, his accompanying expression almost beseeching. The international raised his nose into the air, sniffed slightly and gave a short, dismissive shake of his head before slipping by, wordlessly and ungraciously, to hide behind the tinted windows of the bus. I wondered then what Shankly would have made about such arrogance, such shameful disregard. I like to think he would have hoiked the international out of his seat and stood over him until that photo was signed. Or taken the boy on to the coach and given him tickets for the next match.

The incident crosses into my mind because, when the game is over, Houghton soon leads her players across to the touchline where the crowd are waiting to claim a signature or a selfie. Izzy Christiansen gives advice to one girl who wants to be 'just like you'. Steph Houghton holds a baby aloft, the parents snapping a photo. And Claire Emslie asks a supporter, too timidly shy to engage her in conversation, whether she 'enjoyed the match'. And in reply the girl who missed half of it because of her father's mistake nods her head.

She will be back, for sure.

12 November 2017: Manchester City v Bristol City
Manchester City 4 Bristol City 0

Manchester City: Roebuck, McManus, Houghton, Beattie, Stokes, Scott, Walsh, Christiansen, Emslie (Toone 90+3), Ross (Parris 68), Lawley (Campbell 77).
Subs not used: Bardsley, Stanway, Morgan, Hourihan

Bristol City: Baggaley, Dykes, Matthews, Kerkdijk, Allen, Humphrey (Wooley 80), Arthur, Daniels (Ferguson 68), Biesmans (Palmer 85), Turner, Hemp.
Subs not used: Watson, Wilson

SCORERS

Manchester City: Christiansen 8, Emslie 38, McManus 59, Beattie 87

BOOKED

None

Referee: H. Conley
Attendance:1,010

8

THE SWEET REVENGE OF THE JAMMY BASTARDS

2 November: Stoke City v Liverpool, Premier League, bet365 Stadium

A ground that lacks character can never inspire a lasting romance. When empty, it will always look forlorn and lonely, only a shell of a thing. It is sadly true of Stoke's bet365 Stadium, which was built without grandeur. This is the ingredient that, if missing from the start, can never be added afterwards without drastic rebuilding.

There is no designer chic, no signature creative flourish and no elegant landmark feature about it. The bet365 looks as though it arrived in kit form, the pieces bolted together afterwards. The sight of it doesn't overwhelm. Nor do you gaze at it and feel as though wiping your feet at the front door will be an obligation. The stands are smartly neat but aesthetically boring. The company they keep makes the heart sag further too. It's as if the city's planners, like someone throwing clutter under the bed to forget it is there, decided one day to bundle up all their eyesores and stick them in the same small corner for convenience's sake. The bet365 sits in a landscape so unlovely that the blandness of its own architecture is – temporarily, at least – forgotten when you take in the rest of the neighbourhood. Right alongside the noisy roll of the A50, which is bad enough, is acre upon acre of warehouses and industrial units. Dotted among them is the odd car showroom. Blighting the middle distance, so ugly it makes you gape, is a squat waste recycling factory attached to a thin, skyscraper-tall chimney, which almost constantly coughs out flat slants of grey-white smoke. There isn't twopence worth of wind to carry it further than a hundred yards. In late afternoon, the coldness enough to chafe the skin, the last of the light is about to go and conceal the unsightliness in welcome darkness. Kick-off is four and a half hours away, the match critical to both teams. For Stoke because slovenly form sees them uneasily poised not far above the bottom three. For Liverpool, who are sixth, because losing touch with Champions League qualification now could be so damaging as to become irreparable later on.

I have come ridiculously early to see Sir Stanley Matthews. There are three of him, each sharing the same enormous concrete plinth. It's incongruous almost to absurdity that the finest statue(s) to a footballer in this country – or arguably anywhere else – stands in such a setting. More incongruous still is the fact it doesn't overlook the main entrance, where it ought to be flaunted, but is tucked at the back of the cark park behind the Boothen End. The critic Bernard Levin, opposed to iconography, proposed that a ceremony held to unveil any new statue should be synchronised with another that covered up an existing one elsewhere. Football clubs disagree, having almost become-favourites of the sculptors' union. Commissions are regularly flung out to them. Bronze has been bought and smelted nearly everywhere; a ground, it seems, isn't properly dressed these days without the likeness of a legend to decorate it. At Arsenal, where statues proliferate, Herbert Chapman is in a buttoned suit, a handkerchief discreetly poking from the top pocket. At Wolves, Billy Wright is so lifelike that you think he could be about to drop the ball he is carrying, kick the thing ahead of him and then chase after it. At Leeds, Billy Bremner's face and arms are raised in salute to the sky, a reminder of a United once damned everywhere except on that plot of West Yorkshire.

As the greatest British player of his generation, Matthews warranted something prodigious in public art. He got it. Ambition matches scale. Compared with this, other football statues are like maquettes. A trio of sculptors, working on a figure apiece, broke down Matthews's career into Shakespearean acts: the fourteen year-old boy; the England international; the son of Stoke who, after leaving them for Blackpool, came back and continued to dazzle until he was past fifty. It was some twilight. The different ages of Matthews are alike in their historical accuracy, showing him in collared shirts, long shorts and thick-studded, clod-hopper boots, one pair ankle high. A ball, panelled and laced, is under his command in each of them. The magic of the statue, individually and collectively, comes from the movement conveyed, the craft in the sculptor's hands capturing not only the skill in the footballer's feet but also the dip and sway of his slim body. Stand in front of the last statue, the waste disposal plant directly at your back, and you're convinced that the man made of metal isn't inanimate at all. He's about to sell you a dummy and dribble off into the distance before the angle of his left shoulder slopes again and someone else is beaten.

I spend a long time walking around the monument, the plinth of which is nearly 6 feet high. As I did with women's football, I am thinking about whether it is possible to compare definitively one, particularly far off period with another and then declare categorically that a player from the past would succeed in the present. As a general rule, I would claim it isn't; too much about the game has changed. It has become less languorous for one thing. But I am sure Matthews would prosper now, never overwhelmed, because he possessed in abundance what everyone still craves, which was preternatural talent. He was born in February 1915. This was his only mistake. Had he been a little more patient, waiting seventy years and arriving in the same February as Cristiano Ronaldo, Matthews would have phenomenally outstripped even the level of renown and wealth that came to him in those years that straddled the depression-hit 1930s and the reforming mid-1960s, a longevity based on being fearsomely fitter than his rivals. He was no slave to the ordinary. His friend and one-time playing contemporary, Tommy Lawton, didn't entirely have his tongue pressed into his cheek when insisting that Matthews could judge the revolutions of a floated cross so perfectly that the laces faced away from the centre forward who came to meet it. You could also always recognise the full back Matthews had been torturing; he had grass stains on his arse.

You have probably had your fill of hearing about the 1953 FA Cup Final, which bears Matthews's name instead of Stan Mortensen's, for whom even a hat-trick wasn't enough to make him the hero of his own finest hour. The brimming detail of almost no other domestic match has been so forensically gone over than Blackpool versus Bolton. Revisiting again that sun-warmed afternoon is nonetheless worthwhile for two reasons. The first is about Matthews as an athlete. No one else could have pulled Blackpool back from 3–1 down because no one else had his leg stamina, his lung capacity or a heart that didn't wear out. Injury weakened Bolton's left side towards the end; Matthews saw his chance and took it. The second reason – much more important – is about Matthews as a character. About the way the public tenderly took to him and the affection he inspired. It wasn't purely out of pity that the neutrals wanted Matthews to seize at last the winner's medal that had eluded him twice before. Since he had given so much, his influence for so long all-pervasive, the rush of feeling for Matthews was based on the game being duty bound to give back something to him, rectifying what would otherwise be a gross injustice.

One of my favourite chapters in John Moynihan's *The Soccer Syndrome*, a book still sadly either unknown or under-rated, describes watching the 1953 Cup Final on television. TVs were then a rarity, ranked as luxury goods, and the furniture in most living rooms hadn't been shifted around to accommodate them. The buying boom occurred only because of the looming Coronation. So sets acquired to see a queen crowned saw a king crowned also. Moynihan was invited to a friend's 'tea party' in St John's Wood where the china teapot and the cups and saucers were 'astonishingly' pink; where cigarette smoke gathered in billowy clouds beneath the ceiling; where cake crumbs were widely scattered. The TV, just a postage-stamp screen in a polished wood surround, was switched on twenty minutes before the start to warm up. There were half a dozen others with Moynihan, squeezing on to a well-stuffed sofa and an assortment of chairs. When the picture slowly emerged, he saw the top of the stadium and flags being waved and also heard a chorus of 'Abide With Me'. The commentary was 'monotonous', he said, but the TV seemed to be 'on fire'. Bolton went ahead. Blackpool drew level. Then Bolton went ahead again. 'We joined the tension and became part of it,' he added, remembering plaintive shouts of 'Come on Stan'. But when Bolton scored a third goal, their lead seemingly unassailable, there were low groans of 'poor Matthews' that anticipated his anguish, which Moynihan and his friends began to experience themselves.

Matthews had been 'loitering' impassively, but with twenty odd minutes to go and a two goal deficit to make up, he really 'starts to play'. Moynihan's palms began to sweat, so anxiously committed was he to what appeared to be a lost cause. Moynihan writes of the miracle that followed: 'The pitch even on that small set seemed to push him towards us and into the room so that the tiny, weaving figure was now the prince of the earth. He had literally taken over the world at that moment – our world, everybody's world.' In the last seconds, as Blackpool equalise and Matthews then carves out the late winner for Bill Perry – the net bulging as if 'caught by a sudden typhoon' – Moynihan is aware of the room swaying, of the china shaking, of cake falling on to the floor and of he and his friends on their feet hugging one another and tossing cushions into the air and exclaiming between them: 'It's in, you swines . . . they've won . . . oh lovely . . . good old Stan'. The noise of the Matthews-inspired win echoed 'all over London and in Blackpool and in Stoke and all over the country', said Moynihan in conclusion before flopping down on to the sofa again – giddy, euphoric, exhausted. He was right. That same scene was repeated everywhere. Implacable club loyalties were suspended for an hour and a half to support Matthews, and a few million drinkers went on extended benders that night with their hangover excuses ready-made next morning.

If he had done nothing else except turn the course of that Cup Final, which remains the greatest of them all, Matthews would be celebrated still. That he did so much besides meant his fame was never localised but universal, his feats exported to continents that knew him only from the headlines he made. The least of us are forgotten soon enough – because life grows quickly over death – and even some of the best often get neglected or overlooked. Players also come and go again in your football-watching lifetime. From early years to advanced old age the average fan of just one team will watch more than 1,000 flit by in club colours. Most over the decades become as insubstantial as shadows, their faces half-forgotten as one match blurs indistinctly into another. Matthews belongs to that minute proportion, a different breed altogether, who endure, solidly ever present even if you never saw them play. Their deeds survive them because they were emblematic of an era and so will always be talked about, a fixed reference point in specific spots of time. They achieved distinction, which is different from, and more lasting than, celebrity. In today's world, under the bombardment of all that posturing on social media, we muddle one with the other and so aren't able to separate them.

The finer work on Matthews's monument fades in the winter murk, leaving behind only the hard silhouette outlined against the darkening sky. A young fan, not born or brought up in Stoke and knowing nothing of Matthews' legend, will stand where I stand and wonder perhaps what the fuss is all about. Both the player and the period in which he played will seem antique and therefore irrelevant to him; nothing more than nostalgic whimsy. I'm convinced he will come to understand eventually. Matthews was so grandiloquent with a ball that he can't fail to live on.

The idea of acquiring a memento from someone famous is anathema to me. I don't know what motivates the collector to buy D. H. Lawrence's bedsheet or the butt of a cigar Winston Churchill once smoked. And why, as though longing for some association by proxy, would you want to own a footballer's cup winner's medal or international shirt and display them behind glass or wrap them in polythene at home? The museum is the place for them. When Matthews made his farewell appearance for Stoke, more than half a century ago, there were those who afterwards tried to dig up big tufts of the pitch. And only this morning I picked up *The Times* to discover that some of Matthews's memorabilia had been sold at a Midlands auction house only the previous day. The items were eclectic: the last of his fifty-four England caps (£3,000); a wooden throne, which Ghana presented to him to formalise his status as 'a king' (£850); a tartan golfing hat and a pair of burgundy slip-on shoes (£155). Someone, somewhere is always seeking a piece of Matthews – even if that piece is just kitsch or bric-a-brac.

That's another sign of his immortality, I suppose.

I think the best and most arresting opening line in a football book is: 'On Wednesday afternoon 50,000 grandmothers lay dead'. The writer was Percy M. Young, one of the game's mid-century historians. Young speculated on how an FA Cup replay, staged well before the introduction of floodlights, managed to pull in a capacity crowd on a working afternoon. After discounting the implausible and ignoring the improbable, Young was left only with what he was sure counted as the truth: the excuse of doctor's papers or some made-up family bereavement. Floodlights long ago made both unnecessary, but we take the midweek match for granted when we shouldn't. Especially in early winter, it has a show-beauty about it. The deep burning glare of those bulbs. The inky elongated shadows. The spread of white light evenly filling every corner of the ground. The roof of solid blackness above. Everything looks different, more glamorous somehow, than it does when kick-off is at three o'clock. Everything seems more intense too. Colours are vividly exacerbated, making them seem richer than during some cream-pale November afternoon. Night-time suits the bet365 Stadium, the stands dissolving into it. You don't notice the ordinariness of the surroundings any more than you do the inside of the theatre after the curtain goes up. Your eye goes only to what is lit up.

Liverpool are in a kit of hideous phosphorescent orange. Were the electricity grid to suddenly go down throughout the whole of Staffordshire, leaving only a sickle moon and one of Van Gogh's starry nights to illuminate the pitch, their players would be perfectly visible, glowing incandescently. Stoke City are either uncomfortable with this bilious sight or seriously lack confidence. Most teams, particularly at home, have to be forced back into their own half, foot-by-foot. Stoke, who last won a month ago, simply drop back and let Liverpool pour all over them, spraying passes as they go. Jürgen Klopp doesn't need to be his usual high velocity self. He isn't bustling manically around the technical area or indulging in extravagant hand gestures to gee his team along. He stands, still and calm, like someone who has found a nice view and wants to drink it in.

Liverpool go ahead after just seventeen minutes. The lead, though disputed, is not unexpected. Stoke fail to track the 40-yard run Joe Gomez makes to the goal-line. Those closest to Gomez – in the seats rather than on the field – are convinced that the ball is out before he hooks his boot around it. The cross is flicked to Sadio Mané, a short push of speed taking him past the dopey defence. Lee Grant, the goal-keeper, doesn't winnow the angle either. As he comes off his line, the act almost a shuffling afterthought, Mané spoons the shot over him from 6 yards, his effort a soft caress of the ball. Rather than being furious with their own lackadaisicalness, Stoke are furious only with the referee, Martin Atkinson. He receives a litany of moaning, a display of emotion wasted and entirely pointless. Atkinson ignores it, and is right to do so. The call was close; but, if the lime on the line was wet, the ball Gomez put over would have been marked with a smear of it.

Stoke are so predictable that even someone who has never seen a match before can trace in advance the line of their every attack. Irrespective of the route, usually spreading towards the flanks, the destination is always the same, leading as it does to the head of Peter Crouch. In two months Crouch will be thirty-seven. Yesterday he signed a new contract until 2019. He won't match Sir Stanley Matthews's staying power, but his length of service by Premier League standards is already worthy of a gold watch. The older Crouch gets, the thinner he seems to become. He looks more than ever like a figure who has escaped from an L. S. Lowry painting. Dejan Lovren sticks to him. The two of them jostle to and fro; Lovren gets so close at one point, matching Crouch movement for movement, that he reminds me of Fred Astaire dancing with the hat-stand in *Royal Wedding*. This is Crouch's first start of the season. The ball is thumped high and repeatedly towards that 6 feet 7 inch frame. He is as game as he ever was; you can't help but like his robustness and continued willingness to wait patiently for something to turn up. He gets clattered. He goes over. He tries again. He runs around, often with his back to goal, in the hope that a ball even of dubious quality will eventually find him. When it does, completely against the grain of the play, Crouch makes the most of it, justifying his place.

One team is on the rack and the other is rampant, forcing Stoke to go from 3-4-2 to 4-4-2 to cope with it. Liverpool then unaccountably switch off. That long ball, which Stoke should patent, picks out Crouch, who rises unchallenged in the thirty-ninth minute. He steers a glancing header as accurately as a through pass between Liverpool's pulled-apart defence. Anonymous until then, Mame Biram Diouf gallops after it, surprised to find his anticipation of what Crouch will do has stolen a yard and a half on Joël Matip. Simon Mignolet, well out of his goal, is of sacrificial disposition. Knowing no one else will get there, and also knowing that otherwise a one-on-one duel with

Diouf is unavoidable, the goalkeeper gets his retaliation in first. He sprints towards him and uses his right leg the way corn-shearers once used scythes, the ball bobbling away. Down Diouf falls, crashing and tumbling, when he ought to be sliding in the equaliser. The point of contact, which is at shin height, takes place 2 feet outside the box. Stoke don't appeal for a penalty, but demand Mignolet is sent off as the last man. Referee Atkinson, who had only a rear view of the incident, flashes a yellow card at Mignolet. He is wrong not to produce the red.

I am within sight and earshot of a man of about seventy. His nose is large and port-purple. He wears a Stoke scarf, a Stoke baseball cap and a padded jacket with a Stoke badge fastened on to the breast of it. No doubt at home he drinks from a Stoke mug, sleeps under a Stoke duvet and his alarm awakens him with a blast of 'Delilah', the Stoke anthem. Before the game he had conducted his own quiz about Stoke's history that was based on questions so devilishly recondite that only he knew the answers to them. He has eyes only for Stoke. He is a loyal trooper, the club are the passion of his passion, which is football. He refers to Liverpool constantly as 'jammy bastards'. Mané and Solanke are 'jammy'. The goal Liverpool score is 'definitely jammy'. That Stoke don't score is irrefutable proof that Klopp is a 'jammy bastard' of a manager too. Liverpool shouldn't take this personally. Had anyone not wearing Stoke's red and white stripes – even Lionel Messi – pirouetted past three tackles and, once clear of them, juggled the ball from boot to boot for a dozen yards before volleying into the top corner, he too would have been a 'jammy bastard'. His remarks are peppered with other, four-letter expletives for added emphasis. Asked to chalk these on a wall, rather than shout them out loud, I am not sure he would be able to spell them. He gets most irate when the referee and his assistants don't do the decent thing, which for him is always giving Stoke the benefit of the doubt. Any decision made against them is for him conclusive proof of perfidious conspiracy. When not on the attack, he provides coaching tips. 'Take it wide, Stoke,' is his go-to advice alongside 'Down the middle and up to Crouch' or 'Hold it, hold it'. Already he has worked himself into a pitch of raging indignation over trifles – throw-ins, for example. So, when the real injustice of Mignolet's non-dismissal occurs, I think there is nowhere higher for him to go on the vocal scale. He shows me the stupidity of that first impression. He explodes apoplectically. For a minute or so there is the possibility, like Mr Krook in *Bleak House*, that he will spontaneously combust, leaving behind gunk and ashes and the stench of rancid meat. His eyes swell. His facial muscles tighten. His mouth opens and closes rapidly – even when nothing is coming out of it. When the free kick, the shabbiest of consolations for Stoke in the circumstances, fails to produce a goal, the tantrum is repeated. And when, almost immediately, Solanke thwarts an over-stretched offside trap to put Mané entirely in the clear, he is on his feet again and spitting more disgust at the officials. Mané's shot clatters off the outside of the post. The man doesn't care. 'Offside,' he repeats continuously until the cumulative strain of both this and his previous complaints overwhelm him. Liverpool are the better team by far. The score could be 3–1 or 4–1. He doesn't see that. 'Jammy bastards,' he shouts again at half time.

Stoke City were for so long the subject of a little boasting on behalf of the Premier League. The big boys of Spain, Germany or Italy had either won or appeared in more Champions League finals. La Liga, Serie A and the Bundesliga were nevertheless said to be inferior because each lacked the depth of the game in England. The week-to-week demands made on the clubs in them were claimed to be less punishing. The argument was never watertight, but Stoke, as the everyman club, were held up repeatedly as proof that the Premier League was solid rock all the way through. Stoke's ruggedly pragmatic approach (though not necessarily their personnel) were seen as wholeheartedly English as a cup of strong tea. Unpretentious, but combative. Their skill, while not silken, allied to a clever-clever smartness. Capable enough to beat a top team or at the very least frighten the wits out of them for a while. The superior claim made for them was that Barcelona wouldn't particularly fancy coming to the Potteries on a cold, wet Monday night; for Stoke would be capable of turning them over. Well, this is a Wednesday night and Barcelona wouldn't find much to ruffle their equilibrium against this side.

The average salary in the Premier League is more than £50,000 a week, making the average yearly income £2,642,508. While Barcelona head the wages table in world football, ahead of Paris St-Germain and Real Madrid, nine English clubs occupy places in the top twenty. The money we hand over in tickets and for subscriptions to Sky and BT funds this and also the transfer fees, hiked so exorbitantly in a mad, mad market, that you convince yourself that £10m is cheap, £20m is still an absolute snip and £30m counts almost as a bargain. What something is worth still depends on what someone will pay for it, but no amount handed over – even for a full back – will ever stun us now. Before the last transfer deadline, English clubs spent more than £1b between them. The A-list players will nonetheless always be pulled to the A-list teams, the combination of prestige and better bonuses working on human nature like a gravitational force. This leaves Stoke and others like them among the stragglers, panting to keep up. Their squad includes four players who have won the Champions League. Two of them, Darren Fletcher and Xherdan Shaqiri, are on the field. The other two, Jesé and Ibrahim Afellay, are substitutes. But the Premier League has fractured into three loose archipelagos – top seven, middle seven, bottom six – and the plates on which they stand are shifting, consistently putting more distance between each. Stoke cannot afford the ambitions of stardom. Liverpool are so far in front of them technically that Jürgen Klopp can even afford to warm the bench with his creative wonder, Philippe Coutinho, and the marvellous Mo Salah, scorer of fifteen goals so far. I understand Klopp's desire not to burden them unnecessarily, burning each out halfway through a season, but I still feel slightly cheated.

Stoke probably don't. Their night could become an extremely long one if either Coutinho or Salah appear now.

In the second half, after a short period of relatively claustral quiet, a familiar phrase bursts forth. Leaning backwards and so off balance, Joe Gomez misdirects a defensive header across his own box. Joe Allen, always busy, meets it on the half volley. His shot is torpedoing towards the bottom corner, beyond the unsighted Simon Mignolet, until a deflection from a stuck-out foot sends it 6 inches past the post.

'Jammy bastards,' says the man who is Stoke City. This is the prequel to more swearing and arguing with players who can't hear him.

I have been slow on the uptake. Finally I realise he is a fictional character come to life. In the *Ripping Yarns* episode, 'Golden Gordon', Michael Palin plays Gordon Ottershaw, a fan with an insane obsession with the club he supports. The club are called Barnstoneworth United (coincidentally they play in the same kit as Stoke).When his team loses, which is every Saturday, Gordon goes home and takes out his anger on his own living room. He breaks everything that can be broken, pulling a door off its frame, smashing ornaments and throwing the mantelpiece clock out of the front window. His wife is always either hiding the china or sweeping up bits of it. Gordon, like this Stoke supporter, has an encyclopaedic mind for figures and dates and names, but unfortunately it records only the lows of Barnstoneworth. And so misery is piled on misery. Were Stoke in charge, the man here might reveal some earth-dark humour that has been hidden so far. But Stoke are so plain as to set off exuberantly the colour Liverpool possess. This rankles him further. Liverpool don't look in danger. The ball is pushed languidly about and Stoke seem frantic, as though imminent disaster is ever at their heels. At one point Mark Hughes, their manager, balls his fist and presses it against his chest, as though suffering from acid reflux. His eyes search for small mercies. None is to be found.

If things weren't bad enough for him, Jürgen Klopp brings on Mo Salah in the sixty-seventh minute. He immediately claims our complete attention.

There were only thirteen overseas players in the Premier League when it began. Further back still any 'foreigner' was regarded as Hollywood-glamorous. In the summer of 1978, when Argentina won the World Cup, we admired the busy, accurate passing of Ossie Ardiles, never thinking he'd ever swap South America for England. No one ever did then. When, only weeks later, Ardiles, 'The Little Fellow', came to Tottenham with his compatriot Ricky Villa, 'The Big Fellow', it was considered so extraordinary that nearly 10,000 went to gawp at them during an open day at the club's Cheshunt training ground. In a fantastically hot mid-August, steam almost rising from the pavements, Ardiles and Villa made their League debuts at the City

Ground, where queues formed at 12.30p.m. to witness it and ram the place to the rafters. The Argentinians had travelled only from one continent to another, covering 6,915 miles, but it felt as though you were laying eyes on men who had landed from some far off galaxy. Someone has to bring a particularly exotic talent to these shores to get noticed immediately nowadays. That is what Salah has done.

In the few months since his arrival on Merseyside, he has shown himself to be one of those players worthy not only of the price of your match ticket, but also of a full season's financial commitment. You're compelled to watch him even when he hasn't got the ball because you don't want to miss a moment of what he can accomplish with it. He is dangerous from anywhere – especially wide on the right touchline. Salah only recently became twenty-five and he cost only £35m from Roma. At that price, you can be sure that Liverpool couldn't sign the cheque fast enough and then chauffeured the bearer to the bank to cash it before the Italians realised their mistake. Chelsea had, unbelievably, previously sold him to Roma for a mere £14m, giving the Italians a healthy profit on paper but diminishing their side on grass. You go through the goals Salah scored in Serie A – from distance and from close range, from stealthy back post headers and from the long runs into the box – and you wonder just how many he will claim for Liverpool. They will have been cheaply bought when put beside his transfer fee.

Salah has lovely balance. He could cup water in his bare hands and run without spilling it. He has a quick brain and even quicker heels. A defender's mind is usually still clicking through the long list of skills Salah can inflict on him, working out how to react, when the striker has already performed one of them and is already uncatchable. It is football's equivalent of an earthquake. The opposition feels the after-shock half a second after the seismograph records the original tremor. They can only cling on and wait for the shaking to stop. It is unreal, too, how often Salah unerringly finds the top or bottom of the net. He's able to place the ball in the exact slot no goalkeeper can possibly reach. When one-on-one, Salah looks as calm as someone asked to pop a letter into a post-box. And if he shifts the ball on to his left foot, a team's best strategy is usually prayer. You cope with Salah in three ways. Anticipate where he is going and then match him for pace. Don't give him a free pass to roam around unchecked. Never – on any account – allow him to get into the box with the ball.

Stoke either don't realise how dangerous he is – or are blind to it. How else can you explain why, from 25 yards out, the Egyptian is able to go on a slightly curved run into the area without anyone being aware of his presence? Sadio Mané out-tricks Darren Fletcher before his chipped cross – so delicate as to fall in Sir Stanley Matthews's class – spins slowly through the night sky. Kurt Zouma doesn't know whether to attack it or back-track towards Salah. Dithering means he does neither. The crashing volley, just like the ingenuity that created it, is gorgeous enough to make you forget for a while the ineptitude of Stoke's defending. Salah has been on the field only four minutes.

In May 1948 Matthews was playing for England against Italy in Turin. In the closing minutes, 4–0 up, he took the ball towards the corner flag. The day was oppressively hot; sweat beaded his brow and soaked his hair. Matthews wiped his right hand on his shorts and then used the same hand to sweep perspiration off his forehead, a gesture completed in microseconds. Two decades passed. Matthews, then living in Malta, went to the local butcher's. Recognised by the butcher's assistant, he became a prisoner of the man's recollections. The assistant, who had been in Turin, told him about the 'highlight' of the match: the moment he saw Matthews pluck a comb from the pocket of his shorts and run it through his hair before beating the full back. Matthews had no clue what the assistant meant until, much later, he dredged up the memory of going to the corner flag and realised then how sun and shadow had deceived the assistant's eye. Within weeks he met someone else who spoke ecstatically of the same thing. Matthews learnt that 'the whole of Malta' talked about it. Aware fable can be preferable to fact – for true stories can end anti-climactically – Matthews played along. He knew the myth, which seemed so plausible, had become too established for him to deny it. No one would ever believe him. He found an old comb, put it into a wooden box and presented it to the assistant.

That anecdote flashes back to me in the eighty-third minute. Stoke surrender the ball far into Liverpool's half. Emre Can takes it, looks up to see Salah and then finds him, the pass rangy and high. The defender, Erik Pieters, is like a cricketer under a steepling catch. He isn't sure where it is going to fall and so can't make up his mind whether to step left or right. Salah nips in front of him and is gone, leaving only Lee Grant in his way. You know Salah will score. Only tipping a ton of wet concrete over him could prevent it. There isn't much time to claim the goal, but all great players seem to have more of it than is horologically possible. Salah appears to slow the clock. Had he got a comb and a pocket in which to keep it, he could have done what Matthews didn't. He turns his chest square so that Grant will know the side-footed shot will go to his right. Grant still goes to his left and is down and out when Salah does what he promised with a flabbergasting boldness

It is all over. There is no shouting from the Stoke fan, who is very subdued. Salah has left even him speechless, the 'jammy bastards' exacting sweet revenge for all the criticism he has tipped over them He leaves immediately with a 'bloody hell'. It would sound defiant if the weakness in his voice wasn't so pronounced. I presume his wife, following the match at home, is already packing away the china, taking the doors off their hinges and encasing the clock in bubble-wrap.

Stoke have a flood of worries, which the supporters who have stayed to the end express on the way out. To avoid the crowd I make another stop at Sir Stanley Matthews's monument, saying a little goodbye.

I met Matthews only once and only briefly. He had come to Tommy Lawton's funeral. I stepped backwards to avoid a crush of people in a narrow space. I felt the weight of my heel on someone's toe. I heard the yelp made in response to that. I turned around and found Matthews's lined features contorted into a grimace. He was a white-haired 81-year-old then, but could have passed for someone a decade younger. I had stamped on his right foot – the foot that had crossed the ball for that Blackpool winner in the 1953 FA Cup Final. I began a bumbling, spluttering apology that received no reply, merely a silent half nod of acceptance. I watched him go, ashamed of both my clumsiness and the inadequacy of the explanation for it.

I still am, really.

2 November 2017: Stoke City v Liverpool
Stoke City 0 Liverpool 3

Stoke City: Grant, Zouma, Shawcross, Martins-Indi, Diouf, Fletcher (Adam 85), Allen, Pieters, Shaqiri, Crouch, Choupo-Moting (Jese 74). Subs not used: Haugaard, Wimmer, Berahino, Afellay, Ramadan

Liverpool: Mignolet, Gomez, Matip, Lovren, Moreno, Oxlade-Chamberlain (Milner 67), Can, Wijnaldum, Firmino, Mané (Henderson 89), Solanke (Salah 67).
Subs not used: Karius, Coutinho, Sturridge, Alexander-Arnold

SCORERS

Mané 17, Salah 77, 83

BOOKED

Stoke City: Martins-Indi
Liverpool: Mignolet, Can, Wijnaldum, Oxlade-Chamberlain, Mane

Referee: M. Atkinson
Attendance: 29,423

9

SOME ARE DEAD AND SOME ARE LIVING

13 December: Celtic v Hamilton Academical, Celtic Park, Scottish Premier League

In the Scottish Football Museum at Hampden Park, The Beatles are used as the accompaniment to a short strip of film reflecting the 1960s and 1970s. The track is 'In My Life'. It is about loss and love, the inevitability of change, the inexorability of time passing and also how we remember it. The song is so beautiful, but also so sadly bitter-sweet, that only a few chords of the opening guitar figure and the first verse is enough to send your heart dropping through your chest. The piano instrumental, the bridge that sounds like a harpsichord because it is being played at double-speed, provides the break you need to contemplate properly the lyrics you've just heard and perhaps do some personal reckoning up about the places and people that have come and then gone again in your own life. Whoever decided to use it here, the soundtrack for some games from the past, made the most affecting of choices.

I have the museum entirely to myself. I am the only visitor on a morning so filthy that rain is sluicing down the steep bank of tiled steps that lead into Hampden Park. The steps resemble a huge water feature, some grand piece of hydro-engineering.

I am going at an untroubled pace from one white, low-ceilinged room to another, peering through the thick glass at old boots and old shirts, medals in leather presentation boxes and velvet caps with braided tassels that were won a century or more ago. The best museums – and this is one of them, packing a lot into limited space – always capture the momentum of the big story while judiciously slipping in the seemingly mundane things that make it intimate. What stays with me, for example, from a long ago tour of Edward Elgar's birthplace is not the grand work-tools of the composer: the upright piano, the wind-up gramophone, the nibbed pen and the stacked sheets of music. It is his bicycle clips. Elgar was an avid cyclist and also an avid follower of Wolverhampton Wanderers; he'd bike to Molineux to support them. In Dublin it was Samuel Beckett's hulking black telephone with its conspicuous red button, which he pressed to block irritating callers. At the John F. Kennedy Presidential Library in Boston, beside the official papers, what resonated was his wardrobe: shoes with the imprint of his feet still on them; a pair of gloves; the silk ties and the racks of shirts – so many shirts, in fact, that Kennedy was like another Great Gatsby showing off to Daisy Buchanan.

The ordinary, everyday object brings you closer to the subject because you relate to it. The Scottish Football Museum displays the ball, pale and cracked, that the Wembley Wizards waltzed around England in 1928, beating them 5–1. It has a replica of the Champions League trophy (on loan from Sir Alex Ferguson). It has recreated both the former dressing rooms at Hampden, the polished lockers made of wood darker than ebony, and every swerving, mazy step Archie Gemmill took on his way to that goal against Holland in Argentina. The wee man's boot prints are marked in white on the green-carpeted floor. But I dwell more on the heritage bric-a-brac rather than the crown jewels. The table-top games we played before the computer age made them anachronistic and redundant. The sixteen-page programmes sold for a shilling. The match ticket, just a slight slip of paper, for the first international in 1872. The posters, once slapped on walls with bucketfuls of paste, that advertise in Gothic fonts cup finals and Scotland–England matches. Even the cane walking stick belonging to Bill Struth, the Methuselah of management at Rangers. At first I wasn't sure why I spent such a long time looking at this, tracing the knots along the stem of it and looking closely at the curve of the handle that Struth held at his death, aged eighty-one. The explanation came to me belatedly, so obvious in hindsight that I chastised myself as a blockhead for not recognising it immediately. My father was a Scot, born and brought up so close to the battlefield of Bannockburn that he could roam across it and re-enact 1314 whenever it suited him. In exile he became intensely patriotic, as though over-compensating for his absence. In our home, especially during my early boyhood, St Andrew's Day and Hogmanay were marked traditionally. We loyally took the *Sunday Post*. We did so because it was a homily newspaper – the nostalgic tone and content of it representative of the country my father had left for good decades before – and also because it contained reports of Scottish matches unavailable elsewhere. My education in the game north of the border was conducted during every Sabbath, an article in the *Sunday Post* leading to some reflection of my father's that was contemporary or historical. Eventually, these tutorials included a class on Struth and the success he had brought to Rangers: eighteen Championships and ten Scottish Cups. His era, like his life, was over before Bill Shankly's or Jock Stein's careers as managers began – only Matt Busby's had got underway when Struth was around to see it – but my father argued that he ranked importantly beside that great triumvirate. He was Rangers as much as Stein was Celtic. One of the few things I own of my father's – there was, alas, never much to curate – is his walking stick. Of course, I thought. My unconscious mind had established the link between Struth's walking stick and my father's before I was aware of it. A parcel of other memories followed. Most were of my father discussing the primacy of Scottish players and the game in general, the best of which seemed likely then to flourish forever.

The first sticker album I ever owned, bought only a season or two after Celtic had lifted the European Cup, contains 330 faces. I still have the completed album, which is foxed and brittle, worn at the edges and also down the ragged spine, the staples holding it together rusted a little. Going through it is always worth the effort, satisfying more than the abiding urge to glance over your shoulder at yesterday. What you find there isn't as different in some regards as you might think. The top teams then are almost identical to the top teams now. Power has left only Leeds, who lapsed from greatness so long ago that beer then cost 38p a pint. For them the Championship is a continuing labyrinth offering no way out.

No, the headline story between the album's thin cardboard covers lies elsewhere. You don't have to look too hard to find it either. The focus is on English football, specifically what used to be the First

Division, but the pictures purchased in foil packets told you nearly as much about Scotland once you ripped them open. About a third of the players in the album are Scottish. These Scots, from Billy Bremner to Dave Mackay, held English teams together like a marvellous solvent. You find them on every page. Alongside Bremner at Leeds were Bobby Collins, Peter Lorimer and Eddie Gray. Alongside Mackay at Spurs was Alan Gilzean. There was Charlie Cooke at Chelsea; Ron Yeats at Liverpool; the prodigal son Jim Baxter at Sunderland, but about to switch to Nottingham Forest; Alex Young, the Golden Vision, at Everton. Denis Law and Paddy Crerand at Manchester United. The list runs on because the A1 was a conveyer belt for talent travelling south. It brought the brightest to England, the move seen as a natural progression among those who made it. Even Stein came eventually – if only so briefly that his suitcase remained half unpacked. Scottish names on a team sheet were a crowd draw, props and mainstays of interest, and you went to watch them the way today you would go to watch Paul Pogba and Mo Salah, Mesut Özil and N'Golo Kanté.

The film in the museum preserves Bremner and the rest of them in eternal youth as The Beatles sing with the profoundest of feeling about their friends, some living and others dead, and also about places, some gone and others altered so radically as to be practically unrecognisable. In this context 'In My Life' is being used as a memorial hymn for what, in hindsight, stands as two of the last great decades of Scottish football. The combination of images and music is transfixing and also so sorrowful – some of the players in it, such as Bremner, are dead now – that it heightens your sense of what is lost and irrecoverable. The film lasts only as long as the song does, which is less than three minutes, but the impact of it lingers. I am still seeing it – and The Beatles' lyrics are still spinning around my head like an old vinyl record – not only as I leave, but also hours later when the lights from Celtic Park glow through a belt of wet snow.

Scottish football's struggle to establish itself outside the country's boundaries has become its identity. Inside them Celtic are the only headline attraction since Rangers fell so precipitously, but their dominance, like their wider appeal, has a limited circumference.

On Scottish soil Celtic are 'The Invincibles', winners at a fancy canter of last season's treble. Already this season, they have retained one of those trophies – the Betfred League Cup – and lead the Premier League by five points with a game in hand. Their unbeaten domestic run, stretching back to May 2016, is a handsome sixty-eight matches, a formidable British record whatever the circumstances. Tonight Hamilton Academical, snared in the bottom half of the table and twenty-two points worse off, aren't likely to interfere with a side that under Brendan Rodgers piles up goals like someone stacking wood for the winter. It is true that Celtic experienced something of a narrow squeak last weekend. Only a clearance off the line in added time at Easter Road prevented Hibernian, who had been 2–0 behind, from getting a result so unlikely that anyone who reads nothing but news-papers would have passed it off as a typographical error next morn-ing. The problem for Celtic – and this is emblematic of the problem for the Scottish game – is what happens in Europe. Barely two months ago Celtic went to Paris St-Germain in the Champions League and came a cropper. Pitted against the tricks of Neymar and the teenage vitality of Kylian Mbappé, they did well to lose only 7–1. In the last quarter of an hour PSG seemed to come at them from every angle all at once. Only the French side's rashness – the compulsion to take a fussy extra touch or to shoot weirdly from distance – prevented further slaughter. It was not a wimpish performance from Celtic by any means, but the analysis afterwards of their spirited failure was slanted too generously towards accentuating small positives. The big negative was that – once more – Celtic had not got out of their group, and so Scotland had no flag to fly in the last sixteen. The occasional decent performance in the Champions League soon becomes an irrelevancy when it leads only to the middle stages of the Europa League, a prize also too awesome for Celtic to contemplate winning it.

The decline of the Scottish game counts unquestionably as the saddest thing of my football-watching life. Wild optimists can pretend it is a great opportunity brilliantly disguised as a problem to be solved, but the state into which it has sunk could contain lower depths still. The only way may not be up, and the imbalance of Celtic being unstoppable at home and vulnerable abroad is just one indicator of that.

English jealousy of Scottish football, very real at one point, is long over. Nowhere is that clearer than in the transfer market. In today's sticker albums the collectable stars are European or South American rather than Scots. On arriving in England, the last Scottish-born player to be given a splash headline, rather than a respectable double column, was Duncan Ferguson. He moved from Rangers to Everton for £4m; that was in 1994. Other Scots have come since and cost more even allowing for inflation – among them Alan Hutton and Craig Gordon – but the fees of Matt Ritchie (born in Croydon) and Steven Fletcher have been highest, at £12m apiece, when swapping one English club for another. If the rarest of talents emerged in Scotland you would know him immediately; he would stand out like a bird of paradise among a flock of pigeons. But Scotland continues to look for a transfigurative genius, which is why the national team has been unable to reach the finals of a major competition for twenty years. When it did, Scotland still used to return home before the post-cards. Now a population of 5.3 million has become incapable of producing a squad to reach the World Cup or the European Championships even when the likes of Iceland, which has 150,000 fewer people in it than Edinburgh, can do both.

Explaining why Scottish football's production line has slowed – and also why the quality coming off it has plummeted – will send you into odd and disparate corners of debate. The author James Hamilton Muir (actually, the composite pseudonym of three different writers) once said rather snootily: 'The best you can say for football is that it has given the working man subject for conversation.' Hamilton Muir was wrong. The best it gave 'the working man' was a way out of the tene-ments and the graft of long shifts in dirty industries. In a BBC docu-mentary, screened earlier this year to mark the golden anniversary of Celtic's European Cup win, the survivors of Jock Stein's Lisbon Lions spoke movingly of apprenticeships that were originally begun in 25-a-side games under dim street lamps on whatever scrub land was avail-able to them. These roughhouse matches, which went on indefinitely, have vanished because Scotland, like everywhere else, has become markedly more middle and less working class, and other cultural, social and economic factors have aligned and wrought change unimaginable even as recently as the affluent 1980s, the second period in which we thought we'd never had it so good. No one can offer anything more than an educated guess about where Scottish football will go next, but here doesn't seem to be the place to start if the planned destination really is restoring the reputation it once had internationally.

Celtic Park is a palace, and the magnificence it possesses will intimidate those it does not inspire. Hamilton Academical had been unbeaten for half a dozen games until losing at home to St Johnstone last Saturday. The eye-catching element of the match was not the slim scoreline (1–0), but the paltriness of the crowd. Only 1,451 bothered to go to see them. This was the lowest gate in the SPL, and also lower – by some 300 – than the lowest in England, belonging to the League Two fixture between Morecambe and Coventry City on the blowy west coast. The challenge for Scottish football in general, which that statistic highlights, needs no elaboration. The challenge for Hamilton specifically, coming here after playing in front of gaping spaces, is to buck up rather than buckle under. The crowd is thinned a little by the demands of Christmas, but 50,000-plus is still 20,000 more than Hamilton have enticed through their turnstiles in a total of nine home games so far this season.

Hamilton have a humble way of business about them, content from the start to sit back and hold on. Like a door left ajar, this only invites trouble. Not unexpectedly, the opening goal comes after only twelve minutes. Scott Sinclair is Celtic's inspiration. He provides a chip, nipping in from left touchline to byeline, and Olivier Ntcham, conveniently unmarked, makes electrifying contact with it. He smashes his volley so violently past the goalkeeper, Gary Woods, from relatively close range that you are surprised not to see a plume of sparks shoot upwards as boot collides with ball.

After that late blip against Hibernian, the usual way of things has been restored for Celtic. You wait for Hamilton to offer something, even a glancing blow, in return. Nothing comes. Rakish Bingham fends for himself, riding alone up front, so Celtic start to dawdle because they can. Their build-up is either strangely sedate or torturously slow. In one move I count eleven sideways passes, which claim only 10 yards of Hamilton territory. In another, similarly pedestrian, I count twelve. In a third, I stop counting altogether when Nir Bitton begins strolling around the centre circle ponderously, as though five minutes' worth of cogitation is needed to decide where the ball should be sent next. Celtic can afford to be so leisurely because Hamilton are still so passive, never squeezing the play or applying hard pressure on whoever is in possession until the last third of the pitch. It is as though losing without being absolutely crushed will allow them to tick off tonight as a qualified success – sort of, anyway.

You know another goal can't be far off, and you are quite right; but it is Hamilton who have the temerity to claim it. Going into the Celtic half had seemed too daring for them, but on twenty-nine minutes a raid down the near flank reaches Daniel Redmond. Celtic stand off him and, from 18 yards, Redmond lifts in a surprise drive despite partially losing his footing on the soggy surface. Celtic Park can't take it in.

Since Rangers, currently in second place, remain in rehabilitation and also without a manager, the Championship is again a formality, Celtic's to give away. More often than not you look at their results – games that finish 3–1 or 4–1 or even 5–something – and wonder how the satisfaction of pummelling sides patently weaker than themselves retains their interest for nine months. The formalities must be gone through, I suppose. It isn't Celtic's fault that, without Rangers snapping and biting, what remains worries them only rarely. Motivating themselves must surely sometimes come from a setback like the one Hamilton have inflicted.

The goal is a face-slap, and such an insult requires a retort, which Celtic provide. Half time is approaching when a pass from Stuart Armstrong splits a path that James Forrest races along, swerving around Woods en route, before side-footing Celtic in front again. From the re-start, the clock ticking into the forty-second minute, the Champions look more meanly predatory than ever, pushing Hamilton into hurried and disorganised retreat. The attack, gifted to them, has come with thunderbolt suddenness, the consequence of one piece of careless mis-control and two crass misjudgements from Scott McMann, the left back. These are tiny failures of application. First, he can't nail down a straightforward pass, the ball rolling off his foot. Next, chasing the rebound, he lets Odsonne Edouard seize it before him; Edouard gets there with the long stride of the middle distance runner, and he shrugs off McMann's meek body-check as easily as a man slips out of a winter overcoat. Lastly, McMann's second lunge at Edouard, sending both of them tumbling to the turf, neither reclaims possession nor takes it out of harm's way.

A bad situation becomes calamitous for Hamilton, who are out-numbered. Celtic pour players forward faster than Hamilton can funnel them back. Defenders scatter themselves in likely places, but their strategy, inasmuch as one exists, is merely to hope for the best now. McMann is still picking himself up as Forrest sprints past on the outside, eagerly continuing the raid that Edouard had begun. McMann is no use to anyone; he is watching as Forrest takes charge, the break-ing ball met on the run and struck to Sinclair, lurking beyond the 6-yard area. Sinclair, who is 13 yards out, kills the cross, mastering it instantly. The three defenders Hamilton have managed to muster seem no more than an irritant to him. Sinclair does swiftly with his feet what most boxers do with their hands, intending to bamboozle opponents and provoke them into a fatal move. He shuffles. He feints. He pretends to take a semi step backwards. He shapes to strike but doesn't, the ball remaining dead still. The defenders, trying to regroup, are cagily unsure about whether to go at him or hang tight and unsure also about where to look. At his orange boots. At his gaze. At the ball, focusing on it hard, the way a hypnotist asks his sitter to focus on a pocket-watch and chain. Alex Gogić can't wait; impatience gets the better of him. He tries to close the chance down. Sinclair, lean and with a wide flash of dyed blonde in his hair, capitalises on Gogić's impetuosity. The effort Hamilton are sure will come off his left foot is instead hit with the right. With an easy swing Sinclair scoops the ball through a 3-foot gap. The goal, a thing of great beauty, is Celtic's second in only seventy-five seconds.

The game is over.

While watching here, I have also been listening to the radio reports from matches elsewhere. I am following in particular the progress of Manchester City, dominant leaders of the Premier League, who are making high art out of bloody murder at Swansea. Radio is one of the small and under-rated pleasures of following football. As long ago as

1929, the novelist Winifred Holtby heard her first live commentary on the BBC. Without the 'remotest notion' about the game, she found herself welded to it because 'no one could listen with cold blood and slugglish pulses to the quickening crescendo of the roar preceding the final shout of Goal'. Holtby 'wanted more goals' and 'didn't care from whom'. She explained: 'I just wanted to feel my spine tingle . . . my hair stir gently at the roots with suspense as that voice cried out from somewhere near our drawing-room curtains.' If you didn't grow up with live televised games, the norm was tuning in the transistor, which meant first pulling up the silver aerial as high as it would go. You'd pick up the high whine or the crackle of static, which only digital broadcasting has sharply remedied, and also the interference of other stations, which would drift in and out of range. The sound sometimes filled the room like a gaggle of noisy ghosts. You fiddled with the dial, swivelling it minimally, until the exact spot was found, and only then did the signal register purely, the burst of voices – usually baritone, as though marinated in vintage port – carried you off to Highbury or Old Trafford, White Hart Lane or Maine Road. In mid-weeks such as this one, during the cold beginning of a steely winter, you hunkered down beside the radio, occasionally pressing an ear right beside the grill. The commentators, such as the exceptional Peter Jones, became the friends you never met. You were pulled towards and into a match, the broadcast having a just-for-you intimacy about it. Like reading a book, you made your own imaginative pictures from someone else's words.

The words coming out of South Wales tonight tell of City going at things attractively at full throttle, confusing Swansea with a blizzard of fast, first-time passes. My mind's eye fastens on to the ecstatic descriptions of what City are doing and converts them into still images that almost make up for what I am missing. There is Kevin De Bruyne, skilful enough to plant the ball into a wastebasket from 60 yards. There is David Silva making darting and deftly ingenious runs, always disappearing from his bewildered marker's shoulder and reappearing where he is least expected. There is Raheem Sterling – running endlessly. City under Pep Guardiola seem to have no limits; one assertively domineering show follows another irrespective of the competition or the opposition. Their win three days ago in the Manchester derby at Old Trafford opened up an eleven-point gap, which is an ocean, over the limp-along neighbours, reducing José Mourinho to the supporting role of grumpy loser. What looks effortless never is, that façade hiding the repetitive slog of rehearsal on the training ground, but City make everything look natural and nonchalant and classy. Watching them is a joy.

It is unfair, given the difference in resources, to expect Celtic to be like City, but every goal banged in at the Liberty Stadium only emphasises the discrepancy between what I am seeing in front of me and what I hear being described. Since the formation of the Premier League in England, the game there has inflated in value while Scotland's has dissipated. It is like comparing the conglomerate megastore to the family-owned corner shop. Consider the figures. Celtic spend twice as much on salaries than anyone else in Scotland – around £52m – but it puts them only 203rd in football's world pay league. City's wage bill is almost £250m. Celtic's main shirt sponsorship is worth £3m per season. City's is worth £35m. The prize money for winning the SPL is £3m. In England, a club gets £85m just for turning up for nine months. (Sunderland received nearly £100m for finishing bottom last season.) The sum for TV rights in Scotland, about £30m per season all in, is lower than Norway's, Denmark's, Sweden's, Greece's and even Poland's. Last summer the *Daily Record* featured an XI made up of the 'most expensive' players to have graced Scottish football during its recent, variegated history. The total value of this team, from Fraser Forster in goal to Tore André Flo up front, was £61.5m. De Bruyne alone cost City a few shillings short of £67m. No team since Aberdeen in 1985 has broken the Old Firm's grip on the Championship. Celtic are heading for a seventh successive title. The record of consecutive Championships stands at nine, but booking the ballroom and ordering the balloons for 2021 probably wouldn't be overly presumptuous. The feat, if it comes, wouldn't be good for Scottish football and wouldn't necessarily be good for Celtic either. You can't continually make a big fuss about little matches; and you don't want the Championship devalued to the extent that winning it leaves you looking like the tallest man in Lilliput. For we all know, deep down, when great is really great, and not merely good.

*   *   *

The goals so far at Celtic Park have been first rate. The problem has been the second-rate stuff around them. It has courted banality, letting you see clearly the chief reason why Scottish football is ailing. That Hamilton drew level created only the fleeting illusion that Celtic were in the thrust of a competitive game rather than another of those foregone conclusions that fill the domestic calendar. Even on a rank bad day Celtic are usually good enough to take down opposition of minor ability, such as Hamilton. As the second half begins, and then goes into a soft sleep for a while, the only question is how much Celtic really want to be bothered.

Hamilton, their commitment unflagging, hurry about the pitch and prod and poke for the ball. Bustle should nonetheless never be confused with creativity, nor with strength, and the fact is Celtic hold them off comfortably, the attacks at them not quite up to the mark. Hamilton have the lowest wage bill in the Premier League, their average salary below £42,000, and in October the club fell victim to an 'elaborate fraud' fleecing them of about £900,000. The team, assembled from a relative pittance, isn't malleable but isn't memorable either. There are nonethless still chances for them. Rakish Bingham clips the base of a post. Celtic are flat and rather weary, but endeavour on its own won't topple them. You are left with the feeling that even if Hamilton do score twice, Celtic will spring out of their lethargy and better them. Leigh Griffiths and Moussa Dembélé are on the bench, waiting for such an emergency.

With a quarter of an hour to go some of the stands are emptying. Before the start it had been difficult to walk from the station to the periphery of the stadium. The public paths weren't gritted after the temperature had dropped, freezing the day's early rain. You had to cling to railings or traipse along shaggy grass verges or, as I did, shuffle along as though your feet had been bound. It was the only way to avoid an icy fall. With that in mind, and with the game hardly uplifting, the exit is the logical place to go. I stay on to see the last ten minutes, which are exactly like the preceding eighty. The half finishes as it began, bleakly and in anticlimax. Celtic get perfunctory applause for being efficient rather than impressive.

Scottish football is a lumbering target and you can take easy aim at it, but I want there to be a happy ending, a renaissance of the game. This may be so far off, however, that I doubt – like high-speed trains, the re-opening of public libraries and the introduction of double-summer time – that I will ever see it. There is no gainsaying the future, but a half-century has passed since Celtic won the European Cup and another half century at least will be needed to win another.

On the way out I look up and see what, somewhat bafflingly, I hadn't noticed on the way in: a head and shoulders image of Jock Stein spread across the back of a stand. I stare into the face and remember his abrupt, unexpected death and also the aftermath of it, a week when even grown men washed their face in tears. I am back in the Scottish Football Museum, watching Stein holding aloft one trophy after another, his smile wider than the Clyde.

I hear The Beatles singing again.

13 December 2017: Celtic v Hamilton Academical
Celtic 3 Hamilton Academical 1

Celtic: Gordon, Ajer, Bitton, Boyata (Simunović 71), McGregor, Brown, Ntcham, Forrest (Hayes 79), Armstrong, Sinclair, Edouard (Griffiths 67).
Subs not used: De Vries, Dembele, Lustig, Tierney

Hamilton Academical: Woods, Tomas, Gogic, McMann, Donati, Gillespie (Skondras 49), MacKinnon, Docherty, Imrie, Redmond (Lyon 79), Bingham (Cunningham 84).
Subs not used: Fulton, Templeton, Ferguson, Sarris

SCORERS
Celtic: Ntcham 12, Forrest 41, Sinclair 42
Hamilton Academical: Redmond 29

BOOKED
Celtic: Edouard
Hamilton Academical: Gillespie

Referee: S. Finnie
Attendance: 53,883

10

OLD WATER, OLD BRIDGES

7 January: Nottingham Forest v Arsenal, FA Cup Third Round, City Ground

The past is always with us, folded into the present, whether we acknowledge it or not.

I am aware of it as soon as I walk into Nottingham's Old Market Square, taking in the expanse of slabby concrete that occupies five and a half acres. The white-grey blandness of it accentuates the handsomeness of the Council House: the high, blue dome, which makes the building resemble St Paul's Cathedral in miniature; the round-faced clock, set beneath it like a jewel pressed into a crown; the pediment figure-carvings and the ribbed Ionic columns of Portland stone; the shallow steps leading to dark archways; and also the pair of Landseer-like lions, where courting couples met and meet still, this small spot the shy starting point of a million and more relationships.

The afternoon is pellucid and keenly fresh, the light giving off a mirrored glare. The Christmas tree, its branches stripped bare of decoration, still stands but is about to be chopped down. Even though Twelfth Night is long gone, the fancy illuminations, fixed to the façade of the Council House, wait to be dismantled, boxed up and shut away too. A tram glides by, clanking its bell. The odd scruffy pigeon, pecking for scraps, takes off and then lands again in a fluttering stop. The black hands of the clock nudge 1.30p.m. There is, curiously, almost no one about; it's as though half the city has slept in or gone someplace else. Only a few dozen shoppers, heavily swaddled against the cold, hurry along empty pavements. The odd drinker, desperately thirsty for that lunch-time pint, dashes into a pub. An elderly man and wife, immaculately dressed in double-breasted overcoats and matching cherry-striped mufflers, walk arm in arm, heading briskly, I suppose, either to or from a church service.

You would see all of this and dismiss it as unremarkable – a Sunday of unadorned, ordinary life. I look around, and there are 25,000 people here – perhaps more. It's no longer mid-winter, but a soft early spring, a May evening clammy with heat and dust. The thin trees are tall and in full leaf. I am on the Council House balcony. The crowd below me, jammed shoulder to shoulder, is heaving, the push and press of it creating a constant sway and long ripple of movement. I try, but can't locate, the vanishing point of it, which is somewhere off in the far, far distance. I hear someone tell me that 'not even VE day' in Nottingham was like this. Flags and scarves swish through the warm air. Home-made banners, made from tablecloths and bed-sheets, are stuck on poles, their messages of triumph scrawled in paint with broad brush strokes. The only colours visible anywhere are blood-red and stark white. I see old men in a state of half-disbelief, their faces creased like linen and their eyes watering. I see children, who don't understand the magnitude of the event, being picked up and hoisted high for a better look. And then, finally, I see the open-topped bus. It trundles along, like one of those first-made charabancs with a coughing engine. The wheels take almost a minute to complete a full rotation, the driver making certain everyone gets a decent glimpse of who is on board and also the polished silver trophy. You catch a flashing glint of it. There are still fans for whom this isn't enough. Slightly too eager, and dropping from the kerb on to the road, they reach upwards towards it with outstretched fingers, pleading for someone to lower the bulbous thing into their own hands. You have to shout to be heard – even when speaking to the person next to you. The crowd competes with one another because no one is able to either lead or synchronise the chants, the songs and the general, beery roaring. No one cares about that. Nottingham Forest are bringing home the European Cup.

The scene comes back easily and unbidden, as though time is collapsing in on itself. What I recall lasts a few seconds only, but is briefly as real as anything actually happening around me in the here and now of the hour. In Nottingham, where I grew up, a memory lurks on almost every corner, but few return more powerfully than this one because Forest's feat seemed so fantastically implausible even when it occurred. Now, almost forty years on, it would strike me as totally, utterly and completely absurd – a story of pure fantasy rather than hard fact – if I hadn't been there and lived through it daily and so closely. What it brings is a rush of feeling for former times.

I spent my early life continually writing about Forest – the team Brian Clough built out of nothing with Peter Taylor and also the sides he subsequently built and re-built alone before his abrupt decline precipitated that unthinkable relegation and his premature retirement, aged only fifty-eight. The precise number of Forest games I reported on per season – as well as the precise number of miles I did in pursuit of them – can only ever be loosely guessed at. I could have legitimately given the City Ground as my home address on the census form. I spent sufficient days and months and years there to qualify for residency. Or, at least, to claim squatter's rights.

I left Nottingham fifteen years ago, knowing then that the place to which I would return would always be markedly different from the one I had left. And so it is. Whenever I come back, I go searching for the things that have been lost, which is the city I knew so intimately and also my attachment to it. I can never find either of them because my sense of rootedness in the landscape has gone. It can only ever be summoned again on few and far-between days like this. I am aware nevertheless that the person who remembers these things is not quite the same as the person who experienced them. He altered the way the city altered, the process so gradual and so subtle as to make the change undetectable until the moment came when he looked at things from long distance and paradoxically saw them close up, properly in focus again. He realised only then how time does its work as imperceptibly as water does, chaffing year after year at rock and reshaping it gradually.

I last saw a match at the City Ground more than two decades ago. I have stayed away deliberately. For one thing because I feel, like Thomas Wolfe, that you can't go home again and shouldn't really try. For another because we all need a degree of emancipation from our past – especially something that has swallowed up so much of us. But I had always intended to go wherever the third round of the FA Cup sent Arsenal, not only the current holders but also three-time winners in the last four seasons. To think of them provokes a Pavlovian response in relation to the competition and also to Arsène Wenger, the manager most synonymous with it. To follow them and him seemed common sense.

This week also marked the forty-third anniversary of Clough's arrival at Forest, beginning an eighteen-year era in which he won everything worth winning – except of course for the Cup, which eluded him even when he once got close enough to kiss it. And so it was that one circumstance arranged itself beside another like a rare alignment of planets. When Forest and Arsenal were paired together, it seemed – as daftly pretentious as this sounds – as though Fate had laid its hand on the hollow of my back and was shoving me where I really didn't want to go. I gave in. I bought a seat in the Brian Clough Stand, and I decided from the start to do what I hadn't before, which was to footslog the two miles from the Old Market Square to the City Ground. I would cross Trent Bridge, where I knew there'd be swans, drifting along in a wedge as pointed as an arrowhead, and also rowers, their oars cutting through the water like knives, and also fishermen sitting quietly on the sloping grassy bank of that still, wide river.

So I turn away from the Council House and head off. The Old Market Square remains so deserted as to seem almost ghostly. No one is here . . . except me and those 25,000 fans, alive in my imagination.

A club that needs heroes and has to dwell on history is going through either a desperately lean period or – and this perspective is rosier – a transformative one. Nottingham Forest, fourteenth in the Championship, haven't been in the Premier League this century. On New Year's Eve the board sacked the manager, Mark Warburton, appointing the Academy boss Gary Brazil as caretaker. When the vacancy is eventually filled, Forest will have appointed twenty successors to Brian Clough in less than twenty-five years, the figure only slightly inflated by the fact two men have held the post twice.

Both on the way to the City Ground, and then inside it, Clough's presence is tangible and, since there is nothing modern to celebrate, so are his ancient glories. The scarves being sold on the street have the knitted motif of the European Cup stitched on them or Clough's name and face. The cover of today's programme is one of those over-colourised photographs of the 1959 FA Cup winning captain, Bob McKinlay. He is showing off the trophy, its lid missing. On the big screens, positioned opposite one another and above the corner flags,

McKinlay is there again. He and the other nine men who battled on at Wembley for fifty-seven minutes in those pre-substitute days – Roy Dwight, one of the goal-scorers, had broken his leg – are seen in cleaned-up, crisp black and white. And then Clough appears too. He clips down the tunnel in his signature green sweatshirt. I think of him suddenly sitting in the dugout, stabbing his index finger at someone like a lethal weapon. Or bawling instructions. Or giving the double thumbs-up. He is interviewed too, but only the occasional sharp drawl of his elongated vowels is faintly audible, the substance of his words carried away on a breezy wind. Clough's shadow makes all that follows it at Forest look pitifully inadequate. The two stars, embroidered above the badge on their shirts, are a perpetual reminder of the standards he set during that short, brilliant spell straddling the very end of the 1970s and the very beginning of the 1980s. Perhaps things had to unravel after that; even the strongest heart can take only so much awe-struck excitement.

A team is always a work in progress, but settling on one good enough to get promoted has eluded Forest for so long that frustration hard-ened into rank despair for a while. During some of the most dispirit-ing seasons it was sensible – especially for those brought up on the headiness of the European Cup – to only glimpse matches between the fingers of the hand, so easing slightly the anguish of watching them. The current squad contains the rumour of happier times ahead – providing someone is allowed to stick around long enough to nurture the talent as it grows up in public. The Forest board have been like impatient gardeners, always pulling the plant up to see how the roots are doing.

Today's team is largely home produced. Four players have sprung out of the Academy: the goalkeeper Jordan Smith (23); the defender Joe Worrall (20); midfielder Ben Osborn (23); and Ben Brereton, a striker (18). On the bench is also Tyler Walker, his presence – at a mere twenty-one – putting into perspective for the aged, like me, how time accumulates with you barely noticing it. Surely it was only six months ago that I last saw his father, Des, generate so much pace that he could not only rob an attacker cleanly of the ball but also whip the laces out of his boots without the poor lad realising it. Yes, he was that quick.

However full of brimming potential Forest seem, Arsenal don't look impressed or daunted. Arsène Wenger has taken rotation almost to the limit. He has made nine changes to the side that drew in the final gasp of last Wednesday's game against Chelsea at the Emirates. There is no Alexis Sánchez. No Mesut Özil. No Alexandre Lacazette. Wenger's mitigation will be threefold. First, the cumulative wear and tear of the festive programme in which games came at them in battalions. The Premier League staged matches on ten of the thirteen days between 23 December and 4 January, a physical workload hardly conducive even for pack-mules, never mind thoroughbreds, but necessary because subscription TV is ravenous for ratings and getting them demands that the viewer comes first. The Boxing Day fixture used to be the convivial escape from the house and the turkey left-overs and also the chance to show off what Santa had left you under the tree – gloves, a scarf, one of those Technicolor sweaters or a bobble hat that you might never wear again. Now it's just a minor widget in the perpetual motion machine. Second, Arsenal have to face Chelsea again in seventy-two hours –this time at Stamford Bridge, in the first leg of what I still call the League Cup even though a relatively obscure fizzy drinks company has plastered sponsorship all over it. Thirdly, he has chosen seven players who have already won the FA Cup – including Danny Welbeck and Theo Walcott – and also Per Mertesacker, who has a World Cup winner's medal too. Wenger's selection has the highbrow's sense of superiority about it nevertheless. Even managers who don't sniff trouble tend to prepare for it, but he has not stocked the bench with high profile names capable, if necessary, of hauling him out of a hole. Mind you, the Cup has been a totem for him and for Arsenal, filling the niche where Premier League titles ought to have gone. Wenger has also never lost in the third round, Arsenal are the most successful club in the competition's history and Forest haven't won at all for five matches.

It is still rather baffling when Arsenal begin like a patrician bunch of gentleman gazing lordly down their noses at a plebeian rabble below. Some slight irritation about even being here seems to be bothering them. The ball gets stroked about – calmly and very prettily, of course – but everything about them is half-hearted and listless. It's all so tippy-tappy, as though subconsciously Arsenal believe a win is inevitable for them, which means that simply showing sufficient style will make the substance of the performance irrelevant in the end. The idea seems to be that Forest's novices will be teased first, indulged a little with some ruthless flirting and then punished later on. All too soon Arsenal's presumptuousness is badly shaken.

The afternoon light is finally beginning to burn down when Forest, continually pressing high up the pitch, go ahead. Kieran Dowell's shirt is tugged, a petty sin that gets him a free kick 2 yards outside the area and almost parallel with the 6-yard box. In the turmoil Arsenal, dragging everyone back, slump into disorder. A two-man wall is set, tokenly. It is useless; not only in being unable to block the ball, which Dowell curls in like a hook, but also because the line of it is too high, allowing Forest immunity from offside. Barely able to believe his luck, Eric Lichaj muscles in unmarked from the back, forces his way ahead of the surprised goalkeeper, David Ospina, and nods the ball power-fully into the roof of the net. To judge from their reaction, the goal has come as a strange surprise to Arsenal, who, it seems, had been previously unaware that Forest were actually allowed to score. Mertesacker glances around him with glassy bewilderment, unsure about who should have tracked Lichaj. He then realises it was him.

Going behind wakes up the holders like a bucket of iced water. The equaliser comes only two minutes later. There is another free kick – Walcott delicately scooping it over – and Forest perish because no one has learnt the lesson the Dowell–Lichaj combination just taught Arsenal. The defence is ball-watching – firstly as Rob Holding plants his header against the bottom half of the post and, secondly, after the rebound fortunately finds Mertesacker, who takes it on his chest and pokes his shot on the half-volley through a thicket of legs.

You'd think the shock of going behind to a mid-table Championship side, and then the relief of drawing level with them, would be enough to provoke a disciplined response from Arsenal rather than a dilet-tante shrug. Not a bit of it. Walcott doesn't threaten. Welbeck is a butterfly, flitting on and off the ball. Possession dribbles away from them, leaving Ospina over-worked and Jordan Smith, his opposite number, unemployed. A rule of soldiering is never to interfere with the enemy when it is destroying itself, so Forest, peppery and pugna-cious, only to have come on strongly, their long protracted labours making clear the opening goal was no flashy fluke. Often, breaking in swift avalanches of movement that twist Arsenal's defence out of shape, Forest make Mertesacker in particular look a stranded soul. At 6 feet 6 inches and shorn of fat, he stands like a thin obelisk of bones. And at thirty-three he runs too ponderously to fight off a teenager as broad-shouldered and bullish as Ben Brereton, still a toddler when the German broke into the professional game. Against him Mertesacker frequently gets barged, out-manoeuvred or out-jumped, his long arms flapping. He turns cumbersomely and spends a lot of time either facing Ospina and his own posts or staring at Brereton's back. His limbs can no longer take him where his brain is telling him to go. Mertesacker is casually side-stepped.

Arsenal are harassed and untidy, their back four stretched like a row of ragged washing. They are counting the minutes towards half time, wanting each one to tick by a little faster than usual, when Forest score again. Mertesacker is, for once, an innocent bystander. The fault is Holding's. In the forty-third minute he doesn't get enough power on a high header, which arcs towards Lichaj. Even if you watched nothing of the rest of this tie, and saw endlessly only what happens in the next two and a half seconds, it would be worthwhile. Lichaj will remember it because forty-nine times out of fifty his effort would probably have gone into the top corner of nowhere. On this one occasion, however, he summons a talent that he possibly didn't know he fully possessed. What he displays is control and a grace supplemented by sublime accuracy. When the ball falls from the twilight sky, Lichaj is a foot outside the box and two Arsenal players are closing in on him. He ignores them. He leans back and kills the soft drop of the clearance against his sternum. With almost no back-lift, he times his strike with spilt-second punctuality. Everything is perfect. The weight and pace put into the shot. The loop on the ball, and also the direction and the distance. Lichaj cannot have been more precise in judging each of these. Somehow, just perhaps, he worked them out on paper with some mathematical calculation beforehand, even taking into account extraneous factors such as wind speed and the wobble on the ball. How else to explain it? The shot goes beyond Mertesacker, who turns his head to follow it in lovely flight. In the same moment Ospina moves across his line, knowing as he does so that his dive will only be for show. He sinks to his knees in lame concession to defeat. The ball floats past him, hitting the target Lichaj had aimed for – that tight angle between post and bar.

Not bad for a right back.

At half time Brian Clough is filling those two big screens again.

You see the unscarred features of someone not yet fifty years old, a good portion of life still in front of him. In the build-up to the tie Arsène Wenger spoke of being at the City Ground in the 1990s and coming across him in a corridor. By then Clough was in his early sixties, the illnesses blighting him glaringly apparent. Wenger saw a figure 'lean, very lean,' but nonetheless someone who was for him 'a special person . . . one of the greatest ever (managers) . . . a personality who left a huge print on the history of the game'. Wenger's fulsome tribute to a man he met on only one day almost twenty years ago expanded quite naturally into the era Clough dominated either through winning trophies or simply by being the sum of his many contradictions. Wenger asked the obvious question – could a small provincial city ever win today's Champions League? – and gave the obvious answer. Clubs were originally permitted only two 'overseas' players, such rationing preventing even the better off from monopolising the talent. Nor was football then sloshing about in the TV riches that pour into it now as routinely as tap water into a sink. As Wenger generously conceded, again alluding to Clough and Forest, 'managers had more influence . . . their work really made the difference'. Clough's work was tailored to the age in which he toiled. Wenger didn't offer an opinion about whether he could have 'made the difference' in the modern game too, no doubt because, unlike the matter of the Champions League, he believed declaring so out loud was unnecessary.

The cult of the manager gained momentum during Clough's heyday, developing significantly because of him and his assertive personality. There was a self-magnifying quality about him, and this grew alongside the fame he cultivated. He painted outside the lines of conventional management. There were exceptions, but most bosses who preceded him, as well as a lot who were his contemporaries, had a courteously mannered and civil urbanity about them. They were middle-aged ambassadors, looking ten years older than the date on their birth certificate, who wore pressed suits and ties as thin as a strip of liquorice. Wary of expressing an opinion that might be construed as faintly controversial, they took regular refuge in being allusive rather than emphatic or saying nothing at all. So Clough gusted in and entertainingly took over the back pages even before he'd won so much as a tin button. After he did win something, and then kept on winning, the nagging itch to talk continued unabated, turning him into the Patron Saint of Newspapers, who always had space to fill. It aroused envy and bitter resentments, and sometimes he cornered the market in being his own worst enemy. What he said could also over-shadow, even partially eclipse, what he did, but unquestionably those immense managerial skills, his perception and his nous, would trans-fer to the present day. Being successful in it would nevertheless demand nips and tucks of compromise that were previously alien to him. He'd have to be less antagonistic towards, and more respectful about, owners and directors. He'd have to tolerate being paid less than some of his team. He'd have to put up, under duress, with the sit-down, formal press conferences that take place in front of those boards emblazoned with sponsors' logos. He'd have to accept that television, which he disliked unless being paid lump sums as an analyst, nowadays always calls the tune – and that the music it plays is the repertoire of a military band; you need to be in step so as not to become too conspicuously rebellious. Clough could clear those hurdles and still largely be himself, but his habit of speaking what he believed to be the truth, however outrageous and occasionally at the wrong time, would have to be tempered in regard to criticism of his own players, a degree of self-censorship requiring rigorous application.

Clough was never in danger of losing his dressing room because he bossed it the way Caesar once bossed Rome. It was his jurisdiction, and you were subject to his justice as well as to his whims. In public he could – and did – say with impunity that one player was about as much use as 'a traffic cone' or even that he'd like to 'kick' another on the shins. In private, he could punish – and did too – with a dished-out fine or a fabricated injury, the latter an excuse to bar someone, who had performed poorly for him, from an international call-up. Any manager trying those tricks today would face the sort of mutiny not seen since the *Bounty* broke anchor. The players of that generation generally had too little power. The players of the current one generally have too much. Too many of them demand adoration, infatuation, sycophancy and a loyalty seldom reciprocated. They have rice paper for skin, which makes them sensitive to minor slights, real or imagined, that can end in boot-stomping or hissy fits if . . . a teammate doesn't hug them properly after scoring a goal . . . the club overlooks their birthday or fails to celebrate it with a cake and balloons . . . the manager doesn't pick them . . . or has the temerity to substitute them . . . or casts a sideways glance their way that could be interpreted as darkly suspicious, a silent rebuke or a wordless accusation of some kind.

As Clough's face fades from those big screens, the second half about to start, I look at it and appreciate again that there is seldom genius without a tincture of eccentricity; and also that the best and most interesting individuals are always a great bunch of people. What Clough achieved is old water under old bridges, but how fabulously lucky I was to have seen it, and to have seen him also.

In his familiar hooded, pale grey padded coat, which looks rather worn now, Arsène Wenger is taking his seat in the Peter Taylor Stand, the FA banishing him from the dugout because of disparaging remarks he made to a referee after the Chelsea game. Keeping shtum with match officials, even when your tongue wants to go on an angry run, is something Brian Clough could have taught him. Complaining about a decision you didn't get was, Clough believed, as stupid as a ship's captain complaining about the sea. Having forgotten that, and paid for it, Wenger looks so detached from the action here that influencing the game seems beyond him. That feeling grows as the second half stutters away. Arsenal, expected to tear into Forest after a Wenger pep talk, appear as limply inert as before. They chalk up few marks for technical merit and none at all for artistic impression.

Forest wait sanguinely to pick off what always comes to them, the misplaced pass or the unforced error that ruins one pale Arsenal threat after another. Forcing the game into midfield, where the holders pathetically lack penetrative ideas, suits Forest. As long balls thrust down the channels are beaten back, and as crosses get lobbed into Jordan Smith's hands, you sense Arsenal becoming more irate with themselves. The edge of Forest's area is blurry to them. Wenger sways backwards and forwards in his seat, as though in a rocking chair.

Things, already bad for him, worsen in the sixty-fourth minute. There is some preliminary jousting and jostling between the touchline and fringe of the box, possession pin-balling about erratically. No Arsenal defender latches on to the ball before Matty Cash. Rob Holding lunges at him, and Cash stumbles over his stretched left leg. The referee, Jon Moss, is so well positioned that he gives the penalty instantly, the gesture signalling it decisive. Ben Brereton puts the ball on the spot with ceremonial solemnity, takes five shuffling steps and then lengthens his stride into the sixth. David Ospina gambles, diving to his right. He loses.

Wenger is supposed to be one of the great strategists, but his decision not to bring a substitute or two capable of rescuing Arsenal seems madder, or more haughtily arrogant, than ever now.

When the *Centenary History of the FA Cup* was published in 1972, the opening lines of it read: 'There has never been any necessity to define "the Cup". Everyone knew what you meant. There is no need to define it now'.

That is no longer the case. The Cup retains its regular slot in the fixture list, but not necessarily in the passions of those who play in it. It has come to matter less because other competitions – the Premier League, the Champions League – have come to matter more. Some think of it as a distraction, a nuisance. Others regard it as an anachronism. So the Cup gets mucked around and disrespected. Big and small teams alike field weaker sides, saving themselves for other fights. The semi-finals are sent to Wembley for financial reasons. The dates and also the kick-off times of each round are, like everything else, the prerogative of the TV companies. Even proposals to scrap replays are gathering favour.

The third and fourth rounds were once a store of giant-killing possibilities on icy or glue-pot pitches, some of which were so obviously given an extra hosing of water to create a sticky bog for the benefit of the home team. While the law of statistics dictates there will always be a reverberating shock or two – think recently of Bradford City and Lincoln City – the odds of witnessing one constantly lengthen. The odds of actually winning the trophy itself constantly lengthen too. In the twenty-five years before the Premier League rearranged the order of things, nine different clubs claimed the Cup. Since then, Arsenal, Chelsea and Manchester United have lifted it on eighteen occasions between them. Interrupting that monopoly, the successes of Portsmouth and Wigan look ever more freakish, like lightning forking suddenly across a sky of summer blue.

But the likes of Forest – and particularly their fans – still think of the lustre of the Final even though the expectation of experiencing it is unrealistic. The walk down Wembley Way. The sight of the springy turf. The community singing. The brushed red carpet. The anthem and all the other rituals, as familiarly well established and as fastidiously performed as Parliament's State Opening. It was Danny Blanchflower, twice a Cup winner with Spurs, who said the whole business reminded him of 'some distant religious ceremony . . . a football heaven'. And it was also Blanchflower who added that 'the reality can never live up to the dream'. He was right, but it doesn't stop you pretending. The romantic ideal of that grand day out lives on in those of us who remember, rheumy-eyed, the Cup as it used to be and revelled in the excitement. It lives on, too, in those who want to believe, despite evidence to the contrary, that a solitary afternoon in May with all that colourful brocade will one day be our compensation for year upon year of near-misses and gnawing disappointments. In the meantime, a team like Forest beating a side like Arsenal will have to do; and matches like this one will always mean the Cup is relevant and worthwhile.

The City Ground has never been one of the palatial theatres of the game, but I had forgotten how modestly unremarkable the main entrance seems and also the fact that the Peter Taylor Stand has remained virtually untouched for almost half a century. Its predecessor burnt down midway through the first match I ever saw here or anywhere else, forcing a half-time abandonment. Age has wearied the structure, which looks decrepitly run down. But, with Forest 3–1 ahead, the architecture is immaterial. Four high walls of noise surround the pitch.

The minutes pass slowly, but Arsenal offer nothing until almost the end when a goal comes from a mistake rather than their own ingenuity. Jordan Smith slides out to gather a harmless looking forward pass. It falls from his grip, and Danny Welbeck side-foots the angled chance between two defenders before the goalkeeper can reclaim it. One gift deserves another, and Per Mertesacker is soon the munificent provider. His lazy ball towards the wing is under-hit. The anticipation of Armand Traoré intercepts it 40 yards out. The recovering challenge Mertesacker attempts on him is worse even than his pass. He moves as though his joints are stiff and seizing up, making Wenger's selection of him seem more embarrassingly misguided than before. Traoré is too nimble for Mertesacker outside the box and then too quick for Mathieu Debuchy inside it. He gets hauled down from behind. Forest swap penalty takers: this time Kieran Dowell beats Ospina. Arsenal's unseemly swansong to the tie is a squabble with referee Jon Moss about whether Dowell, who slipped as he struck his kick, hit the ball twice. No one, unless they have the eyesight of an owl, can be sure about that.

The goal brings a false sense of finality, the drama not entirely over. For the last two minutes of normal time, plus four minutes of what is added on, Forest cope with ten men after Joe Worrall gets a red card for an ill-timed, nasty tackle. It makes no difference. Arsenal are out. Wenger is beaten. As upsets go, it doesn't rank beside non-League Hereford's defeat of Newcastle or the embarrassment lowly Colchester once dished out to Don Revie's Leeds. It is still the nearest thing to Cup glory Nottingham has experienced since Clough went to the 1991 final, where Paul Gascoigne was carried off after he ought to have been sent off.

Whoever becomes their manager, Forest know they won't go all the way again – not this season at any rate – but sinking one of the flagship clubs of the competition's fleet will do for the time being.

What the result stirs is pity for Wenger, for whom defeat is excruciatingly painful but entirely his own fault. He has survived longer at Arsenal even than Clough survived here, but that longevity, rather than character, was the chief common denominator between them until now. Like Clough, the more criticism he gets, the more obstinately and intransigently Wenger responds to it. Like Clough, he has discovered that the toughest thing about success is the obligation to go on producing it. And, also like Clough, he has hung around a season or two too long in pursuit of that, either unaware or unwilling to believe that what he seeks – another title, a first Champions League – is already well behind him and out of reach.

As Forest once did, and must do again, Arsenal need to shake themselves loose from their past.

7 January 2018: Nottingham Forest v Arsenal
Nottingham Forest 4 Arsenal 2

Nottingham Forest: Smith, Lichaj, Worrall, Mancienne, Traoré, Vaughan, Osborn, Cash (McKay 87), Dowell (Mills 90), Clough (Walker 56), Brereton.
Subs not used: Henderson, Bouchalakis, Cummings, Vellios

Arsenal: Ospina, Holding, Mertesacker, Debuchy (Akpom 87), Nelson, Elneny, Willock (Nketiah 65), Maitland-Niles, Iwobi, Welbeck, Walcott.
Subs not used: Macey, Chambers, Reine-Adelaide, Dasilva, Osei-Tutu

SCORERS

Forest: Lichaj 20 and 44, Brereton 64 (pen), Dowell 83 (pen)
Arsenal: Mertesacker 23, Welbeck 79

BOOKED

Arsenal: Debuchy, Ospina, Mertesacker

SENT OFF

Forest: Worrall

Referee: J. Moss
Attendance: 27,182

11

WRITING ON THE BACK OF THE LAVATORY DOOR

3 February: Wolverhampton Wanderers v Sheffield United, The Championship, Molineux Stadium

The Black Country, once the fire-red belly of heavy industry, was described by J. B. Priestley as unrolling before you like 'a smouldering carpet' and an immense 'hollow of smoke' to which there seemed to be no end. As late afternoon gradually fades into early evening, you would never know this little bit of England had once been choked with factories and workshop furnaces, forges and also coal seams that were 30 feet thick. You can walk to the Molineux Stadium on one of the serpentine paths running through the shrubbery of West Park, grassy and quaintly genteel. You can pretend you're hiding in a tucked-away corner of a smart London square; Bloomsbury, perhaps. There is a bandstand, a slatted wooden tea house, a clock tower and also a boating lake, where every early morning Canada geese strut about and honk, loudly and indignantly, until someone scatters broken bread and shuts them up. Spring will come late here, as it often does, so there's not even a snowdrop to be seen at the moment; the tilled and well-tended flower beds will hide their buried treasure for a few more weeks at least. Beyond the park's iron railings, there's also a miniature football pitch on which a primary school plays. The upward tilt of the roof that belongs to the Billy Wright Stand is the backdrop to one of its petite goals, giving the modest field a modicum of nobility. The stand, named after the former England captain, is already aglow, a bloom of yellow so intensely bright that you could be looking at it through stained glass. The light leads you like a silent guide towards the ground. There's a shimmer of drizzle, but it has been raining or sleeting on and off for hours, leaving behind puddles that are the colour of tar. The pavements, slick and shining, are narrow and dotted with trees old enough for their big roots to have risen through the concrete, cracking it as though a small earthquake has just occurred.

In a way, of course, it has; and the epicentre is Molineux itself.

Wolverhampton Wanderers took almost a dozen years to get into the Premier League and, like the overnight traveller, passed through without entirely unpacking. Their later return lasted only a little longer before one relegation in 2012 precipitated another twelve months later and an ignominious slide into League One. That lowly position was unfortunate but not false, making the club an object of pity rather than outright derision only because of its heritage. Wolves had experienced plenty of parlous times before, and on each occasion you got the full hour of nostalgic lament for those glory, glory post-war days. In charge on the field was Wright. In charge off it was either Major Frank Buckley, who wore horn-rimmed spectacles and plus-fours, or Stan Cullis. There were three Championships, two FA Cups and also the pioneering, televised floodlit friendlies, called 'little internationals', against Spartak Moscow and Ferenc Puskás' Honvéd that predated the European Cup. What had gone before made Wolves on their uppers appear like the once grandly aristocratic family who had incrementally lost the lot – the silver, the old master oils, the chauffeured Rolls – but didn't quite know why and so struggled to comprehend what downsizing meant. But that head over arse tumble into League One in 2013 still seemed to matter significantly more than the others because it was difficult to imagine the club picking themselves up quickly from it – if at all.

Dropping into the Championship, despite the extensive TV coverage of matches, is like watching your own team disappear. Since the consensus is that nothing but the Premier League can possibly count, it always soaks up nearly every headline going. If the Championship breaks on to the back pages, it's usually in the context of who is likely to be promoted out of it. Finding yourself in League One is more traumatic still. It is like ex-communication. That may be a slight exaggeration, but the division is a dwarf planet in a minor galaxy, spinning so distantly around the sun of the Premier League that sometimes you forget it is there. Once sucked into it, some teams only get out by slipping into League Two. Wolves escaped, and now their startling resurrection is almost complete. The club has pieced itself back together again.

Even though there are another sixteen games to go after tonight's against Sheffield United, it doesn't seem rashly presumptuous to hail them already as Champions. Wolves were eleven points ahead this morning. No one – not Cardiff City, not Bristol City, not Derby County – has been able to slash the lead substantially. The company Wolves have kept at the top of the table hasn't been up to challenging them consistently. After so long adrift in a limbo between past and present, the club seems to be heading into its modern prime. Money is the main reason. It always is.

Every season for Wolves had generally been about keeping an eye open for bargains, but in the year and a half since Fosun International took them over, for around £30m, the Chinese conglomerate have spent a further £50m-plus on refurbishing the team. Fosun and their diverse holdings – the company is into travel, property, tourism (owners of Thomas Cook), healthcare and entertainment – can afford that level of largesse. Their owner, Guo Guangchang, is reportedly worth £5b. Impatient for results, Fosun are already on their fourth manager, Nuno Espírito Santo, and players have come and gone as though Wolves are speed dating. Another relationship – with the Portuguese super-agent, the smoothly suited Jorge Mendes – has been much more binding. Mendes's office is the globe; his clients include Cristiano Ronaldo and José Mourinho. The club simply call him 'an advisor to the owners', a handy catch-all description, but Fosun even owns a stake in his agency, which is convenient when talent becomes available. Wolves bought Rúben Neves for £15m from Porto. Helder Costa, £2m cheaper, came from Benfica. Ivan Cavaleiro, also Portuguese, cost £7m from Monaco.

Nuno is also on Mendes's books, which is handy too. He was a goalkeeper for, among others, Porto, where he won the Portuguese Cup, before becoming a manager and returning to take them into the last sixteen of the Champions League. So far he deserves his full quota of compliments. With that stately balding head, the remaining hair scalped close, that trim beard – more grey than black now – and those heavy-lidded eyes, he looks serious and somehow patrician. You see Nuno and think that, had he been about in the 17th century, Velázquez would have spotted his fascinating face at the court of some European monarch and rushed to capture the character of it *al la prima*. Like Velázquez's other well known portraits of noblemen and saints and Popes, he'd have been dressed finely and his gaze would have brooded back at you in concentrated spots of pigment. Nuno has a strict method, a stern discipline and a work ethic that is all about fixed determination and ceaseless labour. 'Control' is a word he uses a lot.

Wolves had been shaking up the Championship, stomping over all-comers, to such a degree and with such dominance that three weeks ago I went on a preliminary reconnaissance mission (a busman's day out, really) to South Yorkshire. In particular I wanted to see Cavaleiro and the precocious 21-year-old Diogo Jota, sharp-featured and thin-faced, who is on a season long loan from Atlético Madrid until a permanent deal is signed this summer. Also, Léo Bonatini, the Brazilian borrowed from Saudi side Al-Hilal, was the Championship's Mo Salah in regard to scoring. He'd rapped in ten goals almost before the clocks went back in autumn, his tally piquing the interest of other managers. Wolves, unbeaten then for thirteen matches, were at Oakwell, where Barnsley had taken only thirteen points all season and hadn't won for two months. The outcome seemed obvious. It was a cold and overcast afternoon, the sky low and bruised. I waited for Wolves to shred Barnsley into thin strips, convincing me of their high merit. But you don't always get what you want . . .

The first half dragged interminably, a long drip of boredom in which every nerve was deadened. I will always think of it as one of the most dispiriting fifty three and three-quarter minutes I have ever witnessed. There were two long stoppages and numerous shorter ones. The pitch, strewn with prone bodies, looked at one stage like dusty Main Street in a frontier western. The delays piled on top of one another. The game was artless and tedious, barely having a worth-while breath in it. Nothing much happened very slowly. You could excuse Barnsley's performance – their struggling team possesses strictly limited skills – but Wolves seemed to play in the chaos of weary thought or as though battling through a bad cold. There was an utter emptiness about them. What constituted the peaks of that half were a disallowed goal and a semi-squeal for a penalty. There was one shot on target. It was struck with no more force than a firmly pushed back pass. I thought about leaving, unsure about whether I could face whatever came next. I persisted with the match nevertheless, but afterwards wished that I hadn't. The second half was much the same as the first: grim, guideless, goalless. Jota bashed a shot against the bar and then missed a sitter from less than a yard and a half, the sort of chance he would claim 999 times out of 1,000. The misery didn't end until two minutes to five (there were more stoppages and desperate multiple substitutions). I dwelt on the fact that, even if the internet hadn't come along and made the Saturday night football special superfluous, a game such as that one would have killed it off anyway. The paper wouldn't have rolled off the presses and on to the streets until the crowd was already back home for an early tea; and no one who'd seen the match would possibly want to relive it in print. When, afterwards, Nuno implied things hadn't been as diabolical as most of us had thought, he sounded like the delusional Don Quixote trying to persuade Sancho Panza that a skinny nag was really a pedigree steed.

The Championship is watched in 173 countries, from Brazil to Western Sahara and from Djibouti to Australia. If any of them tuned in to Oakwell, and then stayed with the match, it could only have been because the other channels had gone off air. If that game had instructional value, it was only to show us how much of a slog and a scrap the Championship can be. It is a mountainous climb with obstacles. Perhaps Wolves, suddenly short of goals, were in a mid-season rut at Oakwell. Perhaps, after an unrelenting run of fixtures, exhaustion or jitters or complacency were to blame. Whatever the reason, Wolves lost only their fourth league game of the season a week later. Their matches since have been about regaining momentum as much as authority.

Billy Wright said his ambition to play professionally began when he sat in the Molineux grandstand, wedged between his mother and father, to watch Wolves draw with an Arsenal team that included Alex James and Cliff Bastin, then living legends of Highbury. He used to describe the atmosphere here as 'almost overwhelming'. He spoke of the 'hostile glare' of the floodlights and 'the bracing nip of the night air'. He saw lit cigarettes and struck matches, which he thought looked like 'darting fireflies' and heard an 'ever flowing roar'. The ground, Wright explained, became a 'hazy cauldron of unbridled partisanship in which the spectators were the actors no less than the players'. Wright played in front of 55,000, the 'Big Bank' urging them on. The modern Molineux, while holding over 20,000 fewer, demands Premier League status and a side to match it. As a sign of Wolves's renaissance, more than 30,000-plus – their biggest crowd since the year Charles wed Diana – were packed in only last month. Molineux isn't as intimidating as it used to be, but the 'hazy cauldron' of Wright's memory holds true – even if the effect is manufactured. Wolves make such a grand entrance that you wonder how it can be topped when promotion comes. You'd think this was a Cup Final. The teams emerge between a touchline row of black fire-boxes, from which high plumes of gas flame appear. I can faintly feel the heat from them 100 yards away. There are green and silver fireworks too, fired in pyrotechnical salute. In football these days, this is what passes for pomp and circumstance, however elaborately tacky it can seem. The fireworks take off, crossing over and then exploding in synchron-ised splendour. Afterwards the smoke hangs, across the whole of the pitch, like a mucky net curtain in a suburban window. The opening few minutes are viewed in a different kind of haze than Wright remembered. With impeccable timing, it lifts, breaks apart and clears completely when Wolves, commanding from the start, leap spectacu-larly into the lead.

As implausible as this seems, it's said that the TV of the future will allow us to see a game 'through the eyes' of one of the players. The high resolution, immersive technology, called Volumetric Video, will patch seamlessly together body-cam footage and the feed from 5K cameras dotted about the ground. You'll have to wear a virtual reality headset to share in the fun, but the compensation for that clumsiness will be 360-degree coverage from pitch level. You'll know what it's like to not only wear someone's boots but also to run around in them. If so, to see what Sheffield United's Simon Moore saw would be an education in terms of both shooting and the woes of being a goalkeeper.

Under no pressure – United's attack is retreating towards halfway as though out of respect – Conor Coady takes one touch, looks up and picks out Ivan Cavaleiro with a raking pass to the left flank. Cavaleiro, who won every domestic honour in Portugal before moving to France, is one of those players who starts explosively and doesn't stop if he can help it. Parked wide right in the second half at Barnsley, he alone made a decent fist of the match. He is one of the few at Molineux who would have slotted into the team of Wright's more roughhouse era. He has the skill, sure enough, but there is also something strong and physically imposing about him. He is compact and solid, a tidy brick wall, so he can't easily be bundled off a pass, which makes the certainty of his control of it more valuable. But – and fewer still possess this – there is a certain muscular grace and a sculptured hardness about him too. The outline of his chest muscles are prominent against the tight silk of his shirt. At times Cavaleiro looks trapped, snared in a corner, and then he will turn and pivot and sway or lean into the closest defender, pushing him off balance. Some clever roll or small tremble of his boot, or a dropped shoulder, will then open up room into which he can flee.

The speed, the angle and the accuracy of Coady's pass to him adds up to a surprise for United, the line of their back three optimistically high. No one is within 10 yards of Cavaleiro. He shimmies a bit, like a dancer trying to find the rhythm of some music, before heading on the outside. In one of those chance happenings, which occur a hundred times in every half hour of a match, the sliding tackle that robs him of the ball finds its way to Rúben Neves. He's 30 yards out and three-quarters of United's side is now between him and Moore. As soon as possession comes to him, Neves makes up his mind what he will do with it. He pushes the ball a foot and a half in front of him and then goes to meet it, swinging his right boot at it the way a circus strongman would swing a hammer. The shot takes off. United's defenders, on the half turn, have to be sharp to follow the yellow blur of it through the air. The strike hits the inside of the post, directly beneath the bar, with a loud crack, as if the wood might break, and then flies in to the opposite corner. If you had Volumetric Video, putting yourself exactly in Moore's place, you'd see instantly that, even from such a distance, he is a millisecond late in picking the path of the ball because two of his own players block his sightline. You'd also notice the slight bend on Neves's effort, which begins beyond the post; and, doing so, you'd know instinctively where the effort was going but not have a clue about how to get there before it. You'd finally experience the jump Moore makes and also see his left hand grope uselessly for what has already whizzed past him. The goal galvanises Wolves and tranquillises United. Their manager, Chris Wilder, declared beforehand that he would 'have a go', choosing an attacking four-man midfield and three up front. It is a laudable ambition but an unrealistic one when you can't climb out of your own half, let alone into Wolves's box.

At the beginning of Wright's era, under Major Buckley, Wolves were controversially given the 'monkey gland' treatment, administered either through injection or in light-brown capsules half an inch long. The serum, drawn from the testicles of the animal, was supposed to improve stamina. Some believed it did. Some thought it was a placebo, the effect entirely psychosomatic from a quack scientist gone mad and a manager who believed in him. The only stimulant these Wolves apparently need is the whip of Nuno Espírito Santo's words. In the thirtieth minute, as he waves them on enthusiastically, the Championship favourites score again. The goal is far different from – but far superior to – their excellent first. In a slow pouring of rain the team combines to quickly rip United apart down the central seam. The build up begins all the way back with John Ruddy, who rolls the ball out of his area to Coady. From there – after twelve passes embracing seven different players – Diogo Jota, who usually prefers his right foot, finishes from 14 yards with his left. The glittering move has two highlights, and Cavaleiro is responsible for each of them.

The burning kick in his heels over 5 yards is the key to what follows. He's gone suddenly, the defenders in a slapstick chase after him. Cavaleiro can do all this, constantly restating his quality, but he doesn't grandstand when there is a plain job of work to be done. There is an intelligent awareness about his approach. He knows what is happening around him and he also senses, the permutations all thought through, what could be about to happen. Now he retains the ball in midfield, his side-check superb, and then arrives at the business end of the pitch to swap the one-two with Jota. This makes space for the low drive. Moore is blameless again.

Last September United beat Wolves at Bramall Lane and went into second place, a startlingly rapid rise for a newly promoted side with a low budget and limited resources. Ever since United have slowly lost that mooring and are now floating away even from the play-offs. Wilder does have some decent players, the common denominator between them not difficult to locate. The central defender Richard Stearman spent seven and a half years at Wolves. The striker Leon Clarke was raised in the Molineux Academy. The midfielder Lee Evans was in Wolves's promotion team from League One.

United, flushed and anxious, still look far inferior – a bit too timid at the back and prone to shilly-shallying up front. Already, the narra-tive of this match has narrowed to one main story: how many goals Wolves will score in the second half. Wilder, deep in tangled thought, bunches his face into a grim expression, as though about to sink down and confess his troubles to someone. Nothing United do allays that unease.

No child I've known has wanted a referee's kit for Christmas rather than a club's replica shirt. I still wonder why any adult would want one too – even for a wage of up to £70,000 to £100,000 per season. Twenty years ago the remuneration for the job wouldn't have kept a church mouse in cheese for a week; Gordon Strachan, then boss at Coventry City, said his players 'wouldn't take a throw in' for the amount referees were paid. The pay has shot up, allowing the best to make a very decent living, but so, exponentially, has the stress, the hassle and above all the viciousness of the critics who watch either at home or from the stands.

Shortly after the season started, I went to hear a referee discuss the pitfalls and the pressures of his job. He spoke illuminatingly about his weekly routine: training, fitness tests, reports, appraisals, meetings, watching re-runs of games endlessly. In the Q&A segment following all this, he was asked about whether he could hear the provocative abuse he received during a game and afterwards and, if so, whether it cost him nights of sleep. He began with two anecdotes. In the first of them he and his assistants discussed among themselves before kick-off how long it would be before a 'well-known' player swore at them. One assistant chose five minutes. Another chose fifteen. The ref split the difference, plumping for ten minutes. Each prediction was sorely wrong. The player told the referee to fuck off in the tunnel. In the second, the full gamut of industrial language was spewed at him from a voice belonging to a boy who was only eleven or twelve years old. The boy's father, sitting beside him, let the son rage on while remaining mute himself. There was no murmur of disapproval or rebuke. The ref eventually approached the father politely. Why, he wanted to know, didn't the father tell the son to stop or moderate his swearing? Of course, it is the lawyer's golden rule never to ask a question to which you don't know the answer. The ref was about to learn that. The father's reply was tart and angry. The ref deserved whatever he 'fucking' got that afternoon, he said. In hindsight the ref viewed the incident with sangfroid. After all, you can't reason with unreasonable people, and the effort to try is a waste of breath. His hearing, he went on, had to be selective on 'the green bit', his euphemism for the pitch, for the sake of his sanity. Off it, you learnt to tune out social media by simply not logging on to it.

Less than twenty-four hours later, Jon Moss sent off Liverpool's Sadio Mané for a high-kicking challenge on Ederson, Manchester City's £35m goalkeeper. The studs of Mané's right boot went into Ederson's right cheek. The phrase 'outrage on social media' has slipped so commonly into everyday usage that it has become a cliché. Print and broadcast media alike report the public reaction to a breaking story alongside the story itself. Indeed, it often becomes the headline; and this 'outrage' not only adds juicy flavour but is frequently the unacknowledged excuse for running something prominently in the first place. But as Charles Moore sensibly wrote recently: 'Why is this considered news? Outrage on social media is a daily occurrence, like rain in the Hebrides.' Moss's decision certainly provoked 'outrage' on social media. The term 'all thumbs' to define clumsiness or cack-handedness is almost redundant. To be 'all thumbs' in the modern world is to be proficient in tweeting, that great and intolerable noise of modern life. Twitter has made everyone their own Caxton, but the palimpsest it provides has become like the back of the door in a public lavatory.

On it the ignoramuses scrawl, leaving behind any slur or libel, any hate or mockery they like, often anonymously, and then run away without shame, remorse or guilt. Those for whom Twitter brings out the inner troglodyte tend to paddle intellectually in the shallow end of the pool, but also demonstrate something with all their splashing about. We have reached the crazy stage in which some people believe that merely holding an opinion is enough to make it valid and important enough to share. That's why they easily mistake bar-room bawling for cerebral opinion and their ungrammatical, misspelt, unpunctuated and capital-ised sentences as pearls of polished thought. You glance at these messages, usually prefaced and suffixed with expletives, and try to imagine their authors, hunched over whatever device is the conduit for their rage. Your first thought is the obvious one: that nowadays propor-tion, decency, old-fashioned common sense and courtesy have all slipped their anchor and sunk. But your second is that every village must have a disproportionately high number of idiots in it who are also illiterate. On Twitter Moss was condemned and pilloried heinously – all in the very choicest of language. Those hackneyed chants, dating back to middle decades of the last century, about 'the bastard in the black' and the referee being 'a wanker' are the epitome of politeness in comparison. A few 'supporters', convinced there was a grudge that needed to be settled against Moss, even began changing his entry on Wikipedia. Several fictions were stirred among sober, established fact. 'Question marks remain over his ability to referee again at Premiership level,' said one. Another claimed that Moss had been promoted to the Select Group of Referees in 2011 'even though he doesn't know the rules'. A third described him as 'a closet Manchester City fan'. The insults flung at Moss multiplied, appearing at the rate of two dozen per minute, each nearly always viler than the last.

This comes back to me because tonight's referee, Darren Bond, has been as faultless as it is humanly possible to be. Referees frequently take flak for understanding the rules without necessarily understand-ing the game, but Bond has been particularly astute in playing the advantage and allowing things to flow properly, which is to Wolves' benefit. Indulging in ego can be fatal to a referee's career and reputa-tion, but Bond is a diligent stage manager rather than a showy performer. He hasn't interfered fussily to get himself noticed. In fact, you barely know he is here. It's as though, for long stretches, the match is refereeing itself, which is the sign of authority. There are nevertheless some, sitting around me, who clearly believe their ticket represents good value for money only if the referee, whoever he happens to be, is hosed down with insults. Being miserable keeps that type of person going. So there is minor nit-picking about the decisions about throw-ins or corners. Bond has been scrupulously fair and even-handed, but it also doesn't deter one fan from getting to his feet, cupping a hand to his mouth and shouting: 'YOU'RE A FUCKING IDIOT, REFEREE'.

Oh dear. I think about challenging him. I then remember the old maxim about never arguing with an idiot because anyone watching won't be able to tell the difference between the two of you.

Wolves, well into the second half now, remain masters of the match. Sheffield United still can't get up and running despite Leon Clarke, who chases down passes that go astray, and Ricky Holmes, who covers a considerable amount of ground without ever being able to claim much of it for himself. Wolves are sparring with United during this lull and you find your eyes tracking the pitch, searching out Ivan Cavaleiro. His movements are purposeful and interesting. You will Cavaleiro to get possession because he is going to entertain or do the extraordinary. With less than twenty minutes left, however, it is referee Bond who again impresses most of all.

Goalkeepers, once chained to their box, are expected to sweep up, defend and pass a ball as accurately as Glenn Hoddle once did. It has made them ruling lords of the last third of the field. But some – Thibaut Courtois at Chelsea or Joe Hart at West Ham, for example – can overindulge in the rushing out, their legs well ahead of their judgement. Free kicks or even penalties can be given away hastily with only a glancing touch. Out comes the red card, flourished as a consequence of a critical miscalculation – usually the pace of a through-ball hit straight or only slightly angled. Far too often a goalkeeper, getting carried away, thinks it is an obligation to become involved, however recklessly. He always assumes he will reach the ball before his defenders.

There is, however, a flaw in these theories. The average forward detects the merest touch the way a butterfly registers the direction of the lightest breeze. And the striker is adept at making the maximum out of the minimum. You'll see him turn his upper body into a half-corkscrew twist or wrap one leg around the other. The arms will go up. So will the head. The cartoony, splayed dive is accentuated for dramatic purposes. He goes to grass as if someone has just struck him on the back of the head with a sockful of pennies.

Simon Moore is the latest goalkeeper to react in haste and then repent. The ball, pumped forward from 25 yards inside Wolves's half, gets almost as much height as it does distance. It's like something launched from a slingshot. The target is the space in front of Diogo Jota and behind Richard Stearman. The two of them run together for it, the attacker a semi-stride ahead of his policeman. You expect Stearman to push Jota wide and wait for support. Then Moore impulsively decides to be decisive. The ball has still to bounce, and Moore has no idea where it will go after it does, but he commits himself foolishly nonetheless. Stearman peels around the back of his goalkeeper to cover him. Moore can't possibly get to the ball before Jota; he's too far away from it because he began from a standing start, immediately putting him at a disadvantage. He takes a desperate leap forward. His feet are up. His arms flail. He looks like someone who, attempting to clear a five-bar gate, knows in mid-air that his landing is going to be a messy disaster. Moore's gloves barely brush the ball. The rest of him, however, collapses into and then over Jota, who takes the toe of the goalkeeper's right boot on his chin. Referee Bond is well behind the play, but there is nothing wrong with his distance vision. Amid the screaming pandemonium, the 20 or so yards he covers to reach Moore and also Jota, now stretched across the turf, give him enough time to calmly do what is right and proper. He pulls the red card slowly from his left pocket. Moore goes without a peep. On his way to the dressing room, he casually smooths down a flap of hair like someone about to meet a Saturday night date. The man who had previously got to his feet and called Bond a 'fucking idiot' now gets to his feet and applauds him.

Jake Eastwood replaces Moore. He is twenty-one, but looks about eighteen, his face sallow and unblemished. A responsible publican would ask for proof of his date of birth before serving him a pint.

Coming cold to his Championship debut, Eastwood tries to organise the five-man wall, set himself in front of his line and get used to the fact that he has a free kick to save, an idea that couldn't possibly have occurred to him only five minutes ago. Wolves plant three players around the ball. Rúben Neves makes the dummy run, allowing Cavaleiro to test the novice. His low drive takes a deflection off Clarke. Eastwood is halfway through a dive to his right when he realises the effort is heading to his left. He can't recover. His first act is to fish the ball out of the net.

Completely outplayed and now outnumbered, United stagger through the quarter of an hour that is left, simply relieved not to suffer further damage. Wolves take it easy.

Astonishing though it seems, since he wasn't a literary gent, the epigraph to Billy Wright's volume of autobiography, which was published to mark his retirement, came from a verse of A. E. Housman's. Wright used to quote from *A Shropshire Lad*, borrowing what the poet felt about that county to explain what he felt about the Black Country and Molineux. It was for him 'a land of lost content', he said, and he saw the acres of it 'shining plain'.

West Midlands football has seldom made history in the half-century since Wright quit. A few pages would be enough to record its domestic successes. Its last title was Aston Villa's in 1981. Its last FA Cup was West Bromwich Albion's in 1968. Wolves have won only one trophy – the League Cup – since 1980.

But at the end of tonight's game, Nuno Espírito Santo comes on to the pitch and claps the four sides of the ground. Rain, sparkling under the lights, clings to his black padded coat. Wolves could clinch promotion before Manchester City win the Premier League and, like them, do so with a record points tally, beating the 106 Reading racked up in 2004. If you didn't know this, you wouldn't detect it in Nuno's demeanour. He's stern, not ready to celebrate a task only three quarters done.

You have to live in a place to understand its qualities, its mood, its ethics. But I think Nuno is a Black Country sort of chap. After all, he believes nothing worthwhile is ever achieved without continuous labour.

Billy Wright would quite like him.

3 February 2018:
Wolverhampton Wanderers v Sheffield United
Wolverhampton Wanderers 3 Sheffield United 0

Wolves: Ruddy, Bennett, Coady, Boly, Doherty, N'Diaye, Neves, Douglas, Costa (Bonatini 65), Jota (Gibbs-White 81), Cavaleiro (Afobe 77).
Subs not used: Batth, Enobakhare, Hause, Norris

Sheffield Utd: Moore, Basham (Leonard 71), Stearman, O'Connell, Baldock, Evans, Holmes (Donaldson 71), Fleck, Stevens, Wilson (Eastwood 76), Clarke.
Subs not used: Lundstram, Sharp, Duffy, Lafferty

SCORERS

Wolves: Neves 5, Jota 30, Cavaleiro 76

SENT OFF

Sheffield Utd: Moore

Referee: D. Bond
Attendance: 29,311

12

OF SPLENDOUR ON THE GRASS

25 February: Manchester City v Arsenal, League Cup Final, Wembley

It is the twenty-third minute. Arsenal win a free kick 30 yards out. Aaron Ramsey wipes the pale ball against the front of his shirt and then rubs the sweat from the thin furrows of his brow, his head slightly bowed and his eyes fixed always on the goal. Manchester City begin to organise in front of their goalkeeper, Claudio Bravo, who shuffles across and hugs his right post for a short while, as if seeking succour from it. He cranes his neck sideways, peering around the broad back of his own defenders in an attempt to draw in his mind the line and the angle from which Ramsey will test him. Bravo holds up four fingers, waving into position the players who volunteer to become his human shield. The City wall, strengthened suddenly by an extra body, squeezes together. Each man is as still as a chess piece, braced to block what Ramsey is about to blast at him. It is as though Wembley, and everyone in it, is in a state of suspended animation. When a game flows spontaneously, the turns it takes unscripted, you can never frame the scene, which constantly shifts. But in the next two and three-quarter seconds, the picturesqueness of the set-piece pins everyone to a place, perfectly. There's a kind of cathedral hush as well. Even small sounds echo, however faintly. The tread of Ramsey's feet in his four-step run. The crack of leather on leather, the ball pummelled off his right boot. The skip of the low shot as it brushes the turf. The thump the ball makes as Bravo, stooping low, catches it against his chest and then clings on. The attempt and the save are inconsequential once over, a minor skirmish lost soon amid bigger ones. The brief moment will pass us by tomorrow, unreported in the analysis of how the League Cup was won and lost. And it won't, I imagine, even be remembered much, if at all, by those who were directly behind Bravo and saw what he could see – Ramsey's short approach, the ball whistling towards him, Arsenal's attackers preparing to rush in, ready for a slip or a ricochet.

Contained in this sliver of action is nonetheless what a Cup Final at Wembley represents. In that eye-blink you are aware of the stadium's lovely curves and of the tableau of the match laid across it. Lit from above, casting late winter shadows, Wembley looks as though an artist has dressed the set, arranging the players and then telling them to hold the pose so he can trap them on canvas and capture the essence of the occasion before it slides past us. There is Bravo sinking to his knees to smother the danger beneath him. There is City's wall, breaking apart. There is Ramsey, thwarted and throwing his head back to register the fact. The immense spread of turf rolls towards David Ospina, alone in Arsenal's half and wearing a shirt of flaming orange. On the touchline Arsène Wenger winces hard, accentuating the seams of that long, old face. Pep Guardiola slams his right fist into the palm of his left hand. The opposing fans are wide blocks of brilliant colour. At one end City's lean back in their seats, their breath held in case Bravo is about to become – like Dan Lewis or Gary Sprake – a goalkeeper whose whole career will be defined by a Wembley mistake, the ball leaking through his hands or dipping under his dive. At the other, Arsenal's push themselves forward, almost attempting to blow Ramsey's shot into the net.

Nothing else played anywhere else carries, for me at least, the atmosphere of a domestic Cup Final at Wembley. Asked about the stadium this week, Guardiola expressed a personal view that will resonate universally. His reply was only eight words long and Guardiola said it quietly, but anyone who has ever been here needed no clarification about the point being made. Guardiola was talking specifically about bringing Barcelona to Wembley in 2011 and beating Manchester United, the Catalans conquering Europe again. In doing so he alluded to the history and the traditions of the place, now almost a century old, and also what counts about it: the show Wembley puts on. Getting to the final of anything here, absorbing the spectacle and then going home to relive it is a grand thing, never forgotten. Guardiola knows this because he has felt it and was able to articulate the emotion. 'Wembley will always be part of our lives,' he said, which is his way of describing it as a moveable feast, the memory staying with you wherever you go.

From awkward beginnings, the League Cup has emerged with a complicated identity. The competition wasn't born on a high tide of optimism, arriving instead coldly unloved because it was so unwanted. Dismissed as a 'complete waste of time', which qualifies as one of the kinder and proportionate responses, it was considered at the start of the 1960s to be the season's ugly ornament. Establishing itself properly only when Wembley became the Final's permanent home in 1967, the Football League later lost some of the shine the Cup had gradually accrued by eagerly pedalling the thing to suitors like a 19th-century father wanting to marry off his eldest daughter. Ever since sponsors have so quickly followed one another that only someone with eidetic recall can possibly tell you which of them held sway in which season over the past thirty-seven years. The Cup has passed between two brewers, a betting company, a soft drinks manufacturer, an electrical firm, a financial corporation and, most peculiarly of all, the Milk Marketing Board. Ambivalence towards it remains. This was exemplified earlier this season when, with supreme irony, the detractor was Pep Guardiola. He was so unenamoured with the early rounds that his misgivings became a gripe. He called the Cup 'a prize where, when you win, it's OK', the kind of lukewarm endorsement given to something you barely tolerate but are too polite to slate outright.

The latest backer, the energy drink Carabao, will disappear from the Cup soon enough, fading as a shadow does, but its sponsorship is well-timed because this Final, unlike so many others, is different. It won't vanish into obscurity almost as soon as the lap of honour is over. For if the game brings Guardiola his first trophy in England, it is always going to be a pub quiz question. Defeat for Arsène Wenger could also be the beginning of the end for him at Arsenal, a side on the slide.

For months it seemed as though Manchester City had leant on the scales of history and tilted them their way. City are thirteen points clear in the Premier League, needing only another six wins to take the title. A place in the Champions League quarter-finals is a given. Guardiola is too intelligent to be flattered by sycophancy, so being told repeatedly that he had made City practically invincible was always going to provoke derision from him. City were nonetheless scattering so many teams to the breeze that the more Guardiola wrote off the notion of collecting an unprecedented quadruple – 'that isn't going to happen,' he'd said – the more his protests seemed false modesty. But then, at the start of this week, City contributed to the romantic traditions of the FA Cup by losing at League One Wigan. A team costing more than £350m, its group of players a starry constellation, buckled to another which had been patched together for £800,000, including one loan signing and seven free transfers. This was giant-killing *in excelsis*. Guardiola was miffed about it. In the hurly-burly of the last twenty minutes, he shook his head or stuffed his hands inside his pockets and rested his chin on his chest, as if reluctant to fix his eyes on the struggle. Wigan blocked and tackled or let out gasps when the ball, as it often did, slipped across a gaping goalmouth or dropped just beyond a post. With a late breakaway goal, Wigan made City look like mortals, ordinary in their suffering, rather than the supermen we had presumed them to be. But in that defeat, which even Guardiola failed to rationalise adequately in the post-mortem of the press conference, you felt that the real victims of the tie were not City but Arsenal. Surely retribution for City's embarrassment will be meted out on them, making today's match a horror for Wenger.

For City and Guardiola, who has lost only one of the ten Cup Finals in which he's managed a team, the season still has the proportions to become an epic. For Arsenal and Wenger, the next few months are more likely to endorse what that FA Cup exit against Nottingham Forest six weeks ago had heavily implied: that the club, badly ailing, now needs a new direction and new personnel, which also means a new boss.

We were promised that a spiteful north-easterly wind would bring temperatures lower than the Arctic's – something to do with a 'contrary reversal' of the jet stream – but what we've got is a hard blue sky, the hue of it matching Manchester City's shirts almost exactly. A portent, perhaps.

The first chance – a good one – was Arsenal's, however. There was a tangled skirmish near the 6-yard box. For a second or so you couldn't be sure where the ball had gone. You had to watch it again, replayed on the big screen, to acknowledge the fine-line timing of Kyle Walker's tackle, robbing Pierre-Emerick Aubameyang, and also the striker's timidity in allowing the full back to poke the ball away from him. Aubameyang is making only a third appearance since his £56m move from Borussia Dortmund. He is supposed to be nippy, timed at 3.7 seconds over 30 metres. Here, when it mattered, he was hesitant and slow, debating rather than doing.

The opposition generally get so few openings against City that the price the underdogs could pay for Aubameyang's indecision and/or lack of mettle could be the trophy. Ernest Hemingway, an amateur pugilist when he wasn't punching the keys of his typewriter, once recalled a conversation he had with the French boxer Georges Carpentier, who told him of his heavyweight fight with Bombardier Billy Wells. 'Vice, as vice, is bad, but viciousness in the ring is essential,' Carpentier said to Papa. 'What he meant,' Hemingway explained, 'was that Wells had had him in the first round and let him go. So Carpentier knocked him out in the second.' Aubameyang 'had' City and then let them go. Aaron Ramsey's free kick is the closest Arsenal have come since to claiming the lead. And so – and entirely predictably – City smash them to the floor the way Carpentier once smashed Wells.

We are used to City pushing high. The full backs move into midfield or the central defenders go wide, spreading further than the points of their own box, so the ball can be swept to them from the goalkeeper. But their goal, when it comes, is a surprising homage to Route One – a throwback to the 1970s and 1980s when the virtues of the long ball were so fulsomely extolled that it became over-used. The credit belongs to Bravo. Gathering the ball after an Arsenal attack withers in the eighteenth minute, he glances up, barely believing the sight far ahead of him. Wenger has opted for a back three. The pivotal defender in it, Shkodran Mustafi, is meandering back towards his own half. Either the German believes City are decent sports who won't be discourteous enough to launch an attack until he is ready for it, or the jeopardy Arsenal are in simply hasn't occurred to him. Sometimes half a minute can be a mighty powerful thing in a match, and Sergio Agüero proves it regularly. He never gives anyone a moment of complete peace because the creative compulsion in him never rests and also because, with a beady eye, he spots a chance the way a gull spots a scrap of fish. Bravo, seeing Agüero is alone, sends a soaring, sixty-five-yard goal-kick towards him. The ball is played, rather than merely booted, and is as penetrating as a Kevin De Bruyne pass. Mustafi (6 feet) is so complacent that he can't get goal-side of Agüero (5 feet 7 inches). In the challenge between them, which is no more than a bump, he leans backwards, tipping himself off balance. Mustafi is bent over like a stalk of corn. The ball flies above his head, splitting Arsenal down the middle. Agüero, left to his own devastating devices, wheels towards it and waits for Newton's first law of motion to play out. He lets the ball bounce, chesting it down only when he's 20 yards from the posts. Some strikers would get flustered, snatching at the shot too soon. Agüero, on 198 City goals, isn't to be denied or interrupted. He watches with a poacher's patience, aware that David Ospina isn't sure whether to come out or stay back, crouch low or make himself tall. As Calum Chambers and Laurent Koscielny attempt to squeeze the space around him, Agüero dinks his effort casually over Ospina from the edge of the box. The goalkeeper raises his hands towards it like someone signalling surrender.

Human nature is never so generous as when giving advice. We don't mind meddling because we always think we see others' lives as well as, if not better, than our own. Wenger consequently received in advance no shortage of expert tuition about how to muzzle City's superior skill. He was told that sitting back and letting them pour over Arsenal, like rising water, would be to drown, one gulp at a time. He was urged to attack, pressing City as Liverpool had done when winning against them in the Premier League at Anfield, ending City's unbeaten Premier League streak at twenty-two matches. The day afterwards *The Times*, with cheeky and mischievous brilliance, tagged their football supplement *The Game* as a 'Souvenir Edition'. The front page headline read:

City Lose Football Match.

On Merseyside, City were unexpectedly harried and closed down, forced into loose, hasty passing. The supply line to the forwards, if not entirely severed, was disrupted. City's full backs were stopped on or just over the halfway line, preventing them from claiming the touch-lines. Agüero got few moments in the opposition's box. Wenger was urged to imitate that approach. He'd risk being outmanoeuvred in a counter attack, but better to perish honourably going forward than curled up inside your own box. Arsenal's midfield would have to be disciplined and tirelessly energetic, covering so much ground that by the end you'd wonder how any of them still had the strength to breathe. But, of course, the assumption was that Arsenal would get the ball and retain it. This fundamental is beyond them, making every other tip or cunning scheme suggested to Wenger useless.

For the next twenty-five minutes Arsenal are present but don't do anything. Confidence is absent from them, which means authority is absent too. City, through De Bruyne, who strokes short passes, Leroy Sané, who so often receives them and also the gadfly David Silva, who is everywhere, play as though the Cup is their destiny. Arsenal play as though Wembley is a constant torment for them. Mesut Özil wears the cloak of invisibility – hardly the appropriate garb for someone said to be earning £350,000 per week. When he sheds it, which is only occasionally, Özil keeps stopping, as though he's forgotten something. Mostly, it seems, about what he ought to do with the ball. Alongside him Aaron Ramsey isn't much more effective.

Already, Wenger's donnish demeanour has begun to change. At half time, getting up briskly from the bench, he looks at City with an expression of melancholy envy.

A month ago I came on a tourist tour of the 'new' Wembley, curious to know what the interior of it looked like. The surprise was how cramped everything seemed beneath the vast, high stands. The guide – a man in his early seventies – couldn't say much about the bare dressing rooms apart from expressing his slight contempt that 'a hair-dryer' was available to the players. He invited us to inspect it as

though some new-fangled novelty was on show and we were still in
the age when male grooming meant a quick short back and sides and
a tub of lard to hold it firm. I expected to hear him *humph* about
expensive designer aftershaves and say that in his day a bar of shop-
soap did the same job much cheaper. Instead, he led us to the tunnel,
where a bronze bust of Sir Alf Ramsey sits on a plinth. Sir Alf, made
to look a little like Mussolini, is so thin-lipped and grimly expression-
less that you'd think his features had been moulded directly from a
death mask. The guide then lined us up as two opposing teams. He
asked us to pretend that 90,000 awaited us outside (some canned
crowd noise would have been helpful at this point). We came out of
the double doors into weak lunchtime sunlight, finding the pitch
covered in the skeletal iron frames of overhead sprinklers and also a
knot of groundsmen, who looked at us disinterestedly. We were
invited to sit where the managers do and then we climbed to the
Royal Box, where the upholstered seating probably cost more than a
three-piece suite. After our tour ended and the guide escorted us out,
I asked him which he preferred: the old Wembley or the new? 'Oh,'
he said, without hesitation 'the old one, of course.' He reeled off
some of the Cup Finals he had seen, and also some internationals
when England were Champions of the World. Later I thought about
the 'of course' at the beginning of those reminiscences, which the
guide went through like flicking the pages of a history book. I realised
it was a nod and a wink to me, offered because he assumed I would
wholeheartedly agree with his assessment. I don't.

Even in black and white, which is how I saw the 'old' Wembley as a
boy on TV, the pitch was so perfect that bringing up a divot almost
counted as sacrilegious. When everyone else was playing on something that appeared uneven and half-ploughed, Wembley's acres
looked as though the Queen could have used them for a Buckingham
Palace garden party. The stripes on the turf were distinctly shaded
and very broad. The turf itself was so luxuriously lush that you
thought the players would spring up from it the way NASA's astro-
nauts had only recently bounced about on the moon. That Wembley
was sold to us like a fairytale castle with towers rather than turrets. It
was used so sparingly that the place had a mystique about it.

When, however, I finally went and saw it for myself – I'd gone there for an England schoolboy international – I felt let down. Wembley's pitch was exactly as sold – rolled table flat, the grass verdant green – and the wide separation between touchline and stands gave the place an august appearance. But the cinder car park was pot-holed. The grey-white wash of Wembley's walls had flaked and was urgently in need of re-painting. Some of the concrete had worn away too. There had been a rinsing of rain that morning, and the flag atop each tower clung, wet and limp, around its pole. Inside, the toilets stank like a Victorian sewer and the seats were as rough and splintery as a park bench in disrepair. When you sat down, they creaked like the wood of an old ship. Wembley had been completed only half a century ago, but it was already like a stately home crumbling incrementally. The cost of maintaining it outstripped the income generated. Only Wembley's status as a national sporting treasure assured its survival. A few years later, coincidentally after a League Cup Final, I was able to walk up the slight slope of the dark tunnel and go out into the light. I stood in the goalmouth. The surface was blistered from the combat of the match and the stands were empty, but the sense of atmosphere remained and I imagined what playing there that afternoon had been like. The architecture dwarfed me; I felt shrunken beside the banks of seating and terracing. I can still see all that; and I can still feel, too, the hard pitch beneath the shiny shoes I wore that day. I regard the memory fondly, but the past is somewhere best visited briefly; you shouldn't take off your hat and coat and try to settle there again.

The old Wembley was a ruin long before it got pulled down. The new Wembley seemed to take longer to build than Westminster Abbey, but was worth the wait despite the concessions it predictably had to make to the corporate clientele. The steel and stone and tinted glass looks glorious from afar, particularly when you see it from the overland train arriving from Euston. The arch appears suddenly between the gaps of suburbia. The sight is finer still up close, where the nearby hotels and curve of the cloudless sky are trapped as reflections in its big spread of windows. There are things I still miss: the tunnel along which I walked, the huge amount of bare ground behind the goal and the slow parade of the teams emerging side by side There was something noble about that procession, which makes the modern manufactured compensations for it – the huge banners spread across the field, for instance – look meretriciously vulgar. I miss also the thirty-nine steps, which gave you an unbroken view of the teams ascending to and descending from the Royal Box.

I see the old Wembley as I look at the new, jolted out of my dreamy recollection only when Arsenal, even well before the referee, reappear for the second half. It's as though Arsène Wenger has run dry of motivating phrases and has pushed them from the dressing room a minute or two early. Some of the side gather in a wretched huddle in and around the centre circle. They seem to be dreading what's to come.

Manchester City, under Pep Guardiola, aspire to sublimity, so the manager won't be entirely content with his slender lead. Those who can do anything try to do everything – and, if you could, why wouldn't you? – but City, praised superlatively all season, have not been as fluent as usual, more efficient than lyrical. It isn't so much a criticism as a comment on the standards scaled since last August. Nearly every one of their matches has been illuminated with clever surprises. Opponents have needed to show stoicism not to snap completely as City, their movement and passing done with a satin sheen, have made them look leaden and also doltish in comparison. But there's been no enchanted period so far for City, which is a mercy for Arsenal. Somehow Arsène Wenger is still in the game. Saying that out loud, even to yourself, makes it sound a mere technicality nonetheless. City are going to win well. Everyone knows it.

Soon Kevin De Bruyne, capable of launching a raid even with his back pressed against his own corner flag, is showing more creativity than before, collecting the ball and distributing it with firmer assurance. David Silva is, as ever, crackling around the pitch, a live wire connected to everything. And, during those odd half-minutes when Arsenal bother to rouse themselves into activity, Vincent Kompany douses whatever small fire their attack attempts to start. Kompany possesses what Arsenal don't, which is heart and inspiration and also a superabundance of energy and commitment. The treatment table and the hospital operating room have sadly for Kompany – and for

City – become frequently familiar to him in the last decade; he is a 31-year-old who has suffered and recovered from forty-one injuries – strains, tears, pulls – which have made him knowledgeable even about the six-point footnotes in Gray's *Atlas of Anatomy*. Fit again, Kompany owns Arsenal's attack. His broad shoulders barrel Pierre-Emerick Aubameyang off the ball. The striker staggers away like someone struck a glancing blow by a lorry.

City are impatient to claim another goal. The only surprise is that it takes them until the fifty-eighth minute. De Bruyne swings over a fast corner, crisply passed to the outskirts of the box rather than looped in. Ilkay Gündoğan stands in glorious isolation. Eight defenders banked in two lines are between him and David Ospina. Gündoğan throws himself at the chance, miscuing his shot. It skims off the inside of his boot towards Kompany, who reacts to it before Arsenal do. He turns his left foot towards the ball, steering it in from 8 yards. You see how much it means to him. On a celebratory run to the corner flag Kompany leaps and raises his fist into the air. He screams 'Yes' repeatedly, as if reading aloud the last line of *Ulysses*.

Arsenal had carped loudly about Sergio Agüero's goal; indeed, if Shkodran Mustafi had run as hard after Agüero as he did towards referee Craig Pawson to complain about being shoved, Arsenal probably wouldn't have gone behind. Now, briefly, another question is asked. Was Leroy Sané, though half a foot offside, interfering with play in front of Ospina? The TV replays exonerate him. Ospina had already slid towards his right-hand corner, anticipating the path of the original shot and committing himself to it before Kompany's crucial intervention. And Sané, knowing he had trespassed a shade too far, raised his arms and let the shot go past him as politely as a gentleman holding open a door.

Revolution is rarely wrought suddenly in football. On and off the field the game has always been Luddite towards change. The sequence of events, like some shop soiled plot, tediously repeats itself. When any new idea, a gadget-out-of-the-box or some gleaming innovation is proposed, the authorities and sometimes even the clubs seek to obstinately protect themselves from it as though some contagious disease has gone airborne. Deep trenches of opposition are dug and piled into them are excuses, prevarications and at least five hundred and one other reasons why 'it' – whatever that is – can't, won't or shouldn't possibly be done. The resistance continues awhile, occasionally for years, until logical argument wears down illogical intransigence. As far back as the 1930s, Herbert Chapman determinedly championed floodlights as the Football League, equally determinedly, opposed them. In the 1950s there was a haughty antipathy towards participating in the European Cup. In the 1960s some baulked at introducing substitutes, regarding it as rather namby-pamby. In fact almost everything in football that we take for granted now – the recorded highlights of games, red and yellow cards, televising matches live, Sunday fixtures, shirt sponsorship, artificial pitches, the manager's technical area and, most recently, the referee's spray-can and goal-line technology – arrived after opposition swirled up a sea of troubles against them. VAR needs to be smarter and quicker. Communication between the officials and the crowd has to improve fifty-fold. And yes, even after both happen, the process still won't necessarily be uncontroversial – and nor will it be perfect– because interpretation is subjective. But only in football could those philosophically against VAR believe it is better to stick with the wrong decision in haste rather than settle on the right one after a second, third or even fourth examination of the evidence. In last season's final, against Manchester United, Southampton's Manolo Gabbiadini had a goal unjustly disallowed for offside. VAR would have corrected that, confirming technology as a solution not a problem. It robs us of nothing but that perverse pleasure of being able to moan about referees who make mistakes. We will have one fewer excuse to reach for after our team loses. That is called progress.

Arsenal do not confront with passion the conundrum of how to get back into the game. Most teams, unravelling spectacularly against Manchester City, begin first to go wobbly and sweat desperately. Arsenal just seem to accept things, folding passively into themselves. Their performance, already pathetically lame, becomes so dire that a stethoscope would barely find a heartbeat in it. The size of the pitch at the Emirates is slightly longer and slightly wider than Wembley's. Mesut Özil, who was supposed to take City on, is nevertheless like

Eric Lichaj ecstatically celebrates his goal against Arsenal in the third round of the FA Cup. He can't quite believe it either.

The goalkeeper's misjudgement. Simon Moore, of Sheffield United, has come to claim the ball – but brings down Wolves' Diogo Jotta instead. He is sent off for it.

Billy Wright, captain of Wolves and England. He described the atmosphere at Molineux as 'almost overwhelming'.

The prince of Wembley. Vincent Kompany, outstanding during the League Cup final against Arsenal, has shot Manchester City further in front and now knows the trophy is theirs.

Pep Guardiola, claiming his first trophy in England, becomes more animated than before as Manchester City stretched their lead in the League Cup final.

A kiss for the trophy. Sergio Aguero, goal-scorer, doesn't want to
let go of the League Cup.

From close range Gabriel Jesus thumps his header past Kevin Trapp, the force of the
effort pushing the goalkeeper towards his own net.

The Greatest of the Great. Pele is worshiped after Brazil win the World Cup in Mexico's Azteca Stadium in 1970.

The Olympic rings suspended from the twin, sky-scraper-like towers on the way into stadium which hosted the 1936 Games.

Blue Moon rising. The City fans, sure the Championship will be theirs on derby day, toast Sergio Aguero's opening goal at the Etihad.

A player vindicated. Paul Pogba, whose two goals rescued United against City, accepts the adoration of his own supporters.

Proof that Hardwick Social's opening goal against Gym United did cross the line. Gym's Stewart Walker can't hook the ball clear.

A world made of football pitches. Hackney Marshes, circa the 1950s, was then a Sunday home to about a hundred teams and around 1,000 players.

Field of Dreams: The modest strip of land on Liverpool's Loudon Grove is imaginary Anfield or Goodison Park for youngsters.

someone nervously lost in a room too big for him; he clings to the skirting of it as though for protection. Jack Wilshere alone doesn't want to lose so meekly; he runs when others walk, he tackles when others only stick out a leg in pretence. Arsenal's supporters, occupying the West End, can't watch such a shamefully supine exhibition from their team. With more than half an hour left, and despite the cost of the ticket, an enormous swathe of those in red and white get up, turn their backs in protest and head for the exits. Row upon row is wrapped in silence now, the seats there deserted or with only the odd, hardy soul in them still.

We are all capable of believing things that are not true. Beforehand Arsène Wenger did so. Wenger, who has never won the League Cup, said that his record at Wembley put history on Arsenal's side today. Pep Guardiola called that bluff by refusing to give it credence. It is always sensible to do what's necessary before it becomes unavoidable, but even at 2–0 down Wenger only wanders into his technical area, looks about him and wipes his runny nose with his hand. His compatriot, the poet Baudelaire, thought: 'Life has only one real attraction – the attraction of the gamble'. Wenger clearly doesn't agree. He makes no changes, which is another reason why City score again. David Silva, picked out by Danilo in a packed box, goes around Calum Chambers and hits his left-footed drive into the far corner. There are still twenty-five minutes to go.

You always think about the number of goals City rack up (79 in the Premier League to date) and seldom hear of how few they concede (20). But no side is more accomplished in regaining possession once it is lost. Arsenal, strolling after it, can't get the ball. Between the seventy-second and seventy-fourth minutes City stitch together thirty-nine passes without Arsenal getting a touch – or even coming close to it. Halfway through, City's supporters cotton on and begin to salute the sequence the way a bullfighting crowd salutes every swish of the matador's cape with 'Olé'. Arsenal look inelegant, uninterested, crushed.

It is easy to analyse City but difficult to copy them because their short passing, which looks ridiculously straightforward, is simple only if you have honed and sharpened to a point skills that are learnt nowhere else but on the training pitch through constant and fatiguing repetition.

Guardiola has a penchant for 'boxes', the discipline in which two play-ers have to out-pass a third. This game is now an exercise in that, and you begin counting up the one-twos. This is splendour on the grass, which City glide over. You're reminded of what that rugged forward-cum-attacking-midfielder, Sandro Mazzola, once said about Johan Cruyff's Ajax. 'Everyone in the team had beautiful feet.'

Arsenal had one chance, early on in the half, when Claudio Bravo took a haymaking swipe at a through-ball and only made contact with fresh air. Their only other significant attack ended with Granit Xhaka shooting a foot and half over the bar. As a perfectionist, Guardiola still isn't satisfied. More animated now than earlier, his black coat flapping, he tries to make sure City don't slacken, retaining their clean sheet on a point of principle. He is too preoccupied with that to contemplate the miseries of others, such as Wenger. The Arsenal boss looks as though every part of him is hurting. His is a struggle against personal despair. Losing is forgivable. Giving up, which is what his side are abjectly doing, will demand a pound of flesh afterwards from someone. Probably him.

Even the final whistle does not come as a relief for Wenger. He knows the wider implications of this defeat for him. For now he will stumble past the consequences and on to another match, but this one has raised so many emotions in him that you can see each chase the other around his worried face.

There is usually, and sometimes undeservedly, too much made of bosses and not enough made of players. There are also few people, especially in football, who are worth pursuing the way that Boswell once pursued Dr Johnson to discover the multitudes in him. Pep Guardiola is an exception in both cases. His Boswell, Guillem Balagué, shows in *Another Way of Winning*, which I re-read this week, how Guardiola lives his life in a fever of commitment to the game. Managers are constantly reworking their teams – adjusting, read-justing, buying and discarding. Guardiola still understands that, despite nineteen major honours, anything worth doing remains devilishly difficult to do, which is why he devotes himself so completely to the task. You don't have to go far into Balagué's book to find the words that define his subject. These are 'intense' and 'complex', 'detailed' and 'obsessive' and 'tireless' and 'passionate'. The phrase 'care for the smallest detail' creeps in as early as page 11. Two paragraphs down you discover that Guardiola had twenty-four assistants at Barcelona, but was almost incapable of delegating the analysis of matches to them in case something, however infinitesimal, dodged his own eyes. 'Players,' writes Balagué, 'say they are sure he would love to spend more time with his wife and kids, but can't because he dedicates the vast majority of his time to winning games'. Slightly further on in the text Guardiola is remorseful, reproaching himself for missing his daughter's performance in a ballet. He instead sat through recordings of matches that his assistants had already seen. Effort, always effort, defines the portrait of Guardiola, the 'football freak', that emerges like a photograph slowly developing. What *Another Way of Winning* also shows is Guardiola as the players' manager, doing more for them than for himself. In a particularly piquant passage Balagué says that 'right from the beginning' at Barcelona, Guardiola was 'establishing a camaraderie, forging a bond'. He cannot 'understand or accept that a group doesn't shout, hug, give their all,' adds Balagué, noting how Guardiola 'constantly' does these things simply to make his players 'feel loved'. You see this as the presentations begin. Arsenal trek sullenly up the steps for their loser's ribbons, a souvenir unwanted and, given their rank inadequacy, hardly deserved either. When it is Manchester City's turn, Guardiola stays on the pitch rather than collect his own winner's medal. He wants to see his team enjoy themselves, so he watches them like an ordinary fan. Later, as the Cup is eventually passed to him, Guardiola is caught in wistful contemplation of it. He holds the three-handled trophy aloft and a little away from him, like Hamlet contemplating Yorick's skull. Guardiola could have been thinking about anything. A fiction writer worth so much as a pinch of salt would nevertheless craft a hook that has him in that moment going through the list of little-Englanders who doubted his ability to prosper in the Premier League. The culture here was so different, they said, that he wouldn't be able to impose his style on it. The physical demands of the game and also the remorseless pile of fixtures would undo his best efforts. It's taken eighteen months, but this Cup is the first of many vindications to come for him.

Guardiola has taught us a lot already, but the paramount lesson is this. People who say something cannot be done ought not to interrupt those who are already doing it.

25 February 2018:
Manchester City v Arsenal, League Cup Final, Wembley
Manchester City 3 Arsenal 0

Manchester City: Bravo, Walker, Kompany, Otamendi, Danilo, Fernandinho (Silva B 78), Gundogan, Silva D, De Bruyne, Agüero (Foden 89), Sané (Jesus 77).
Subs not used: Ederson, Stones, Laporte, Zinchenko

Arsenal: Ospina, Chambers (Welbeck 65), Mustafi, Koscielny, Bellerin, Ramsey (Iwobi 73), Xhaka, Monreal (Kolasinac 26), Ozil, Wilshere, Aubameyang.
Subs not used: Cech, Elneny, Mertesacker, Maitland-Niles

SCORERS

Manchester City: Agüero 18, Kompany 58, Silva D 65

BOOKED

Manchester City: Kompany, Fernandinho
Arsenal: Chambers, Bellerin, Ramsey, Wilshere

Referee: C. Pawson
Attendance: 85,671

13

FROM SEA TO SHINING SEA

10 March: Fleetwood Town v Plymouth Argyle, League Two, Highbury Stadium

One of my favourite football books, so precious that I wouldn't lend it out whoever begged at the front door, is Simon Inglis's *The Football Grounds of Great Britain*. First published in 1983, the publicity blurb called it 'an essential reference work', which was true then but counts as a gross understatement now. The second edition arrived in 1987, which is poignant because we recognise it in retrospect as the mid-point between the horrors at Valley Parade, Heysel and Hillsborough. By then Inglis had travelled 'some 9,000 miles' and walked, notebook and pen in hand, through the gates of 150 grounds.

The legacy of his magnificent wandering is football's equivalent of Baedeker's 1937 *Guide to the British Isles* or those slim volumes of the English counties, which were sponsored by Shell to promote motoring and sell petrol. When motorways existed only as drawings on a draughtsman's easel, and almost no one travelled anywhere, the poet John Betjeman and his friend, the artist John Piper, tucked themselves into a Morris Cowley and chugged through the countryside to explore the landscape and the landmarks in it. The pair were like foreign correspondents reporting back from spots that, if not exactly unknown, were just names on a map to most of the population, who lacked the money and the means to go there. These travelogues were meant as ephemera, constantly in need of updating, but have since become time-capsules on paper, each valuable in showing us the way things were in the world in which our ancestors lived. Baedeker and Betjeman are voices from history, preserving for posterity what has since been lost and is (occasionally) irrecoverable except in photographs and the words each of them left behind. To read them is to feel sometimes like

a stranger in a half-strange land. Corners of the country are so radically different, either because of circumstance or alleged progress,
that you find it hard to credit that either Baedeker or Betjeman are
describing a place you know. *The Football Grounds of Great Britain* can
provoke the same response.

Inglis is a very knowledgeable writer and his great labour has ardent
love behind it. You know what motivates him from these two sentences:
'The experience of visiting a football ground is inseparable from the
game itself. Every ground provides a different atmosphere which
colours ones entire appreciation of the match.' He set out to explain
why and did so in a work that for me is a masterpiece, scholarly but
always thoroughly entertaining because the author's erudition is
lightly worn and never self-consciously clever or condescending. Inglis
is the game's Nikolaus Pevsner; he does for football's architecture what
Pevsner did in forty-six volumes for the buildings of England.

The book, being just thirty-five years old, shouldn't be a period
piece. The fact that it is adds to its worth. In capturing what football
used to be like Inglis also captures the subsequent scale of the changes
to it. For someone of my generation, as well as any earlier one, *The
Football Grounds of Great Britain* creates a little stir of memories on almost
every one of its 367 packed pages. But for anyone who came to football only when the Premier League had already begun coining the
money in, Inglis's account must seem archaeological. How fortunate
we are that he got there in the nick of time and recorded everything
before the revolution happened.

Manchester City are still at Maine Road, Southampton haven't left
The Dell and teams such as Huddersfield Town, Hull City, Oxford
United, Brighton, Rotherham, Wimbledon, Doncaster Rovers and
Reading (I could go on) remain at addresses that are nowadays sites of
shopping centres, supermarkets, factories or flats. Even clubs who
haven't shifted since, among them Manchester United and Aston
Villa, were playing in front of stands that look as though ninety
minutes spent in them would be hard going on the bum and terracing
that could predate the steps of the Parthenon. At the bottom, and also
in the nether regions of what was then the Football League, stood
structures that seemed even older, barely existing as shabby ruins
where wood decayed, plaster peeled and lumps of concrete fell off. Of

Newport County's Somerton Park, Inglis says categorically that it will 'simply rot, rust and waste away' unless 'hard cash and bright ideas' rescue it. Of Exeter City's St James Park, he looks around him and laments the way it seems 'held together by poles, wire and a coat of paint'. And of Scunthorpe United's The Old Show Ground, he remarks with superb tartness that the place seems 'remarkably untouched by the glamour of League football'. Inglis frequently discovers a 'hodge-podge' of mismatched stands and unroofed terraces, the grounds assembled piecemeal through financial expediency or lack of ambition. Each reminds you of men without an iota of dress sense who pull out and put on clothes from a jumble, unaware of whether any item remotely matches. The Shay, belonging to Halifax Town, would register a one or half-star rating if Inglis stooped to such vulgarity. It is 'undoubtedly' the 'worst' for spectators, he explains. You instantly realise what that means – how really rotten it must be – since almost everything elsewhere is barely adequate.

In all its classy Art Deco finery, the ground I most miss is Highbury. I miss the 'impressive façade' (Inglis's verdict) of the East Stand on the Avenell Road, where the 'clean, unfussy' frontage is 'dependent on understated detail'. I miss the sight of the cream walls and the grey and green metalwork. I miss the tall windows with their iron mullions, the flagpoles and the moulded recess that showed off Arsenal's emblem, placed high above the wide main door. I miss the six short stone steps to that door and the ornate lamps flanking them. Inglis asks us to think of Highbury as coming from the same era as 'Bakelite encased wireless sets . . . Odeon cinemas and Ovaltine'. There was certainly nothing anywhere else like its marbled hall, which shone on match-day like the lobby of a swanky hotel of the 1920s and 1930s. I miss that too; it was very white tie and tails. I also miss Jacob Epstein's dark bronze bust of Herbert Chapman. Walking past it, after coming down the curve of the stairway, the banister splendidly polished, I always felt duty-bound to nod respectfully towards the old boy in silent but reverential tribute. Inglis celebrated Highbury's 'symmetry', the linear design of the stands opposite one another. The architect, Claude Ferrier, was described as someone to whom 'untidiness was anathema'. Inglis acknowledges it in declaring of Highbury: 'There is not a line out of place; all is in total harmony'. Ferrier sadly never got to see it completed; he was run over and killed by a motorcyclist before the workmen finished.

For the purposes of balance and fairness, Inglis points out that some saw Highbury as 'a cold, outdated, dusty mausoleum of long-past glory' that was 'caught in a time trap'. I never felt that way, and I maintain that anyone who did can only have had a peculiar aversion to beauty. Today beauty, as far as football grounds are concerned, gets confused with awe. The ultra modern stadium tries to knock us out with scale and novelty. The experience, which used to be solely about the match, is now also about immersing yourself in what happens around it, a desire grounds are designed to satisfy. Tottenham's new home, which won't return much loose change from £700m, will have a skywalk across one of the roofs, a food court, heated seats and a retractable pitch. At the Etihad, Manchester City already have their Tunnel Club, where you can gawp through glass at the players lining up and then walking on to the pitch. It's not unlike watching fish in a giant aquarium. Somewhere – and it is arriving shortly too – there will be a screen stuck into the back of the seat in front of you, replaying what you saw just five seconds ago. Technology is even promised that will allow pictures and statistical data to be beamed on to the surface of the pitch. All this innovation will come at a price, lavish luxuries for the corporate customer alone.

At Highbury, where the architecture meant the pitch wasn't the only place to have an aura about it, anyone could see a lot of Ferrier's best work for free without passing through a turnstile. No matter how many times you'd been there before, Highbury always made you stop and look at it awhile before going in. You appreciated the prowess of it all over again. Highbury represented what I thought a football ground ought to be. When Arsenal left, moving to the Emirates in 2006, it was slowly turned into flats and so the grass, which everyone from Buchan to Brady and McLintock to Henry had graced, became a communal garden. Both the façade of Ferrier's East Stand and the marble hall imposingly remain, but the atmosphere Highbury once had naturally disappeared into the ether, leaving the nostalgic amongst us a little bereft.

Six years later Highbury was back on the main fixture list. Not in north London, but on the extremities of the Lancashire coast.

Fleetwood Town don't appear in *The Football Grounds of Great Britain* because the club didn't qualify for an entry. When Inglis began his book, Fleetwood were in Division Two of the North West Counties League and their Highbury Stadium, named after nearby Highbury Avenue, was patched together so modestly that it made even the tumbledown eccentricity of The Shay look like the Azteca or the Maracanã.

Fleetwood, who coincidentally play in the same kit as Arsenal, didn't begin their ascent from the low plateaus of non-League football until 2005. It was the start of six promotions in a decade, a rate of speed and progress that only rocket fuel normally achieves. Now, as though proving one of life's most reliable laws – that what goes up will inevitably come down again – they are fighting to stay in League One. Today's opposition, Plymouth Argyle, are pushing to get out of it.

I decided to come here months ago, inking the match into the diary, not just because I wanted to see the alternative Highbury (capacity 5,327) but also because it will demonstrate the loyalty of the true fan.

Get beyond Lancaster and the land levels out. It is flat and smooth and predominately bare. The soil, softened to mud, is almost black after being soaked day-upon-day in snow and rain. The spires and the towers of the most far away churches are as conspicuous as in the Fens of Norfolk or Lincolnshire. The country roads are narrow too, and the corners of them can be as tight as right angles. It is particularly gloomy. The clouds are inky, swollen and depressingly low – it's as if some of them are about to sink into the damp earth – and the wind is chopping them into odd shapes. On the verges scraggly clumps of daffodils, their petals ragged and blown into disarray, look to have arrived too prematurely ever to prosper and the early spring lambs in the fields huddle alongside one another for shelter. The further you go into all this, the more you feel as though you are heading towards the edge of something. And Fleetwood is the end, the last stop before water, which today is so still you'd think it was half frozen. Fleetwood is so out of the way of things, not quite remote but hard to reach nonetheless, that you have to want to come and see it. You don't pass through the place on the road to anywhere else unless you've got a date, several hundred fathoms down, with Neptune. The town sits on the 2-mile wide Fylde Peninsula. To the north is Morecambe Bay. To the east is the River Wyre. To the west is the Irish Sea. Blackpool's Tower is only 8 miles away and can be seen, rising grey and skeletally, on the horizon.

This is what Sky Sports is calling Rivalry Weekend, the games being screened geographical and historical private wars, among them Manchester United v Liverpool, Celtic v Rangers, Aston Villa v Wolves and Nottingham Forest v Derby. The only thing in common between Fleetwood and Plymouth, apart from their status as ports, is the desperate need for points. On a rainy and blowy afternoon, the difficulty of grabbing the attention of even the locals becomes apparent. The town's population is under 30,000, a miniscule catchment area from which to recruit for the Cod Army. On Lord Street, a man in his late sixties – white receding hair, the face beneath like a pale walnut – stands on the steps of a pub taking long, slow drags on a cigarette, as though nicotine is a bracing alternative to sucking in oxygen. He is wearing a Manchester United shirt beneath his bomber jacket. He's been watching the first half from Old Trafford and is about to go back into the beery warmth of the bar. For him the Premier League on television beats the stone-coldness of the terrace, partly explaining why Fleetwood's League gate (unless Blackpool sail the boat over) is usually 2,000 or 3,000-something even though Highbury is good enough to warrant bigger, better crowds.

Simon Inglis looked into the future and a made 'a plea for imagination, colour and a bit of pomp'. He feared newly built grounds would become 'soulless concrete stadiums with no identity', prefabricated things put up on urban brownfield sites where the land is cheap and a motorway is close by. If he embarked on the mammoth task of updating *The Football Grounds of Great Britain*, I am sure he would approve of what Fleetwood have achieved. The Parkside Stand, open for only seven years, catches the light. The feature curve, the pleasing drop of the roof and the panes of clear glass more than satisfy Inglis's criteria for distinction, ambition and also unquestionably add that 'bit of pomp'. The rest of Highbury, from the facing stand and the covered terracing at either end, is trim and plainly well tailored. The only incongruity is the Highbury Soccer Social Club, which looks like a residential bungalow from the 1960s. It will have to go.

The back page headline in the current edition of the *Fleetwood Weekly News* reads:

'Sooner Town Win the Better for Survival'

which is stating the bleeding obvious but sums up the team's perilous position without the need for elaboration. Fleetwood, fourth from bottom, haven't won in the League since mid-January. Three weeks ago John Sheridan, appointed until the season's end, replaced Uwe Rösler, his sacking the consequence of seven consecutive defeats. Sheridan is nearing 600 games in management at Oldham, Chesterfield, Newport, Notts County and also at Argyle, where he spent almost 1,000 days before losing in the League Two play-offs. The Italians have a saying: 'In life you meet everyone twice.' Football, being such a tiny world, makes sure that you criss-cross everyone's path six dozen times at least. Sheridan's successor, Derek Adams, has just collected the League One Manager of the Month Award for February, during which he stretched Argyle's unbeaten sequence to six matches. It continued not so much a comeback as a Lazarus-like resurrection for them. In early December, Argyle were bottom after taking only seventeen points from twenty games. Offering odds that even then looked generously short in the circumstances, the bookmakers jokily made them 1,000–1 to go up. A flurry of small bets then, made either on the basis of unshakable faith or the wildest optimism, could lead to some big wins later. Having lost just one game in fifteen, Argyle are sixth in the table, thinking ultimately of Wembley in May.

But in the opening quarter of an hour of this match, you can't tell the difference between promotion pushers and relegation candidates.

Had it been scheduled for last Saturday, this game like almost every other below the Championship, would have been called off. The bad weather, forecast to sneak in during the Sunday of the League Cup Final, arrived in a prolonged white blizzard forty-eight hours afterwards, smothering the country in snow that piled 8 feet high in the remotest and most exposed areas. The country did what it always does when the climate goes on the attack. Sense of proportion went awry in a panic. Some whippersnapper reporter on the BBC – he was in his mid-thirties – unilaterally declared the snow storms to be the 'worst in living memory'. The statement suggested one of two possibilities. Either his further education skipped mathematics and British history altogether or he'd dozed right through them. He must have assumed, as if we were in the mid-19th century when surviving past fifty was considered lucky, that no one had come through the winter of 1962–3. Back then you could build a snowman in late December and still be looking at it in early March. Conditions were monstrous. Snow up to the eaves. Roads and railway lines closed for weeks. The sea frozen at Whitstable, imprisoning ships. The Thames frozen at Oxford, allowing someone to drive his Austin Seven across it. A Scottish Cup tie, between Stranraer and Airdrie, was called off thirty-three times. The Pools Panel was created and put in long shifts on blank Saturdays, declaring the results of matches that hadn't taken place. The thaw finally set in, but in the beginning the football seemed stiff, almost still refrigerated.

Fleetwood and Argyle have had only a fortnight off – hardly much of an interruption – but neither of them settle gracefully into the match. The very early scuffles are a road of trial and error. Neither a shape nor a pattern emerges, and the passing is scattergun. The ball is repeatedly whacked high and long from the Memorial Stand to the Percy Ronson Stand and then back again. For Argyle especially the break was unwanted. It was like being shut up suddenly in mid-sentence when the momentum of some fine speech was underway. This is all about getting slowly into the flow of it again. Fleetwood make that task easier than it ought to be. Moses Makasi, a 22-year-old midfielder on loan from West Ham, is making his debut. In the sixteenth minute he savours it.

In that game at Molineux six weeks ago, Wolves beating Sheffield United, I watched the return of Benik Afobe, re-signed until the end of the season. Afobe had scored twenty-three goals in forty-eight appearances for Wolves before Bournemouth arrived with a £10m cheque to buy him. He never broke successfully into the Premier League. When

Afobe knew the deal to bring him back to the Black Country would go through, he sat in his car weeping copiously. These were tears of gratitude. There are some players who, for whatever reason, establish a rapport between themselves and the crowd. That affinity and that affection creates a bond that just *is*. As complicated and indefinable as romantic attraction, it can be based on personality, commitment, effort, energy, respect or longevity as much as a bundle of talent. When Afobe warmed up along the touchline and then trotted on as a late substitute, you knew he had it. You also knew that what Wolves felt for him was reciprocated; Odysseus wasn't given a homecoming as rousing.

At Fleetwood, Nathan Pond is established as a bona fide cult hero. He's in *The Guinness Book of Records*, the only man to have played in seven different divisions with one club. He is more than captain of Fleetwood; he's the spirit as well. At thirty-three, Pond is about a season away from 500 appearances for them. When Fleetwood were drawn against Leicester City in the FA Cup earlier this season, it was Pond to whom the media turned to talk, not only about Jamie Vardy and the relatively recent years in which the striker scored promotion goals for £850 per week at Highbury, but also to supply a potted history of exactly how Fleetwood had come so far, so fast. Pond's name was acclaimed more loudly than anyone else's when the announcer read out the team sheet before kick-off today. His appearance on the pitch repeated it.

So when Pond is to blame for Argyle's goal – he weakly heads a harmless punt up-field directly to Ryan Taylor – Fleetwood's faithful are sympathetic and even forgiving. Pond tries to clear up the mess. The defender, aware immediately of the peril he has put himself in, does what he can to chase the Portuguese attacker Rúben Lameiras, who once appeared in the same Tottenham Under-21 side as Harry Kane. Pond is too pre-occupied to realise the danger on his blindside. Makasi steals around him. Lameiras stokes a short pass forward and Makasi takes it in his lean stride. From the edge of the box his shot curves around Alex Cairns and into the bottom corner. Pond is angry with himself. He shakes his head, scrunches up his face and raises his hands. Fleetwood's fans, who like Pond so much, see no point in getting angry too, knowing that even his failures are wholehearted.

Width means adventure, and you expect Argyle to use it and flay

Fleetwood. It is slightly deflating for the contest when the form side sit back, tentatively withdrawing into themselves a little as though scared some secret weapon is about to be deployed against them. Fleetwood do have their moments. Ashley Hunter holds the ball close to him, his skill expressed in tight spaces. There are intermittent squalls of rain now, some of them quite heavy, but he buzzes about like a fly on a hot summer's day, always an irritant to Argyle's defence. Hunter goes inside and outside them and, put clean through, surprisingly nudges possession wide rather than take on the opening himself, which means it is squandered. So, too, is a near post chance that Conor McAleny can't get over, lifting it instead almost above the roof of the stand. As though jealous of Pond, and wanting their own entry in *The Guinness Book of Records*, Argyle have played seven different goalkeepers so far this season. The current incumbent, Remi Matthews, strives for permanence with a clawing save to make certain McAleny doesn't atone for that previous clanger.

At half time Argyle are fortunate to be ahead rather than behind.

The *Shorter Oxford English Dictionary* defines the fan as 'a keen and regular spectator of a (professional) sport' and 'a devotee of a specified amusement'. It is a pathetically inadequate description.

For most of us being a fan is, like life itself, a pursuit of happiness that we seldom find. Indeed, on match days we live in a flustered, agitated or outright anxious state. The few moments of pure pleasure we get are fleeting. We care so much that we can only ever relax during a game when our team is a certain number of goals up with a very limited number of minutes left. For we are safe then – aware blissfully that the worst, which is the opposition fighting back and overwhelming us, can no longer happen because mathematics makes it impossible. Our weekend or our midweek can't be spoilt. I can't actually enjoy a Newcastle match, for example, unless the side is winning 3–0 in the last quarter of an hour or is two ahead with ninety seconds or so to go. As a football fan, especially of an under-achieving or perpetually unsuccessful club such as my own, the dread prospect of defeat and the possibility of victory (however unlikely) co-exist in the build-up to a game as well as during the game itself. Always, you forgive the trespasses your team makes against you. And, also always, you trick yourself into harmless delusions about them too. You're certain the next match, the next month, the next season will be different and more successful. You rationalise disappointments, convincing yourself that experiencing them is some weird endorsement of suffering. Even when you're celebrating, the points and the plaudits secured, what looms soon enough is the forthcoming fixture, the thought of it popping up like a gremlin. All this is a constant torture and we willingly submit ourselves to it. No wonder non-fans consider us either slightly loopy or downright deranged. The length to which fans go is sometimes bizarrely extreme. It can leave you doubting their actions while simultaneously admiring the conviction of them.

There was the Dutch fan who had a 'best ever' national XI tattooed on his back. The team appeared in formation – and on a pitch. There are several husbands around the globe who have persuaded their wives to call a new-born daughter Lanesra without necessarily telling them what it spelt backwards. Other babies have taken a while to be baptised, the christening font echoing to every name in Liverpool's 1965 FA Cup winning side (plus manager and assistants) or the Chelsea team of 1970 or Leeds United's 1992 Premier League Champions' squad. The convenience of the deed poll has allowed one grown man to switch his surname to White Hart Lane and another to suffix his with 'United' – after he'd already prefixed his Christian name with 'Manchester'. In the 1960s there was a Rangers fan who took the council to court when it wanted to paint his front door green, the colour of Celtic. He won his case. And a householder somewhere in Coventry once sprayed every coverable inch of the exterior of his home in shocking sky blue. The neighbours were not impressed, apparently.

The poet Dannie Abse, a Cardiff City fan, said that, apart from 'the drama, the theatricality and the unpredictability' of football, he liked the fan who would describe losing as 'a tragedy', but went to home matches each week and travelled further afield sometimes even though another loss would possibly befall him. We're familiar with fans as pilgrims. They expensively cross continents and oceans to spend a solitary Saturday watching a Premier League team, their love for it fostered originally on TV. On the tour of Wembley that I took, there were four middle-aged men who had planned a six-week holiday from Australia entirely around Liverpool's fixture list. England's country houses and National Trust properties counted as nothing to them beside the Shankly Gates at Anfield. I remember, too, a 21-year-old Brazilian who chose to coach Blyth Spartans on Football Manager – in his own computer world he won the Champions League – and subsequently developed an obsession with the club. To satisfy it, he travelled to Croft Park to watch them in the Evo-Stik League.

Being a one-off, which guaranteed it a lot of publicity, that kind of sacrifice is less impressive to me than another, which is made regularly by fans who spend big fortunes without fanfare to follow their team around the country. Earlier this season there was a man who bought fifty-six different rail tickets – twenty-eight for himself, another twenty-eight for his girlfriend – to reduce the cost of watching Newcastle at Oxford United. He didn't see the game; his girlfriend had a bad fall on the journey and needed treatment in hospital. There were also 115 Blackpool supporters who, defying traditional common sense but clearly not their own, went to Plymouth on a Tuesday night in mid-September and arrived home again with Wednesday's dawn. And today there are over 600 Plymouth fans occupying a flank of the Parkside Stand and also the away-end terracing.

It is 325 miles from Plymouth to Fleetwood, an explorer's expedition from sea (well, the English Channel) to shining sea that takes almost eight hours on the M5, the M54 and the M6. Sitting next to me on the front row – we are practically at pitch level – is someone who made exactly that journey. He has grey hair, thin bristles for a beard and heavy-framed dark spectacles. He is nudging eighty, he says, declining to specify his age. I am too polite to press him for it in case I sound indelicate. He arrived last night. He explains that setting off on the supporter's bus at 5.30a.m. and returning the same day 'would have been too much for my old bones'. He proudly tells me that he first saw Argyle shortly after the Second World War, pushing through the 'cheap' turnstiles and being passed to the front. He often used to go away, but doesn't travel much now because new-built stadiums are sometimes steeply constructed and his legs 'aren't fit' to climb the steps to a high seat. He's come to Fleetwood to see Highbury, proving as accurate something else Simon Inglis wrote in *The Football*

Grounds of Great Britain about our attraction to places we haven't been to before: 'That feeling of excitement as one approaches a ground for the first time, walking calmly at first, but quickening as the turnstiles beckon. There is always that wonderful elation at seeing the pitch, the stands and the faces spread out before one's eyes.'

Outside Highbury I'd arranged to meet another Argyle fan, Toby Jones. Football is blood-deep for Toby. He 'inherited' the club from his father, who grew up on the South Bank at Molineux, watching Wolves in the 1950s, before making Devon his home and adopting Argyle as his team. Toby's father saw the Santos side – containing Pelé, Carlos Alberto and nine others – that went westward three years after Brazil had won the World Cup in those electrifying Finals of 1970. Pelé pulled him and nearly 38,000 more into Home Park. In their previous game, against Fulham, Santos were contractually entitled to half the gate receipts. At Plymouth, presuming the crowd wouldn't amount to much, the Brazilians had agreed in advance to a flat fee of £2,500. On the night, the sight of heaving terraces and the queues outside sent them into a hissy fit. If Argyle didn't agree to hand over a further £2,500, Santos wouldn't play; it was a stand-and-deliver hold-up without the highwayman's mask. Argyle, three ahead at half time, won 3–2 and the extra cash came afterwards in cellophane packets containing £50 notes. Toby was still a baby then, the story of how Argyle whupped King Pelé passed down to him.

He lives in London nowadays, but Argyle perpetually bring him back to the city and send him around England. About a dozen years ago he totted up how much he spent supporting them. It came to more than £2,000 per season. Toby, despite working in finance, has stopped counting the cost of his passion. He knows the total would be ridiculously high, but won't become an armchair supporter. 'I find it impossible not to go to football matches,' he says. A home game for him is like an away match for the rest of us. The fastest weekend train from Paddington to Plymouth takes three hours. The drive to the West Country is four hours. One wintery Saturday he went to Darlington only to find the game postponed at a quarter to two because of snow. There have been motorway crawls, closures and breakdowns. There have been slow trains, signal failures and an assortment of clutter on the line. He's arrived home at black, godforsaken hours of the morning because of all of them. Nothing puts Toby off. He treats Argyle's triumphs and disasters with remarkable equanimity. He's seen managers come and go again. He's seen promotions and relegations and uneventful seasons during which the football was 'terrible'. He's seen Argyle smash in eight goals at Hartlepool, concede seven at Brentford and fondly recalls facing Manchester City, well before their riches made them different from everyone else. He's danced on the pitch at Spotland too, a jig for promotion. Only last summer, he went on the pre-season tour of Holland but never saw a game. Local mayors, preposterously nervous about the possibility of witnessing English hooliganism, decreed that Argyle's friendlies should be played unannounced and behind closed doors.

I also spoke to Tony Cannan, a member of Argyle Fans' Trust. He's driven from Plymouth, starting at 7a.m., to be here. His Devonian accent is pronounced; you'd guess where his home is after hearing him speak just one sentence. Tony believes firmly that you should 'support the team where you're from'. He's done so 'forever', once seeing only the last quarter of an hour at Nottingham Forest after the car he was in blew some gasket at Bristol.'When we got there,' he says, 'the stewards were staggered that we wanted to go in. Argyle were winning 3–0 and our end was yelling "We Want Four". We'd missed every goal and so we started shouting "We Want One". Nobody but us knew why.'

As I dawdled about before going into Highbury, I was struck by two things. Firstly, the Argyle fans seemed genuinely to know one another. It's as if a huge, extended family had come together – shaking hands, slapping one another on the back, asking about this friend or that, chatting about the match to come. Secondly, I noticed the profusion of club colours. At the men's fashion show in Milan last month, the football scarf became what one newspaper called designer 'catnip'. An editor at *Vogue* called them 'peak tribal'. Some of these catwalk creations cost between £215 and £225. The cheapest scarf in the club shop at Plymouth is £12. Everyone seemed to wear one, as though not doing so meant you were improperly dressed. Plymouth's chic is way ahead of Milan's.

Inside Highbury, the 'family' element became even more apparent. Not only because of the way the players, warming up beforehand, spoke to or signalled towards the fans, but also the waythe fans communicated among themselves. A group sitting behind me picked out someone each of them knew beside the goal and began calling out to him. When finally he picked up the message and responded in kind, those on the terraces directly around him began to respond as well.

The fans have made Herculean efforts to get to Fleetwood and are exuberant about being here. I hope Argyle won't let them down.

A month ago Fleetwood were flaky and would have cracked apart after going a goal behind, the act too much for them to bear. But John Sheridan's new management has generated new resilience.

So the equaliser, which they ought to have claimed before the interval, arrives only ten minutes afterwards. It is rooted in an Argyle mistake far worse than Nathan Pond's. Fleetwood, attacking down the left, don't have any option but to float the ball into the area and towards the back post. This is what Ashley Hunter does. His chip isn't even tricky; Yann Songo'o need do nothing more strenuous than balloon a header well clear. For the first half hour of the match, above the goal at that end, thirteen seagulls were grouped closely together, making a cross-hatch of dives and upward swoops, barely missing one another. You thought the birds might be attempting a mini-murmuration, coming together as one mass like starlings. It isn't clear whether Songo'o has spotted one of these gulls making an absurdly low approach in his peripheral vision. The only other plausible explanation is that someone, somewhere has shouted 'LEAVE' in his ear. Whatever the reason – much to Fleetwood's astonishment – Songo'o deliberately ducks under Hunter's diagonal centre. Running behind him, the same way Moses Makasi ran behind Pond, Paddy Madden meets the ball as it drops, stubbing a toe at it. He scores from 6 yards. Remi Matthews is so shocked that he doesn't budge from his line.

From the tannoy blazes what I assume is the traditional accompaniment to any home goal: the jaunty sea shanty from the children's cartoon, *Captain Pugwash*. A million childhood memories float by.

The best of the rest of the chances – the second half is a skirmish

rather than shower of bright sparks – belong to Argyle. Oscar
Threlkeld doesn't exploit one of them, shooting over the bar. Graham
Carey, cutting inside, is denied by a low save from Alex Cairns. The
goalkeeper can't hold the shot, but the ball is whisked away. Fleetwood
twice feel aggrieved and Sheridan is on his feet to let referee Darren
Handley know about it. He is angry when Handley refuses to give one
handball in Fleetwood's favour. He is dumbfounded in stoppage time
when another gets turned down. The first looks like ball to hand. The
second falls into the twilight zone, the decision dependent on the
referee's perception of it.

A draw seems just about fair, I suppose. That Manager of the
Month Award, still hot in Derek Adams's hands, can be like receiving
the black spot for the next match, but Argyle have dodged defeat. The
run – and, perhaps, Wembley – awaits them.

At the beginning of the season, the Football Supporters Federation
published a report in which two-thirds of almost 9,000 fans complained
that the richer clubs – in the Premier League, of course – were overly
pre-occupied with polishing their global brand rather than catering to
the wants and the needs of those who went to watch them. Those
results come to mind on the way out of Highbury. I am also ponder-
ing something Toby Jones said to me: 'I much prefer the lower league
game.'

When he can't get to Home Park, Toby swaps green for blue, going
to watch Wingate and Finchley in the Bostik League Premier Division
against sides such as Dorking Wanderers, Dulwich Hamlet and
Kingstonian. He likes the social atmosphere – as I do at Guiseley –
and being able to swap ends at half time if the inclination takes him.
He also likes the connection, the condition of shared intimacy, that
exists between the fan and the club. So it is at outposts such as
Fleetwood and Plymouth too.

There is a short sketch, from the TV series *Alas Smith and Jones*,
in which Mel Smith takes the part of the broadcaster who reads
the results at five o'clock on *Grandstand*. He reaches the Fourth
Division (as it was then). The first three scores are perfectly enunci-
ated, the practised pause between team and score is precise,

polished. His intonation is very James Alexander Gordon. Only when he reaches Burnley v Colchester United does his character go off script.

'Oh dear, oh dear,' he says, wearily. Torquay 2 Wrexham 1 comes out in an elongated yawn. It is followed by a plaintive, despairing: 'God, who's interested in this stuff?' He begins to articulate aloud his boredom with his job and his patronising disdain for what he thinks is the inconsequentiality of small, out of the way 'backwaters'. He describes them as he sees them. So Hereford becomes 'some boring old market town in the middle of nowhere'; Mansfield is an 'obscure coal mining village'; Southend is a 'dreary seaside resort'; Peterborough is 'some anonymous barnacle off the A1' and Tranmere becomes a 'depressing huddle of one up, two downs . . . dwarfed by a derelict dockyard'. I particularly liked his sarcasm about Stockport – 'some deadly dull suburb of some northern industrial city' – and also Hartlepool, curtly dismissed as a 'godforsaken fishing port'.

These places are much different now – the sketch is thirty years old – but the look-down-your-nose snobbery of them, which made the joke work originally, still exists. For those only interested a lot in the Premier League and a little in the Championship, League One and Two can seem like a flea circus compared to the big top. But I know why Toby and so many others prefer them. The clubs are locally rather than globally owned. The chairmen aren't Russian oligarchs or billionaires in bespoke suits based in New York or the Middle East. (Fleetwood's owner and chairman Andy Pilley was born, brought up and lives on the Fylde coast.) The players are accessible and also approachable. If, on match day, there is more space where nobody is than where anybody is, then it merely allows you to get to know one another better. The whole experience is more informal, less corporate and glossy and you don't have to take out a bank loan to buy a season ticket.

I leave Fleetwood convinced I would come to Highbury regularly if I lived here.

After all, who can resist Captain Pugwash?

10 March 2018: Fleetwood Town v Plymouth Argyle
Fleetwood Town 1 Plymouth Argyle 1

Fleetwood: Cairns, Coyle, Eastham, Pond, Dempsey, McAleny (Burns 89), Madden (Hiwula 90), Glendon (Biggins 80), Jones, Hunter, Sowerby.
Subs not used: Neal, Grant, Maguire, Diagouraga

Plymouth: Matthews, Sawyer (Taylor-Sinclair 70), Songo'o, Ness (Ainsworth 64), Carey, Lameiras, Makasi (Grant 86), Threlkeld, Taylor, Vyner, Fox.
Subs not used: Letheren, Fletcher, Law, Sangster

SCORERS

Fleetwood: Madden 56
Plymouth: Makasi 16

BOOKED

Fleetwood: Coyle
Plymouth: Fox

Referee: D. Handley
Attendance: 3,079

14

WHAT WE TALK ABOUT WHEN . . .

27 March: Germany v Brazil, International Friendly, Olympic Stadium, Berlin

Yesterday, as Easter week blew in greyly rather than spring-yellow, I caught the U-Bahn closest to the ruined beauty of the Kaiser-Wilhelm Gedachtniskirche and travelled six swift stops. At the end of an upwardly sloping and slightly twisting concrete path, through pedestrian underpasses and past graffiti-daubed red-brick walls, I found the most depressingly gloomy and coldly austere ground I have ever seen.

I walked up Olympischer Platz and wandered in front of the East Gate, where two obelisk-like towers rise 165 feet high. The left is the Bavarian. The right is the Prussian. Between them, suspended on knotted wire, hung the Olympic rings, dangling forlornly like Christmas decorations left up months too long. None of the rings had even a blush of bright paint on them. On the Bavarian tower was a clock, the once shiny gold gloss of its face and hands chipped and dull now. The clock had stopped; it was permanently twenty-five to two in this corner of West Berlin. And in the middle distance, behind high railings and narrow turnstiles, the Olympic Stadium looked squat and dark and also a little sinister in its plainness. There were no flags atop the white poles dotted on the roof of the stands. There was no feature relief – no lovely niche or ornate carving, no sweep of modern, green-tinted glass – to break the hard, uniformity of neoclassical columns and balconies. A gaggle of security guards, wearing thickly padded jackets, hopped from one foot to the other or blew hard on their fingers, desperate for a brazier to warm them from the whip of the wind.

I dwelt on what I'd left only twenty minutes ago. In the heart of Berlin, the flower shops and the street stalls were selling tulips that glowed, each a hot shot of pink or blue or red, and the linden and the chestnut trees had a few fledging leaves on them. Sparrows appeared suddenly to sit on the branches or to flutter around you. The fashionable cafes on Kurfürstendamm, their crimson curtains harking back to the bohemian flavour of the 1920s, pulled in patrons prepared to ignore the iffy weather and take coffee and brandy in bulbous glasses at pavement tables, where the pages of *Die Welt* or *Morgenpost* were being slowly turned. Nearby, every department store-front was a festival, lavishly ribboned and bowed and dressed up for the holiday weekend to come.

But the Olympic Stadium, and the vast acreage around it, was desolate and miserably barren. It was a lonely spot that seemed to belong somewhere else: to another and quite different city entirely. I felt I had walked into some monochrome world. The level land was devoid of colour – even of scrub-green or earthy brown. It was as if those colours had somehow been leached out of the landscape like blood from a body. Left behind was something pale and creepily lifeless. That morning there had been rain, sleet and also faint flurries of snow. The puddles were wide enough in places to see almost the whole curve of the sky reflected in them. Having the bruised clouds dragged down to your feet only accentuated the maudlin condition of the place.

I saw a few games behind the Wall in the early and mid-1980s. I was advised, when phoning back copy, to refer to East Germany as the German Democratic Republic; I was assured someone, somewhere would be listening in on every call. The Western-style hotel, which – of course – accepted only Western currency, especially dollars and pounds, sealed the traveller off almost hermetically from the locals apart from chamber maids, bellboys, bar-staff, waiters and cooks. Beyond the hotel's plate-glass doors, Berlin was like a stage set. The roads were absurdly clean, as though scrubbed and brushed perpetually. There was no litter and the light grey walls of block buildings contained not even the merest chalk-smudge of graffiti. In the air was the stench of disinfectant and also the exhaust of Trabants, some of them shaky enough on the move to suggest a door might abruptly drop off or a wheel would come loose. On the first morning I went out tentatively to explore and got drawn towards the near-1,200 ft tall Fernsehturm, its steel-plated dome glinting in the sun like a bauble. I hadn't gone far when, after turning around, I noticed two figures loitering not far behind. Each was dressed like a character recruited from Central Casting. Long black buttoned-up leather coats. Wide-brimmed hats, tilted downwards. Cigarettes burning between index and second fingers. It was as if someone had, after reading one le Carré novel too many, determined that Cold War fashion should remain forever exactly as described in Cold War fiction. I realise now that these men, who stuck with me for almost half an hour, deliberately made themselves conspicuous. Their purpose was to deter me from succumbing to a temptation I hadn't even considered. At the time, however, each seemed too comic to be a menace. I went on my touristy way, eventually towards the Brandenburg Gate and Checkpoint Charlie.

On first sight, the Olympic Stadium was far more unsettling to me than the streets of the old East had ever been. It does not stand on common clay. It was impossible to look at it and not feel a shiver as the shadow-stain of history fell across you. I saw the gigantic, swinging bell in Leni Riefenstahl's documentary of the 1936 Games. I saw the fire cauldron that held the Olympic flame. And I saw, above all, the swastika fastened to the Prussian Tower. The stadium was architecture as Nazi propaganda, and Hitler demanded it should be monumental and powerfully intimidating; something made out of block upon huge block of limestone, granite, basalt, travertine and marble that would equal for the eye − in scale and swirling achievement − what Wagner built for the ear from notes of music. Hitler specified it should evoke the landmarks of ancient Egypt, ancient Greece and ancient Rome, envisaging in his delusion that soon the Games would always be staged in it. What he got was a coliseum oval in which character, such as it existed, came from precise symmetry and the simplicity of clean-cut lines.

In the day's wintery murk, the stadium reminded me of a mausoleum − undecorated, awfully unbeautiful and ghost-haunted. I recoiled from it with a great and snarling distaste. I even questioned whether I wanted to watch a match here and also how I could possibly enjoy it.

But that was then and this is now. Tonight I know differently.

From the outside, the stadium was impossible to like, which made the prospect of actually loving it seem utterly preposterous to me. From the inside, sitting in block 3.1, everything is a spectacle. The lushness of the turf. The running track, a vividly deep and rich blue. The high, horse-shoe cantilevered roof, illuminated on a starless night. The teams appearing side-by-side from the tunnel-mouth at the Marathon Gate and then covering the 90 yards to the centre circle so slowly that it takes them almost a minute and a half to get there. Everywhere the flash-bulbs from phones – coming and going again in white needles of light – accompany that long, circumspect walk. The klaxons and the horns. The waving flags and also the rippling banners. The native Berliner, novelist Peter Schneider, author of *The Wall Jumper,* admits his city is 'not beautiful', lacking as it does the 'soothing' structural splendour of other great capitals. But Schneider thinks that Berlin's enduring appeal exists partly because of its history – 'both the good and the atrocious . . . the dark episodes' and partly because of the current of energy running through it. The Olympic Stadium personifies this in microcosm. The aesthetics of it become immaterial in the razzmatazz theatre of a capacity-house. The energy that Schneider describes is thumping away here. Were the charge giving off electricity, you'd be calculating it in terawatts.

It's almost 9p.m. in Berlin and nearly 5p.m. in Rio. I think about the Brazilians gathered at this moment around TVs at home or crammed into sweaty bars and gazing up expectantly at big screens, every one of them wishing they were here. I also think about the England game I saw at Wembley six months ago when the crowd was relatively sparse, unexcitable and eventually so bored and irritated that the ground became swamped late on with those makeshift paper aeroplanes thrown from the stands. Here, there's a huge rectangle of blank paper beneath each seat – it's white, yellow or black – and you're asked to hold yours up on demand, the move synchronised so we spell out in letters 20 feet high some pap message about German football being united. We comply, obediently, but immediately afterwards everyone is equally synchronised in scrunching the sheets into balls and chucking them towards the pitch. As the Brazilians put their guts into their national anthem – 'our hearts shall defy death itself' – paper is avalanching all around them in the grandest of ticker-tape parades. It is a peculiarly beautiful sight.

England's match was a World Cup qualifier so low key that it could have been a Sunday beer match at the end of a season. This, 'only a friendly', has as much going for it and arguably much more riding on it. Not only because it's number one versus number two in the Fifa rankings, but also because Brazil haven't met the World Champions since being obliterated by them in that national humiliation almost four years ago, a result triggering such profound and heaving grief that an entire country wept and kept on weeping. With the World Cup finals only seventy-nine days away, I realise that a game of this scale for them needed a venue to match it. The Olympic Stadium isn't a bad place to gain a little revenge.

Even in the fragile beginnings of the match, as each eyes the other comprehensively, it is Brazil who seem the more assured of them-selves. The ball being used is the Adidas Telstar 18, Fifa's choice for the World Cup, and Willian, Paulinho and particularly Philippe Coutinho get as much practical experience with it as possible, each of them dominant. With passes slung from touchline to touchline, Brazil seem to elasticise the width of the pitch and force the Germans into all sorts of desperate measures to survive. Jérôme Boateng is soon scampering about, frequently at full pelt, as though he might actually pull off the unlikely trick of being in four places at once. Sometimes Boateng, the ball flicked around or over him, has to spin in small, puzzled circles to cover the slowness or the inadequacies of those around him. You can also almost hear the defender's heart hammer-pound in minor panic whenever Coutinho grasps possession. There isn't much physically to admire in the Brazilian's build – he fills a super-slim shirt and boots that are only size seven and a half – but the way he uses it is spectacularly effective. In one raid he merely has to lean gently to his right, a minimal tilt of the shoulder, and the Champions' defence buys the dummy wholesale, clearing a path into the box for him. In another, despite being marked so tightly that you worry all the breath could be squeezed from his body, Coutinho accepts a pass, makes a liquid twist and wriggles through a gap so narrow that most of us would have to tackle it sideways. In a third, after winning the ball near halfway, he combines feint, step-over and foot-to-foot control with a change of pace that sends him through midfield in a scorching yellow streak. Coutinho, full of misdirection and surprise, does not have an excessive dependence on anyone. Germany have no one like him.

The Champions, though unbeaten for twenty-two games, spluttered unimpressively four days ago against Spain, escaping fortunately with a draw. Their fans, who expect and have come to understand only success, were narked then and are peeved now. On the touchline, Joachim Löw is already in a state of constant exasperation. Dressed in a bespoke grey suit and a polo neck sweater, the fringe of his long, anthracite-black hair almost flopping over his eyes, Low resembles a very 1960s follower of fashion. You can imagine him swanking into and out of the boutiques of Carnaby Street, a wannabe Beatle. He has made seven changes to his side, the most significant of them the decision to give a night off to Thomas Müller, back home in Munich with Bayern. Without him, the attack looks a little lost and threadbare. Löw watches it scavenge for chances. In midfield Toni Kroos and Ilkay Gündoğan are labouring to create them. On the flank Leroy Sané can barely poke his nose into the game. Up front Mario Gómez drifts ineffectively. The Germans – too ponderous, too uncoordinated in their approach – generally seem to lack the impulse to make something properly meaningful out of the match. And this, remember, is against a Brazil without the £200m Neymar, last seen in a wheelchair before an operation to repair his fractured metatarsal.

Brazil ought to take the lead in the thirty-sixth minute. Willian, a versatile player of immense gusto, strokes a straightforwardly angled 20-yard pass from the right flank. It's as if he's tugged on one thread and unravelled the whole fabric of the German defence. The hole through which Gabriel Jesus darts is gargantuan. His run glides him into the area and also around the pincer trap which Boateng and Antonio Rüdiger try to lay for him. Rüdiger is so comprehensively confused and outwitted that he stumbles, going over face-first. Germany have been without Manuel Neuer since September – his fractured foot has still to heal – and no understudy could possibly compensate for his absence unless Löw convinces David de Gea to change nationality and then Fifa to change their rules.

Kevin Trapp is no Neuer. With Boateng and Rüdiger blocking his way, the goalkeeper isn't sure which position to take. He shuffles a yard or two off his line and waits passively to make a save. He is grateful when Jesus, who has a lot to aim at, unaccountably loses his composure, belting his shot not only over the bar but also towards the second tier behind the goal. Löw shrieks. Tite, the Brazilian coach, is stunned into near-speechlessness. Jesus, horrified at his own prodigality, sinks to his knees and hides his face behind his spread fingers, as if what he can no longer see won't hurt him.

Brazil have still always looked on the edge of something, and Jesus has only a minute to wait before redemption arrives neatly gift-wrapped for him. It is typical of the Champions' performance so far, all apprehensive ums and ahs, that neither they nor the ball get entirely free of the box. Boateng and Rüdiger have barely regained their bearings after the previous attack and support for them is widely scattered. Again, the provider is Willian; he has always mucked in and gone where the hard work is. His cross is top spinned with loop and curve, the distance on it measured to the half-inch. Trapp takes a step forward and gets hopelessly stuck there. When Jesus, bravely diving, smacks a header at him from 6 yards, the goalkeeper flaps his left hand at it weakly, as though the panelled leather could burn him. He tumbles inelegantly backwards, arriving in his own net a millisecond before the ball does.

A total of 1,366 days have passed since that 7−1 humiliating defeat in Belo Horizonte, so your gaze goes first towards Brazil's celebrations; Jesus is mobbed. In his technical area, Tite clenches a fist and shakes it. The coach is not far off fifty-seven, but he looks slightly older and certainly more weather-beaten than that. A wide neck sits on a sturdy body. The head, often entirely still as he looks at the match, is as solid and as dignified as an Epstein bronze. He watched that semi-final defeat at home. His wife cried when Germany scored their third goal. He cried after their fourth.

The more revealing reaction, however, is Germany's. The players – and Löw – seem genuinely perplexed. Boateng is talking and pointing, picking over the goal. It's a rehearsal for the conversation that will take place in the dressing room in another ten minutes from now. He is acknowledging that Brazil, who at the start had seemed only a difficulty to Germany, have blown up into a full-size problem. Solving it will take effort rather than simply waiting, as the Champions have previously done, for the opposition's sheer exuberance to run away with them and lead to a mistake.

No two football nations have occupied English thoughts more in the past half-century than Germany and Brazil. We have measured ourselves against one of them and marvelled enviously at the other.

I have read accounts of the 1966 World Cup that claim few in England saw it at all in the context of the two world wars and that fewer still considered winning imperative to national pride. Perish the thought and pull the other one. If you believe that, you can only have followed Saturday, 30 July from another country or, perhaps, another planet. Vincent Mulchrone was the star writer of the *Daily Mail*, a consummate columnist and reporter who conjured the one image of Sir Winston Churchill's funeral that qualifies as a marble monument of words. 'Two rivers run silently through London tonight, and one is made of people.' On the morning of the match his piece was headlined 'World Cup or World War?' and the opening sentence declared: 'If Germany beat us this afternoon at our national sport, we can always console ourselves with the fact that we have recently beaten them twice at theirs.' Reading that cold and in isolation, you'd conclude that Mulchrone was clearing his throat in preparation to scream his lungs out jingoistically. He wasn't. His whiskery antennae were keenly sensitive even to the subliminal and, where the World Cup was concerned, he thought sarcasm would best convey the fact. The next nine paragraphs may have been too subtle for some, but the distaste Mulchrone expresses for football camouflaged as war is unmistakable. 'Win or lose, tomorrow's papers are going to be sheer hell. The shame of a defeat will be exceeded only by the horrors attendant on victory. The deductions that will be drawn about the future of the British nation are already terrifying,' he said.

Even as a young boy I understood soon enough that the final wasn't only about a squat gold trophy; 1966 was only twenty-one years after the Second World War had ended. This isn't even a blink in geological time. (As I write, twenty-one years ago was 1997 – the year of a land-slide election, the transfer of Hong Kong to China, the death of Princess Diana. It seems as if only a fortnight has passed.) Every adult I knew then had either fought in the war or lost someone during it, and so every third conversation seemed to bring up experiences of it and then the consequences. My generation was blessedly immune from the death and the bloodiness of the conflict, but not the immensity of it. What came at us were hundreds of battles we understood nothing of, a hundred more place-names we couldn't pronounce and score-upon-score of high-ranking, moustached men with ribboned medals and braided uniforms who told us of their part in Hitler's downfall. The Sunday newspapers were full of the serialised memoirs of generals, admirals and squadron leaders. Novels and histories about the war were forged at an industrial rate. The weekend matinee on TV always seemed to be *The Dam Busters* or *In Which We Serve*, *The Cruel Sea* or *The Great Escape*. There was also *All Our Yesterdays*, the Second World War replayed in half-hour weekly instalments from Pathé and Movietone newsreels and, much later on, twenty-six episodes of *The World at War*. There were vast fictional sagas too, such as *A Family at War*, and all manner of other dramas and documentaries in which slipping 'war' into the title guaranteed a bumper audience.

At the beginning of this year, the departing German ambassador in London, deciding there was no further need for niceties, ditched the diplomacy. On his way out of the Court of St James, he rebuked us for being unhealthily obsessed with the war – specifically on how we had 'stood alone' and also 'stood against' a 'dominating Germany'. The remark was arrogant, offensive, patronising and also wrong. The ambassador confused legitimate remembrance with preoccupation. He saw a minuscule minority, for whom stoking the memory of war has nothing to do with the need to preserve history and everything to do with its extreme glorification, and from them misguidedly concluded that the majority thought the same way. You digested what he had to say and wondered how someone obviously so intelligent could also be obviously so stupid on something he ought to have known much more about.

During Euro '96, when football was supposedly 'coming home', one tabloid newspaper's build-up for the England–Germany semi-final at Wembley was to roll off the presses a front page that read 'Achtung: For you Fritz, the Euros are Over'. It was illustrated with a stock-shot in which, like some *Dad's Army* foot-soldier, Stuart Pearce had an army tin hat superimposed on to his head. It was a bad and puerile aberration, but I like to think we've gone past that stage and – I hope – another in which England fans wore T-shirts that pretended Hitler's War was a pop tour, the last gig in London 'Cancelled'. But there will always be full-blown bigots, with wood shavings for brains, who lean on the old and pitiful excuse that their nationalism is really patriotism, and also the merely dim-witted who can't differentiate one from the other. Each believes not only the dumb conviction that their country is superior to all others – simply because they were born in it – but also that everywhere else is practically contemptible, which justifies whatever mockery, abuse and disrespect is thrown at them. When England faced Germany in the Westfalenstadion a year ago, there were 'fans' – the oldest of them surely born thirty years after VE Day – who sang songs such as 'Ten German Bombers' or 'Two World Wars and One World Cup' (to the tune of 'Camptown Races') or chanted 'Stand Up if You won the War'. You shrivelled with revulsion when these began and then curled up with shame when they continued. That we still pump this sewer-effluent on to the 'terraces' of the world is unforgivable, perpetuating as it does what we expected would be long behind us by now. The only and very slight consolation is that comparatively so few join in that even the Football Association ought to identify them easily and then be able to sluice them out of the game.

Tonight I will remember the Olympic Stadium for more than the match. I'll take with me the sight of supporters in the aisles and on the stairwell entrances, preferring to stand rather than sit. I'll take with me the stench of strong beer, sold from the end of each row and poured into plastic plots with handles, and also the acid tang of cigarettes, the dusty blue fag-smoke swelling sometimes into chubby clouds. Segregation will always accentuate tribalism, so I'll take too, and most significantly, the way in which Germans and Brazilians are sitting together, sharing the experience without a rancorous word or gesture. It is rooted in parity of achievement, which excludes England. In World Cup terms, Germany and Brazil breathe the same rarefied air, making them different from the rest of us and forming the basis for the mutual respect that is transparent here. Germany have won three World Cups since we won our own. They've been runners-up three times too. And, since that 1966 lap of honour, we've beaten them on only six occasions in twenty-four games. You can play a lot with statistics, massaging them conveniently towards whatever interpretation suits your agenda, but figures as incontrovertibly stark as these can't be slanted. England look like no-hopers in comparison, always clinging on to one summer of success like a baby to its blanket.

If the German ambassador had talked about football rather than war, and 1966 rather than 1945, you'd have little choice but to concede his point.

There are bookmakers already offering short odds on Germany winning the World Cup again. No manager has retained it since Vittorio Pozzo, who was in charge of Italy in 1934 and 1938 and in between also won the Olympic gold medal in this Olympic Stadium. (Hitler went to Germany's quarter final, watched them lose 2–0 and never saw another ball kicked in the tournament.) Joachim Löw has a chance of imitating Pozzo. In reaching Russia, Germany scored forty-three goals, leaked only four, won all ten qualifying matches and finished eleven points ahead of the group. But the German fans, who sit around me, are flushed and agitated during half time. One of them, a man in his seventies with a nose the shape of Mr Punch's, has not stopped talking, the words rolling off his tongue in tides. He makes me regret that I don't speak German because those alongside him hang on to his opinions and mostly nod in agreement; but, like most of us, I grew up thinking that English should be spoken to me overseas as an entitlement.

Even when factoring in the changes Löw has made, Germany ought to be more efficient and less uptight than this. Alisson, the Brazilian goalkeeper, has punched away the occasional cross and parried a shot or two without becoming an integral part of the match. Germany, trying to rev themselves up through Toni Kroos and Leroy Sané, can't manufacture anything more substantial than a half-chance or something that might have been and also don't ever get the ball on to the right spot. Brazil do, cleverly retaining possession with simple runs and simpler passing. If another goal comes, it will be theirs.

One of the most conspicuous Brazilian banners, draped from the top tier of the stand, celebrates another side rather than Tite's. Pelé's face is stencilled on to green silk and LEGEND 1970 is printed below it. A week before coming to Berlin, I watched again the highlights of the 1970 World Cup in Mexico. Outside, the sky was as cold and as flat as a slice of quarried slate. The remnants of early spring snow still hugged the hills and the sight of neighbours' gardens brought to mind that last report the *Guardian*'s Donny Davies filed before he and The Busby Babes left Belgrade in 1958. The melting snow there, wrote Davies, 'produced the effect of an English lawn flecked with daisies'. Inside, on the screen, everything was a fantastic blaze of colour, as if Matisse had painted it. The still air was sauna-hot. The grass was summer soft. The pictures sizzled. That World Cup was short, lasting barely three weeks, but what happened during it left a mark that has endured for nearly fifty years, which is only the very beginning of its longevity.

When Pelé used the phrase 'The Beautiful Game' in the title of his autobiography, he was unknowingly borrowing it from H. E. Bates, who had called football 'the most beautiful game in the world' in *The Sunday Times* a quarter of a century earlier. Bates was, in turn, unknowingly borrowing from another writer, Jimmy Catton, who wrote in *Athletic News* of 'the spread of such a beautiful game as association football'. He did it a year before the Great War. And Catton was borrowing from anonymous authors, who had said the same thing before him about billiards and bowls, golf and cricket. It became attached to football, and is too established to be snatched away now, because of Brazil and what was showcased in that June belonging to Pelé. To Carlos Alberto. To Gérson and to Jairzinho, the Hurricane. To Tostão and to Rivellino. To the under-rated Clodoaldo. What we talk about when we talk about 'the beautiful game' is Brazil. History seldom seems like history when you are living through it. Events roll out fragmentally and in a rush. It means that making sense of them, or remotely coming close to some definitive judgment, is nearly always impossible on the hoof. You can't usually take the random bits and slot together something entirely whole out of them because without hindsight, which only time grants us, there can be little perspective. Mexico 1970 is an exception. The momentousness of what you were watching was apparent as it took place. Every match for Brazil was the instalment of a story that could lead to only one possible end. Those who sell souvenirs produced commemorative goods that celebrated Brazil's triumph well before the final. As Hugh McIlvanney wrote: 'It was not much of a risk.' With each pass, neat trick or wondrous goal, you appreciated them as unquestionably The Greatest, unmatched in the past or the present and probably in the future too. The sun-bright team in the sun-bright shirts were not merely gifted but divinely blessed; and we felt divinely blessed also to see them late at night or in the blurry early hours of a British morning.

A small publishing industry has risen up and is thriving around the origin, evolution and analysis of football's tactics, satisfying those specialist connoisseurs of strategy and planning who know not only every formation (and who operates it) but also talk sophisticatedly of 'false nines', 'zonal marking', the 'raumdeuter role' or 'gegenpressing'. Often it is done in the way master victuallers speak of wine, the language becoming eruditely elitist. But sometimes you don't want to know how a wine is made. You're not interested in the soil in which it was grown, the barrel in which it was stored or the glass into which it ought to be poured. You just want to get it down your neck and savour the taste of it, gorgeously, on the tongue. Watching Brazil in Mexico is the equivalent of that. Who cares about formations? The team moved instinctively and seamlessly from one to another, sometimes swapping from 4-4-2 to 3-3-4 in one fluid movement just because it could. No rearguard could have stopped them unless the rival manager had sneaked a couple of extra players on to the pitch. Suppose you could have scored six goals against them? Brazil would have scored eight or nine in reply. They even managed to win without someone between the posts. Félix, of Fluminense, looked as though he was self-taught as a goal-keeper, but had used a manual from which there were a few vital pages missing. Brazil conceded only seven goals in Mexico; Félix should have stopped all of them.

Brazil inspired what ought to be officially rated as Kenneth Wolstenholme's second most quotable line of commentary. It wasn't as pithy as the number one in that chart, but Wolstenholme's response to the ten-pass move that led to Carlos Alberto's late goal in the final against Italy – 'that was sheer delightful football' – was imbued with shock and awe. This was detectable in his pronunciation of the words 'de-light-ful foot-ball,' each syllable stretched and given identical stress. Wolstenholme summed up simply enough Brazil's magic and what was achieved with it, but Gérson did it better still. He delivered an epithet of such witty insightfulness that Wilde would have plagiarised it if he hadn't already been long dead. 'Those who saw it, saw it. Those who didn't will never see it again,' said Gérson. He was right, but it hasn't stopped us looking. The Brazil of Mexico '70, however, were so full of riches and had so much raging beauty about them that subsequent Brazilian teams – even the two who have since won the World Cup – look pasty-pale and plain.

What we always crave from Brazil is the unexpected, a moment that forces you to the tip of your seat and then on to your feet. It's another burden we place upon them because of that 1970 World Cup. We see Pelé almost scoring against Czechoslovakia with an audacious snap shot from inside his own half, the ball soaring over the bewildered goalkeeper before dropping only a foot wide after wobbling in the shimmering heat. We see Pelé again, facing Uruguay, striding on to a left-footed through-ball from Tostão that bisects two defenders and forces the goalkeeper to leg it out of his box at the speed of a commuter afraid of missing his train. You gasp the first time when Pelé lets the ball go and the sliding 'keeper is flimflammed completely into missing it. You gasp the second time when he cuts on the inside, then suddenly switches back to find the running ball and send his shot goal-bound on the angle and without apparently lifting his eyes to look at the target. And you gasp a third time when the ball skips across the far post, the 'keeper just about on his feet at last.

It's strange how the mind can bend a memory. For several years, until I saw that scintillating move again, I would have sworn on oath that Pelé had scored from it. I had benignly willed his finish to be as perfect as his preparation and then I convinced myself that it had been.

*   *   *

The current Brazilians do not have the same blithe spirit, but there is an easeful grace about them that almost twice inspires something comparable. Outside the box Philippe Coutinho takes possession from Marcelo, jumps past two tackles and lays off to Paulinho. He holds things up, waiting for Coutinho to peel quickly around him before delivering a short square pass. Coutinho, aware that Willian is stampeding in from the back, lets the ball go. The German defenders are in as much disarray now as that Uruguayan 'keeper had once been under Pelé's spell. Willian puts his laces through it. I imagine the ball booming off the boot and filling the back of the net. I see it as a goal, carved out in a dozen seconds, that can be remembered for a lifetime. But Germany are spoilsports; Jérôme Boateng, who seems to have illimitable energy, gets across brilliantly, throwing himself at the drive in a long, horizontal stretch to charge it down.

The other highlight is a piece of improvisation, an eye for what no one else even recognises as an opening. Douglas Costa takes the ball down on his knee near his own box. He is tight to the touchline. Four German defenders are ahead of him. You wait for Costa to pass back or sideways, assuming there is nowhere for him to go. He opts to attack, running 20 yards before Niklas Süle challenges on the halfway line. Costa outflanks him, forcing himself between the bulky-chested defender and that white strip of lime, the space hardly bigger than the width of the ball. He powers on at such pace that no Brazilian has yet caught up. Costa is undone only when he has to change course, pulling inside abruptly and giving the advantage to Süle. The recovering tackle is impeccably timed, avoiding the catastrophe of a clumsy penalty given away.

The Germans are shuffling their team repeatedly in the second half, one substitute coming on after another. It's as though the management are shaping their excuse for defeat; perhaps it will be that the game is only a 'learning experience'. No new player makes a difference. Brazil allow the Germans possession but not dominance. In a game of word association, you wouldn't select the phrase 'disciplined and organised defence' to describe them ahead of, for example, 'attacking flair'. Even after exhausting every synonym for that, you wouldn't necessarily alight on anything else either. You automatically think of Brazil scoring goals rather than stopping them. Disciplined and organised defence is nevertheless exactly what Tite has brought. Germany can't break the double bank – four players and then four more – that Brazil build.

Brazil have swapped coaches five times in the dozen years that Joachim Löw has been in control of Germany. But Tite, summoned almost two years ago after an insipid Copa America, energised them into becoming the first team to qualify for the World Cup apart from the hosts. He is not the sort of coach who thinks a team will obey and alter simply if he jumps up and down and shouts at it. He is an organised fellow but relies more on intuition than rationality. He concentrates on the team ethic ahead of individual whims, so Neymar, the sort of player who wants to be seen by everyone and do everything all at once, has had to be yanked into line. And Tite demands absolute control. Pelé calls him a 'serious person', which is meant as a compliment. This, his nineteenth international, is a good example of all the aforementioned.

The German fans, accepting the outcome but not wanting to witness it, start to trudge towards the U-Bahn ten minutes before the end. Those who stay see Julian Draxler crash a volley from 18 yards that Alisson punches away as though contemptuous of it. The distant chance is nothing but a straw at which Germany try and fail to clutch. The truth is that not only have Brazil been better, but also Tite and his team have wanted the result more passionately, which is why they got it. Their performance came with feeling. The game wasn't a waltz, but nor did it test them overmuch.

At the end I watch Tite run his hand through his silver hair and look about him as casually as a man who has just ticked off something on his 'to do' list. If he hears the German crowd, whistling in palpable disappointment and some alarm, he doesn't noticeably react to it. On the way out, walking down Olympischer Platz, the mood is subdued even among those who are now using Germany's flag as a cape but brought it to salute goals. The World Cup Finals are not going to be as easy for them as some had assumed.

I turn and glance briefly at the Olympic Stadium. It is ringed in light and looks ravishing.

In the morning, I know it will look ugly again.

27 March 2018, Germany v Brazil, International Friendly, Olympic Stadium, Berlin
Germany 0 Brazil 1

Germany: Trapp, Kimmich, Boateng (Süle 68), Rüdiger, Plattenhardt, Gündoğan (Werner 81), Kroos, Goretzka (Brandt 61), Draxler, Sané (Stindl 61), Gómez (Wagner 62).
Subs not used: Hector, Ginter, Hummels, Khedira, Leno, Rudy, ter Stegen

Brazil: Alisson, Alves, Silva, Miranda, Marcelo, Fernandinho, Casemiro, Paulinho, Willian, Jesus, Coutinho (Costa 73).
Subs not used: Coquette Russo, Ismaily, de Oliveira Augusto, Fred, Marquinhos, Murara Neto, Firmino, Conserva Lemos, Ederson, Taison, Da Silva

SCORERS
Brazil: Jesus, 38

BOOKED
None

Referee: J. Eriksson
Attendance: 72,717

15

THE LITTLE DEATH
OF DEFEAT

7 April: Manchester City v Manchester United, Premier League, Etihad Stadium

All you can hear is the boom of 'Blue Moon', the anthem of the Etihad's mass choir, who scream rather than sing it. All you can see are waved silk flags and woollen scarves, every one of them held high or twirled like an old-fashioned wooden rattle. In this upheaval of movement, and the pandemonium of roaring noise and rippling colour, small fists of smoke suddenly appear on the topmost tier of the South Stand, each a swirl of Prussian blue, as though we are in Milan for derby day rather than Manchester. Heady is the air here.

There are some fans performing jerky dances down the aisles. Others yell, their words unintelligible, while throwing their arms wide and aloft. Some embrace a neighbour. A father lifts his young boy on to his shoulders and shouts at him to 'Remember all this, son'. A man in a replica shirt is on his knees, rocking to and fro and tilting his big, sweaty face heavenwards; he mouths the words 'thank you' repeatedly. The woman beside me rubs away tears that slowly fill the shallow crow's feet around her eyes, already dark from her runny mascara. Someone on the opposite side of the stadium lets go of a single balloon, which gets snared beneath the glass and steel of the saddle-shaped roof before escaping into the cloud-heavy sky.

This is football as a mad fiesta, a consequence of disbelief about what City are so close to achieving and also what it will mean now, and far into the future. There have been 175 derbies before. None has attained the status of this one. The usual spoils, which are Manchester's bragging rights, get passed about in the churn of regular competition, making them an ephemeral prize. On this cool spring evening the fluke of the fixture list, and their domination of the Premier League in the last eight months, offers City an opportunity that is deliciously rare. You can't imagine it occurring again. Fiction is obliged to avoid freaky coincidences to make it seem plausible. Real life isn't bound by such conventions of plot, which is why City, a whopping sixteen points ahead of second-placed United in the table, can claim the title on their own pitch and against their rivals, a kind of one-upmanship imperishable because it is historic. Neither would ever forget it. I bought my seat months ago, while the possibility still appeared slightly fanciful, something make-believe, but when I spoke to someone in midweek who makes a more than decent living from flogging them, he told me I could re-sell mine and finance a week's holiday of epicurean luxury with the profits. His phone, he said, was 'boiling hot', but anyone expecting to spend 'only £1,000' would 'get no further than the gents'. A place, even low in the corners of the ground, would cost £1,500 – 'at least,' he added. He couldn't give a precise figure. The price was rising as he spoke.

I arrived in Manchester in the early afternoon, bought a copy of the *Evening News* and wandered out of Piccadilly Station. The pavement was shiny with morning rain. I found myself on Cross Street and then in Deansgate. I walked about Chinatown and lingered in the city's squares too. The place was quiet; there was a bottled-up tension about. In the pubs, where the Merseyside derby was being shown on wide screens, I found United fans huddled over pints and pessimistically concluding that a draw 'just might' be possible, enabling them to save face. None dwelt too long on the lifetime purgatory to which defeat would condemn them. Most instead bemoaned the fact José Mourinho hadn't produced a team to get the blood pumping at Old Trafford this season; another title of their own seemed to lurk around a very distant corner indeed. The semi-finals of the FA Cup, coming in a fortnight, represented to them nothing but the outskirts of real success. On the tram from Piccadilly Square, the passengers squashed against one other, City supporters traded predictions, each of them unequivocally upbeat. No one thought the broiling atmosphere of Anfield, where on Tuesday Liverpool had ferociously given City a three-goal belting in the Champions League, would cause lasting psychological harm. At the Etihad, tinselled up for the occasion, I saw City's coach arrive and Pep Guardiola climb off it. He wore a long, unbuttoned black coat and carried a leather rucksack over his shoulders like a backpacker on a hike. Clipped prominently to his pale grey sweater was that familiar loop of yellow ribbon, worn to signify his support for those activists and politicians imprisoned over Catalan independence. Guardiola seemed oddly pensive for someone whom a truly big match is a monthly date on the calendar. His look was glassy and a little far away. He shook hands almost mechanically and without staring directly at the City fans who queued to meet him behind the low metal barriers at the main entrance.

What a difference in Guardiola now. You see bliss in his expression and relief in his body language. A minute ago, on the half hour and in an act of uncharacteristic sloppiness, David de Gea sprayed a 30-yard ball straight to City's Leroy Sané. United, forced to turn an incipient attack into a full retreat, floundered on the back foot, unable to shut off Sané and then to close down Ilkay Gündoğan, all but anonymous against Brazil in Berlin only ten days ago. His back was awkwardly to goal. To fashion anything from the chance, he had to simultaneously slide possession beneath his left boot, pivot gracefully on a dot of turf and then take swift aim. What Gündoğan produced was an angled toe-poke. The ball De Gea had given away came back to punish him, beating his dive and slipping 6 inches inside his far post.

The goal lengthens City's lead. For in the twenty-fifth minute, meeting a pacey, in-swinging corner, Vincent Kompany had showed enough muscle to get in front of Chris Smalling, who claimed such a handful of his shirt, tugging so hard and doggedly, that you thought the number would be torn clean off it. Kompany's header blew past De Gea, hitting the net with a wild rip.

Guardiola, like City's fans, is in paradise. Two goals up. Only an hour – sixty measly minutes – separating him from the title. With six games to spare, this would be the Premier League's earliest ever coronation. With another three points to add to the eighty-four already accumulated, City would soon smash past the record of ninety-five, which Chelsea set in 2004–05 – ironically under Mourinho – and then go further on, breaking three figures. Other statistics in the reference books, previously considered almost impregnable, could topple to Guardiola too. No one is unaware of all that, which is why the preliminary celebrations sound like a detonation. There are those of us who still prefer the poetry that Champions write ahead of the accountancy of totting up passes, assists, possession, the number of goals plundered and even the winning margin at the top of the table. We take all our nourishment from the exhilarating and elegant way in which City play. Their approach appeals emphatically to the senses. You don't mind that the title race hasn't been a contest, Guardiola constantly in command, because you've seen football of such debonair sophistication, such style. Cty's official kit ought to be a tuxedo and a white tie.

'Blue Moon' finally dies away, replaced with a chorus of that ancient standard: 'Now you've got to believe us . . . we're going to win the League'. United are stuck for words and so remain gravely silent, knowing no reply can currently build a counter argument to it that would seem even faintly convincing. In his technical area, Mourinho doesn't know where to look except at the watch on his wrist, the face of it the size of a kitchen clock. Guardiola, taking precautions before City's Champions League return against Liverpool four days from now, has left more than a third of his side on the bench: Kevin De Bruyne, Gabriel Jesus, Kyle Walker and the fit-again Sergio Agüero. What City have got, however – the two Silvas, David and Bernardo, plus Fernandinho and Raheem Sterling – is sufficient to make United seem amateurishly inept. This doesn't look like a game between Champions-to-be and probable runners-up, but instead top versus a team gasping for breath at the bottom of the table.

Even now City ought to be so far in front that it would be humane to take United off and end their suffering quietly in the dressing room. Early on Ashley Young, slipping in the box, touched the ball on the floor with his trailing hand, the wobbling deflection created taking it away from Sterling. The referee Martin Atkinson gave City nothing. De Gea used his legs to deny another possible goal. As the half wears on United continue to deteriorate, the defence caving in as City give them trouble from touchline to touchline.

A striker, when clean through, needs only to be a fraction off in the contact he makes to send the chance a foot too high or too wide. Sterling twice did the thing he was supposed not to do. From prime positions he powered shots so unhandsomely off target that you wonder whether he'd hit a whaling ship if one docked in front of De Gea's posts. The cries from the faithful at his wastefulness were still expressed more in anguish than disgust. The assumption is that City can delay humiliating United properly until the second half when other goals – an awful lot of them too – will put them more firmly in their place. Already the total could be three or four – and possibly even as many as six. United have only been able to operate within the crushing limits City have imposed. It has inflicted on them an effect comparable to concussion. Dazed and ragged, the team staggers around. You can't be sure if it realises any longer where it is or even why. Smalling and his partner, Eric Bailly, hardly seem to know one another's name, let alone where each ought to be in relation to the other; City whoosh between them, the gap so wide that no pass to take advantage of it needs to be surgically precise. Smalling and Bailly aren't alone in their confusion. The usually reliable Jesse Lingard and Ander Herrera aren't in it. Neither are Nemanja Matić and Alexis Sánchez, currently poor curators of their own talents.

And as for Paul Pogba . . .

In his play, *40 Years On*, Alan Bennett remarks on T. E. Lawrence's irresistible need to be the centre of everything even when doing absolutely nothing. 'Clad in the magnificent white silk robes of an Arab Prince he hoped to pass unnoticed through London,' wrote Bennett. 'Alas, he was mistaken.' Like the Prince of the Desert, for whom much was vanity, Pogba seems to want all eyes to look at him all of the time. Since he's 6 feet 2 inches tall and an ambassador for hairdressing as living sculpture, Pogba draws the attention when his contribution to a game doesn't go much further than standing still in likely places. A hairdressing magazine claims Pogba has had twenty-seven different hairstyles since United bought him. These include Burst Fade Fohawk, dyed Mohawk, curly bleached blonde and an assortment of patterned buzz cuts, each as meticulously designed as the formal gardens at Versailles. Today, Pogba has had the sides of his head shaved, leaving a long, narrow thicket on top. One half is streaked City blue. The other half is supposed to be white, but has gone slightly yellowish in the wash. This is Pogba being cheeky. With an ostensible nonchalance that didn't disguise its premeditation, Guardiola dropped into his pre-match press conference the claim that Pogba's agent had offered his client to City during January's transfer window. The shock disclosure was predictably denied, but the original statement fulfilled Guardiola's purpose. It raised the delicate matter of Pogba's future and the possible shape of it. Pogba's contribution to United has been so sparse of late that it is impossible to tell whether Guardiola's gamesmanship or his own spluttering form is responsible for another below-par performance.

The beginning of 2019 will mark the fortieth anniversary of Trevor Francis becoming the first £1m buy in British football, a deal doubling the previous highest fee. An average house then cost £13,500. The average car cost £3,000. Beer was 35p a pint. Someone calculated that, weighing 11 stone 7 pounds, Francis was three times more expensive per ounce than the price of gold. Someone else, writing to the *Daily Mail* and possibly doing so in green ink, condemned the amount paid for him as 'a disgrace'. He launched into the matter of underpaid 'social sector workers', confusing the public purse with private investment. When Pogba arrived at United from Juventus for £89.7m, creating a new British record in 2016, the reaction was mostly shrugs and so-whats. We're so blasé about how much money clubs spend now. In Munich's Olympic Stadium, where he dived at the back post, Francis justified his fee only three months after it was paid. His header won the European Cup. The investment in Pogba has produced a scratchier yield. You are aware of him today paradoxically because he is absent from so much of what is going on. As he figures in only streaks and flashes of the match, the City fans taunt him as an over-rated show-boater, his skill superficial. You can still only say of him what could also be said of eight of his colleagues. Mourinho might profitably substitute any of them. In his isolation up front Romelu Lukaku is proving that a man can be an island, but just he and De Gea, the most impressive United survivor of the half, can be certain to reappear from the tunnel.

With a minute to go, there is another prolonged serenade of 'Blue Moon', lustily sung. It was written as a slow ballad in the mid-1930s by Rodgers and Hart. More than half a century later City revealed impeccable taste by borrowing it. Even someone with a tin ear will recognise that the short ditty chosen to follow it does not similarly belong to The Great American Songbook. City sing at United: 'You're Fucking Shit'. You can damn the crudity of the chant for considerably lowering the tone, but not challenge its factual accuracy.

The whistle goes, and Mourinho spins on his heels. He heads towards the dressing room, making sure he will be there well before his team. United look clawed to pieces, their skin in urgent need of saving. Mourinho has a quarter of an hour to do it. The obvious question has no obvious answer, however. What can he possibly say to make a difference?

Not long before he died, Brian Clough paid José Mourinho a compliment that was like a personal blessing. The venerable ex-manager, referring to himself in the third person, said he liked 'the look' of Mourinho because 'there is a touch of the young Clough about him'. The similarities in achievement – each turned unfancied clubs into Champions of Europe – have been broadly matched in approach, attitude and attributes: the gift of vivid speech, the swagger and the bombast of ego (nearly always quite outlandish), the showmanship (everything coming with a little dressing) and the brusque outspokenness. Their personalities are alike right down to unsolicited kindnesses, which are frequently done privately, for friends and strangers. Mourinho does not have the eccentric quirks that contributed so much towards building Clough's image – the flat cap, the dog, the walking stick, the familiar emerald sweatshirt – but he does employ a similar methodology under the spotlight's halogen glare. Like Clough, Mourinho learnt early on how to use psychology to motivate his team or indulge in niggly mind-games with his rivals. Also like Clough, a natural talker, he can either embrace the media or react sourly towards it. More than occasionally, he gives the impression no clean hand ought ever to touch a newspaper and that a TV interview constitutes a particularly irksome job of work for him.

In looking at Mourinho, and seeing a reflection of himself, Clough identified the common denominator between them. The managers were born almost thirty years apart, but Mourinho acts out one of Clough's core beliefs. This is: It is no consequence what others think of you; what matters is what you think of them.

Mourinho was sixteen years old when Forest won the first of their two unlikely European Cups. He discovered the team and its mercurially maverick boss. During Euro '96, then at Barcelona with Bobby Robson, he travelled to the City Ground to watch a game between Portugal and Turkey. Mourinho rode the train from London and spent the day meandering around Nottingham, a trip that became part-pleasure as well as business for him. He did what day-trippers do, such as visiting the Castle and the statue of Robin Hood beneath it, and then strolled towards Trent Bridge. As his eyes slid across it, the compactness of the City Ground astonished him. 'Are you kidding me?' he asked himself, taken aback that such a small stadium in such a relatively small city was home to a side that had made the biggest possible splash. The modesty of the bricks and mortar explained anew to him the magnitude of what Clough had done.

Clough didn't live long enough to witness Mourinho win his second Champions League or to develop a friendship with him. If he had, Mourinho is certain the two of them would have 'got on'. The problem is that the slightly more mature Mourinho at Manchester United – he will be fifty-six next birthday – has started to resemble Clough a lot less than he once did. It isn't only that his hair is greyer or that the bags beneath his eyes have become like painted semi-circles. He seems to have forgotten what Clough never did: that you should always charm as you disarm, and also that the most brutal of truths can be more effective when wrapped in a joke. Even when indulging in a diatribe, Clough could be funny, spiking with humour speeches that he'd thought about deeply and rehearsed in his head in advance. His repartee crackled with a fake spontaneity, the pretence being that the punchline had only just occurred to him. His pauses also had a comedian's eloquence and timing about them. He knew the difference between a smart-alec wisecrack and bad-tempered facetiousness. Any year of Mourinho's career is eventful enough to produce a biography; he is always the man to which 'something' happens. But he has also become the contrarian who seldom seems to enjoy himself much anymore. The smirk or the sneer appear to be his two default facial expressions; if he smiles, it is almost a back page headline.

He has begun to sound too crabby and too cynical, and often comes across as angry, disgruntled, miserable or ungracious. So much that goes wrong is a gross injustice against him; and nearly everything that requires an excuse or explanation turns into a histrionic whinge. You consequently find yourself stripping the indignant nonsense out of his sentences as he speaks them.

Rudeness can be the weak man's imitation of strength, and Mourinho sometimes resorts to it not only because he can, replying with a petulant snap or the disparaging curl of a word in his mouth, but also because the answer gets buried 6 feet below, deterring attempts to disinter it. He can deliver the death-ray stare too, as though what he has been asked is beneath his dignity. Mourinho has become hard to understand and harder to like because of it. His voice still commands the ears, but he does not necessarily hold them any longer. He seems the sort of person who will look at additional evidence only if it confirms the opinion he already holds. Mediocrity clearly maddens him too, but dealing with it appears to bring out the worst in his character. You tune in to his press conferences only because, like rubber-necking on a motorway, you can't stop yourself from looking. You wait for the awkward question to be put, knowing whoever asks it could just have clipped the wrong-coloured wire attached to the bomb. Mourinho starts ticking. You squirm and want to take shelter even from the security of your sofa while pitying those who are actually there.

Mourinho often gets asked the same question, which comes at him in gently roundabout ways or in flimsy disguise. It is about his caution, a preference for sending out sides prepared to occupy their own half in hours of tedious endurance. The kind of philosophy someone adopts depends on the kind of person they are. It was Clough's avowed intent never to 'bore the arse' off spectators if he could avoid it. He and Mourinho evidently differ on that point. The neutrals among us would readily take a free season ticket at the Etihad before accepting one at Old Trafford. Mourinho arrived at Old Trafford positively, like someone about to energetically sweep the dust out of a room, but his United aren't nearly exciting enough. The vision he had then and his expression of it now are different. You can't claim the last eight months have tumbled around United, but second place won't be enough for them and Mourinho has far fewer opportunities to satisfy his ambition for a title in the near future because of the pots of dosh Sheikh

Mansour bin Zayed al Nahyan will invest to stop him. You aren't sure whether he will ever win it for United or in the end succeed only in trampling down what he was supposed to improve.

Whatever happens, you do know that Mourinho's self-belief, protected by more armour-plating than a tank, won't take a dent. In prefacing public appearances George Bernard Shaw would immodesty declare that he'd kindly agree to drag his 'astonishing self' to an event. Mourinho has never used Shaw's phrase, but the spirit of it lives on in him. He speaks as though almost each utterance deserves its own blue plaque. We are in public what we pretend to be, but how much of what Mourinho says and does is play-acting – and how much counts an expression of real emotion – is difficult to know exactly.

But we are about to find out if Mourinho, simply through force of personality, can steer United away from what is threatening to become a private apocalypse for them.

The atmosphere during half time is mellow, and the City fans luxuriate in it. Someone is sure United have already got changed and are now sneaking out of a side-door, slinking back to Old Trafford. Someone else can't wait until a T-shirt with the final score emblazed on it gets designed and printed. He promises to wear it 'all bloody summer'.

The question, asked and answered with airy certainty, is whether City warrant the Premier League's *egregia cum laude*, recognising them as the best of the best in the competition. More worthy than Liverpool with Dalglish and Souness in 1983–4? Or Arsenal's 2003–4 Invincibles under Arsène Wenger? Or United's treble winners of 1998–9, the feat earning Alex Ferguson his knighthood? While fat sums of Abu Dhabi money have been enabling for Pep Guardiola – more than £450m spent so far – no one questions the difference his management makes. No piano, even a Steinway, will play itself.

City won't be presented with the Premier League trophy until their final home match, staged next month. The supporters don't mind. It will be like having two big parties to mark one big birthday. The consensus is that the game represents a once and forever tipping point. The reasoning isn't complicated. City aspire to become under Guardiola what United became under Ferguson. The club already has the more modern ground. The better training facilities. The thicker wallet to entice the most expensive players. The manager for whom beauty in the pursuit of silverware matters. It is United's turn to feel inferior.

The surprise, when they emerge, is that José Mourinho has substituted no one. Even Paul Pogba remains with us, a decision that brings derision. Perhaps, as Brian Clough once did, Mourinho said only this to his team: 'You've got us into this hole – now you get of us out of it', which would explain the reprieve. You expect to see United finished off quickly. It almost occurs within five minutes. Ilkay Gündoğan sends a shot twanging against David de Gea's left post, the 'keeper nowhere near it. This, marked down as just one more let off in a long sequence of them for United, fails to fluster City's fans, who suppose the law of averages will favour them eventually.

Changes then occur in the match almost faster than the mind can process them.

No one knows the origins of the phrase 'a game of two halves' and whether whoever wrote it did so with a po-face. The earliest reference I have found comes from the *Arbroath Herald and Advertiser for the Montrose Burghs* of 1911. Since it appears in such a small publication, the logical conclusion is that someone else minted the thing first. It was possibly already a cliché by then. Nowadays we trot out 'two halves' only as a bit of fun, everyone knowing the joke.

Nothing, though, is more appropriate than these five words in summing up the next half hour or so.

The happy bubble which City are in lasts only seven minutes more. The pop is spectacular. Alexis Sánchez dribbles and wriggles his well-knit body free on the right – a complicated thing easily done – and then crosses for Ander Herrera on the edge of the box. Herrera, revealing remarkable foresight and then an even more remarkable deftness of touch, chests the ball into the empty space in front of him. Pogba, who has spent almost an hour doing United no good and City no harm, reacts quicker to the opening than Vincent Kompany, who can't bustle him away. Pogba waits until the ball bounces and Ederson commits himself. He pushes his shot over the goalkeeper's lunge, scoring his first goal for five months. The finish contains all the poise which Raheem Sterling has previously lacked.

CITY 2, UNITED 1

City regard it as an aberration that will be cancelled out soon and then forgotten. The goal is dismissed as a token, mildly appeasing United's disgruntled fans. But Pogba has woken up and is a changed man. Only two minutes later he starts another move. He lays a pass to Sánchez and then ploughs straight on, unencumbered by any tracking midfielder. His languorous stride-pattern matches the progress Sánchez is making. In the past I have seen Pogba lift a hand towards whoever is in possession; he always looks like a haughty diner demanding that the waiter deliver service to his table immediately. As though each is reading the thoughts of the other, he doesn't need to signal at all to the Chilean. Sánchez sees where Pogba is going and holds the play up a little. The flighted ball is for him alone; and any battle is over before it has been engaged because Nicolás Otamendi, who should be eternally on the look-out for danger, is distracted. He watches the cross rather than Pogba, who thrusts ahead of him and powerfully beats Ederson with a downward header from 8 yards. Pogba carries on running and plucks the ball out of the net as his reward. He then boots it high into the air and cups his hand to his ear to register the numbed silence of City's supporters.

CITY 2, UNITED 2

The Etihad pitch is one of the Premier League's biggest at 7,140 square metres, but it suddenly looks too small to contain all the drama going on within it. Few moments of the match go on quietly. Guardiola likes the surface well watered, so passes move quickly, and cut to slightly below half an inch high. City have begun to travel sluggishly with the ball, as though the grass is growing around their boots, and all the slickness has gone from the dry turf. Nowhere counts as a place of safety either. United attack from every direction and City, instantly becalmed, can think from only one minute to the next because their strategy is shot. United's fans, packed around the corner flags, are in a kind of exhilarating fever dream. City's fans, packed everywhere else, look askance at one another and then across at Guardiola, expecting him to do something.

Pogba has had more of the ball in the last ten minutes – he is calling for it now – than in the whole of the first half. No one, apart from Sánchez, can hold a tea-light to him. He is transformed from misfit to master. City's fans, searching for someone to shout at, barrack him. Whenever Pogba comes within 20 yards of the touchline, he is given earfuls of abuse. The mildest of it is: 'Fuck off you wanker'. We've become depressingly accustomed to such boorish vulgarity in football, but this comes with a vicious snarl and involuntary showers of spittle. The words bounce off Pogba. He offers hardly a half-glance or a facial twitch in response to them. If he looks at his accusers at all, his face is oddly free of judgement. His impassivity under attack makes those insulting him madder and more virulent still. City are displaying the several stages of football grief: frustration, incomprehension, anger and depression. All these are accentuated in the sixty-ninth minute.

Danilo inexplicably mis-controls and takes down Sánchez in his attempt to get possession back. In case Martin Atkinson hasn't noticed, Sánchez ekes out the maximum theatricality from the resulting dive, plunging into a double roll, like a gymnast across the mat. He is about 10 yards from the touchline and well into United's half. In memory I know I will always see the way in which he exploits the position he's been given one frame at a time, as though stop-motion photography recorded it. Each stage – the tender placing of the ball, the short run towards it, the ball itself going up and over the feeble defence City arrange ahead of it – is slowed or frozen altogether. City are preoccupied with Pogba, their main person of interest. It allows Chris Smalling to do what Fernandinho ought to have stopped. The defender escapes him and goes into space. The volley, from five and a half yards, is crashed in.

CITY 2, UNITED 3

The scoreboard makes a brutal impact on the eye for City. For them the game has taken the kind of wrong turn that seems hallucinatory. They stare at what is going on without really seeing it. *Private Eye* used to publish a series of paperbacks called *The Bumper Book of Boobs*, a collection of misprints and mistakes from newspapers across the world. The best of them comes back to me in the hubbub. The *Ghanaian Times* once ran the headline:

Nizam of Hyderabad is Dead

Next morning readers lifted the newspaper off the mat and discovered this had been a teeny exaggeration. That day's headline read:

Nizam of Hyderabad Slightly Better

As it was with him, so it is with United; but City, who really believed their neighbours had died out there in the first half, can't rationalise what is happening to them. The promise of winning the title here and now, which had been within a finger-tip of their possession, has not only slipped away, like something precious lost through a hole in someone's pocket, but is now less important than saving the match because doing so will also save them from a terrible and shocking embarrassment. The fans' misery is so severe because their joy had been so great. No one, thinking this was possible, had prepared for it. And the situation can't be accepted in dignified silence or with a sheen of civility. Amid the ordeal some City fans begin verbally squabbling among themselves, blaming complacency or even Guardiola's decision to exclude Kevin De Bruyne and Sergio Agüero from the off. It now seems like a botched plan. One woman, sensitive to slights, insists that a United fan has infiltrated the block and is filming the distress around him on his mobile phone. She points at him and gives a prolonged scream of banshee proportions, piercing enough to shatter wine glasses in the hospitality suites. The stewards lead the man away. The woman is still wailing 'GET HIM OUT'. The stewards have to intervene again when something – who knows what? – is said or done on the front row. It is all becoming a bit messy and distracting.

In Manchester's city centre I had passed racks of half-and-half scarves. One street seller attempted to sell them as 'a souvenir of the derby,' knowing only football tourists without heartfelt loyalty to either side would ever consider buying one. His hair hung in clotted lanks, like short grey rope, and his fingers were covered in an assortment of gold rings. He held up a scarf, as though he was inside the Etihad, and the collapsing softness of his face took on all sorts of imploring shapes, desperate for a customer. None appeared. You are either blue or red in Manchester. The two tribes are territorial and passionately polarised. You are attached to one or the other as if by umbilical cord. So who belonging to City would dare wear – or even want – Mourinho's mug inked on to wool? And who belonging to United could possibly be seen with Guardiola's face around their neck? In their technical areas, the mangers strive not to glance at one another. You can only piece together what you know of them and extrapolate from it the interior monologues each must be speaking. United have only twenty minutes to hold on – Mourinho seems assuredly calm about doing so – but City's bench does have that 'Break Glass in Emergency' look about it. And, since this is an emergency of tearing panic, Guardiola brings on first De Bruyne and Gabriel Jesus and then Agüero.

City rely on De Bruyne, who can perform with spontaneous eloquence, to make something for the two forwards. The best command you to remember them. He is in that category, the play-maker's play-maker. Posterity will know him after his career is over. When Guardiola, calling De Bruyne a 'complete player', recently said that he was capable of winning the Ballon d'Or one day, the reaction of anyone who has watched him regularly was merely: 'Of course'. De Bruyne appears with spots of colour on each cheek. He would look more cherubic still were it not for the thin shading of stubble on his jaw. Fairly slight and slim shouldered, he is not an overwhelming physical presence, but a cerebral one. In the visionary role in which he operates, even an ostensibly penny-plain pass has often an exceptional luminosity about it. Talent finds a target no one else can hit. Genius hits a target no one else can see. You could be in Oxford Street during the Boxing Day sales and he'd still find you in space. The height of his art – first in picking out a player's run and then in planting the ball perfectly to meet it – appears as some ontological trick, baffling until the camera reveals the secret of it to us. Earlier in the season, contained within City's 7–2 trouncing of Stoke, De Bruyne gave a virtuoso performance of passing that someone at the Etihad had the wonderful sense to tapestry together as a film lasting five minutes and three seconds. Each frame contains something that is useful, instructional or beautiful and coaches everywhere ought to download it immediately. The film, recording all the touches De Bruyne had in that game, is more valuable than a library of technical manuals. You don't need to be one of the game's connoisseurs to appreciate the aesthetics of this one-man show: the immaculate balance, the nimbleness, the poised movement and fleetness of foot in those orange boots. On occasions De Bruyne looks lighter than a dancer in pumps as he glides, almost ethereally, or pivots sinuously on the ball even when the rest of his body isn't in exactly the right position to do so. Some of his passing is like watching liquid gold being poured into a cup.

But there is none of that today. De Bruyne has arrived too late. The tempo and the pattern of the match are well set and he can't influence either of them. In their epic collapse City, so articulate all season, have been struck dumb. There is a worthy shout for a penalty. Ashley Young slides into and takes down Agüero, his studs rattling high into the Argentinian's shin pads. The card count has mounted quickly – you can't tally them up without a pencil and a notebook – but Young, pushing his luck to the limit, escapes both a possible red and a penalty. Martin Atkinson dismisses City's appeal emphatically, the nadir of a shockingly bad afternoon's work because the offence is so blatant.

The rage of City's supporters is blowing itself out. Resignation has set in instead. No one sings 'Blue Moon'. Even the stalwarts leave before the whistle, wanting the Etihad to be well behind them when United's comeback of comebacks is confirmed. There are a lot of empty seats when David de Gea, as late as the eighty-ninth minute, dashes Agüero's ambitions from close range, diving upward and across his goal to tip away a glancing header from beneath the bar. You're usually not surprised by anything De Gea does – he is so consistently impeccable and genuinely ambidextrous – but this is the season's greatest result-saver in the season's greatest match. United can now whittle down the left-over minutes.

The game was billed as a 'no win' one for Mourinho. Since even denying City the title would only minimally delay their lap of honour, it was considered that any success he garnered here would be humble and pyrrhic. Not any longer. The win, which is honey-sweet, is a declaration of intent for next season. Mourinho has also left City with something no one at the Etihad wants to remember but will find impossible to forget. The record book, out soon, will confirm City as Champions, but United will always think the feat should come with an asterisk that guides you towards a footnote and today's date. The defeat United have inflicted is like a little death for City – and the bereavement will be long endured.

I wait for the rest of the crowd to clear, watching Pogba rush towards the small section of United fans, where he attempts to communicate with them through sign language. In football you always know that your heart will be broken time and again. Some City fans, still sedentary, can't stop sobbing, their eyes red with distress. Near the club shop I come across a man who is the sum of City's suffering. He looks too old to cry, but laughing would hurt him too much. He is being physically propped up by a friend, who pats him on the head and promises to take him for a long drink. You calculate by the barrel how much beer will be needed to anaesthetise his pain away tonight.

Eventually I join the ragged ribbon of City fans who form a shuffling, miserable queue for the tram. On the congested platform, the timetable apparently all out of kilter, there is shoving and pushing and mournful curses. A guard – broad, burly, bearded – arrives to bring a semblance of order. He makes small talk with a fan, who is moaning about United, about City's defence and also about Guardiola. The guard, solicitously attempting to add perspective to the sombre occasion, tells him he will only have to wait 'a week or two' more to uncork the champagne. The fan looks up and tells him to mind his own business; he doesn't drink champagne. The guard, as though he hasn't heard the rebuff, cheerfully asks whether he will be going straight home. The fan looks up at him again. 'No,' he snaps. 'I'm off to find the nearest bloody canal, and then . . .'

The rest of the sentence dies on his lips.

7 April 2018: Manchester City v Manchester United
Manchester City 2 Manchester United 3

Manchester City: Ederson, Danilo, Kompany, Otamendi, Delph, Gündoğan (Agüero 76), Fernandinho, Silva D (De Bruyne 72), Silva B (Jesus 72), Sterling, Sané.
Subs not used: Bravo, Walker, Laporte, Toure

Manchester United: De Gea, Valencia, Bailly, Smalling, Young, Herrera (Lindelof 90), Matic, Pogba, Lingard (McTominay 85), Lukaku, Sánchez (Rashford 82).
Subs not used: Rojo, Mata, Martial, Pereira

SCORERS

Manchester City: Kompany 25, Gündoğan 30
Manchester United: Pogba 53 and 55, Smalling 69

BOOKED

Manchester City: Sterling, Fernandinho, Agüero, Danilo, Kompany, Jesus
Manchester United: Herrera, Lukaku, Pogba

Referee: M. Atkinson
Attendance: 54,259

16

TO THE INFINITY BRIDGE AND BEYOND

29 April: Gym United v Hardwick Social, FA Sunday Cup Final, Bramall Lane

In February, when this season's FA Sunday Cup was still to get past the fifth round, the holders Hardwick Social had to part with the trophy, returning it to the Football Association as protocol decreed. The trophy is no piece of plain silver, but a thing of subtle beauty. Resembling in shape a vase from Middle Eastern antiquity, it has no handles and, without its plinth, the lip of the top is ever so slightly broader than the base. The silver is gorgeously engraved. The filigree patterns of whirls and swirls, which decorate almost the whole surface, were achieved with the kind of painstaking labour that can only have taken months and gallons of midnight oil to complete. The trophy was a gift from the Shah of Iran, the 'King of Kings' and also a minor football obsessive. He presented it to the FA to mark the organisation's centenary as far back as 1963. When its 150th anniversary clicked around, the FA displayed his handsome contribution to the English game alongside the FA Cup. It did not look out of place.

Sending the trophy back was the responsibility of Andy Westwood, Hardwick's manager. He doesn't so much run the side, which plays in the Stockton Sunday League, as live it on a daily basis. Westwood does everything from choosing the team to washing the kit. He picks up the tape to bind shin pads and socks. He sorts the drinks bottles. He arranges the practice and the match balls. He does some of the online form-filling and the other shuffling paperwork to comply with the league's regulations. Westwood is thirty-six, which makes him barely older than most of his team. He became boss, slightly reluctantly, just six years ago and only because of a family tragedy. His father, Alex, who showed the same devotion to duty in exactly the same cause, died of cancer. He was fifty-eight. It is said you can tell the character of a man through his deeds. Alex Westwood once saw a street-mugger steal a bag from a 72-year-old woman. He set off instantly in pursuit, chasing the thief into a dead end. He then sat on top of him until the police arrived to make an arrest. He was so popularly well known, and so highly esteemed, that the League established a Memorial Trophy in his name. Last season Hardwick won it for the fifth successive time, a success not entirely unexpected. Since son took over from father, Hardwick have claimed five consecutive championships. A sixth will be secured once a small backlog of fixtures is cleared. There have also been cups galore for them, bringing doubles and trebles and quadruples. Nothing, however, equals the achievement of taking the Sunday Cup, coveted by so many but possessed by so few. It is to the weekend amateur game in England what the Champions League is to Europe. According to the FA, there are around 37,000 grassroots clubs in the country, but only the best of the best are eligible for the competition. The demands of it, as well as the standards in it, are consistently high. In making the cup theirs, beating formidable Londoners New Salamis at Sheffield United's Bramall Lane, Westwood's side became Sunday aristocracy. 'The greatest day in our history,' he says, as though still not quite believing it happened.

Hardwick have won so much under Westwood that it is a squeeze to show everything off on the same shelf. But since the Shah's benevolence is conservatively worth about £20,000, and also because the club didn't want to risk scratches or dents, the trophy was hidden away once the celebrations of winning it were over. When the FA asked for it back, Westwood considered dropping it off at Wembley in person, doing so before the League Cup Final. He decided against it after discovering that buying a seat for the game (£100), on top of the train ticket from Teesside, would have been a pricey extravagance. Hardwick's chief source of revenue is a weekly raffle with a first prize of £50. It usually reaps a three-figure profit for them. Each player buys £2 tickets, an alternative to a match-fee. Westwood arranged instead for a private courier. The cost was £76. He put the trophy into its padded wooden box, which the FA had given to the club after the final, and then locked it. There was some short and polite wrangling over the postcode. It was though Wembley was a lost or entirely unexplored land that no delivery driver could possibly find unless HA9 0WS was clearly written on a label. So off that exquisite example of Persian craftsmanship went, tucked in the back of a white van, anonymous among stacks of other parcels.

Now, back again at Bramall Lane, Hardwick bid to become only the third team in the Sunday Cup's 54-year history to reclaim it immediately. No one has won the trophy back-to-back since the early 1990s. Twelve months ago Hardwick, grateful to be in the final even as underdogs, denied New Salamis that honour. After 120 minutes, and a goal apiece, only a penalty shoot-out could settle it. 'I thought beforehand that our chances were zero,' confesses Westwood in contemplation of the fact that New Salamis' parent club are Nea Salamis Famagusta FC of the Cypriot First Division.

This afternoon is a complete role reversal for them. Last year's small fry are this year's big fish. Hardwick are solid favourites against Gym United, the champions of the Bury and District League. From that quaintest of market towns, Bury St Edmunds, Gym draw most of their talent from Thetford Town of the Thurlow Nunn Premier Division. Westwood can still trump that. Hardwick don't have to scratch about for prospective recruits. There are fifty-seven players on the books, but the team is close-knit, community-based and, most importantly of all, a collection of friends who simply want to play football. No one thinks of it as moonlighting or pot-hunting. All bar two live locally too. One is based 17 miles away. A second is in London, gladly returning to appear occasionally. The players hold down an eclectic range of jobs. Among them are electricians, builders, plasterers, a window cleaner and an air conditioning engineer. Their goalkeeper, Michael Arthur, who saved two penalties and then scored the winner during that shoot-out with New Salamis, works as a retinal screener for the NHS. Westwood is office manager for a construction company. He is a former midfielder for Stockton Town, from which the basis of his strongest side is forged. Stockton are currently ninth in Division One of the Northern League. Arthur plays for them. So do three other mainsprings of Westwood's squad: Jamie Owens, nicknamed the Hardwick Messi, Sonni Coleman, a former England schoolboys international, and Nathan Mulligan, once part of Middlesbrough's Academy. In the summer of 2003, aged only sixteen, Mulligan thought a spluttering cough was a chest infection. Doctors diagnosed leukaemia. In 2009, recovered at last, he made his debut for Darlington in League One. In another three weeks Mulligan, along with at least eight of Hardwick's team, will be beneath the arch at Wembley, where Stockton will try to win the FA Vase. 'Sometimes I'm asked how much I pay the Stockton lads to turn out for us,' says Westwood. 'I tell them the truth. We don't pay them anything. They buy their raffle tickets like everyone else because (he pauses) . . . that keeps the club going . . . each of them wants to play for us and be alongside their mates . . . and for the simple enjoyment of football. Mind you, we're all like that. We're football people.'

Hardwick normally arrive separately for matches in their own cars. Today Westwood has arranged a spot of luxury for them. He has borrowed Hartlepool United's team bus – high-backed seats, tables and tinted windows – for the 107-mile trip southward. You appreciate his organisational bent. He covers all the squares, clearly feeling that the little things are infinitely the most significant. Each player was sent a printed itinerary for the final and also reminded to take eight to ten hours' rest and drink 5 litres of water on the eve of it. The team met at 7.50a.m. for breakfast at Stockton Town's ground. The coach set off at 8.45a.m. It stopped en route at Woolley Edge for a comfort break. The team arrived at Bramall Lane an hour and a half before kick-off. Appearances count for Westwood too. 'We need to look professional,' he reminded his players.

Hardwick listened to him. From the Hauling South Stand, I watch them warm up on the opposite touchline. Their control, poise and demeanour are impressive. Westwood looks on from a distance, his hands jammed into the pockets of his dark tracksuit. It's a cold lunchtime in Yorkshire. The sky is obscured by high, ribbed cloud and a strong south-westerly blows the flags on top of the far stand almost flush. It makes the fabric look stiff, as if each flag has been dipped in starch. As Hardwick's fans start to come in, abandoning the pub just across the road, you get the first shouts of 'Andy Westwood's Green and White Army'. Don Revie, neurotically superstitious, thought green so unlucky that he banned anyone at Leeds United from ever wearing it during his decade and a half in charge. He was born in Middlesbrough, next door to Stockton, but he'd blanch at Hardwick's choice of emerald and wouldn't go near Gym's kit either. On the team sheet it is described as 'volt green'. Bright pale lime-yellow, the colour of a cocktail experimentally mixed, it shines as though lit from within.

To their credit, the Football Association strives to make the Sunday Cup Final as much like the FA Cup Final as possible. There is no red carpet and the Shah's trophy is still snug in its box, where Westwood last saw it, rather than on display. There are nonetheless the pre-match preliminaries of a big production. There are the hand-shaking presentations. The national anthem is sung. Bramall Lane is a scrupulously clean and spruce stage. The tiers of mostly post-box red seating, empty on three sides of the ground, make the place look more grandly cavernous than usual. Less than twenty-four hours ago Sheffield United lost to Preston here, a defeat that extinguished any prospect of reaching the play-offs. But you wouldn't know the pitch had been played on so recently. It is smooth and close-cropped, fit for the occasion.

For Hardwick, this represents heaven.

A week ago I went to watch Hardwick Social against Norton George and Dragon, a pub team. The temperature had been hot and sultry for a few days, more reminiscent of the end of July than the last quarter of April. In the little known book *This England*, W. S. Shears came to Stockton at the end of the 1930s and wrote of the smoky 'great industries': iron and steel foundries, shipbuilding, 'chemical-producing factories'. He wouldn't recognise it today. In the town centre white blossom lay on the kerbsides like freshly thrown wedding confetti. The forty-three spouts of the sparkly, crescent-shaped fountain shot up from the pavement; and squealing children ran between the tall jets of water, deliberately getting themselves soaked. Their parents silently baked in the fine weather. The High Street would be a decent place for Stockton Town to prepare for their FA Vase Final. Reputedly the widest in England, it is 6 feet wider than Wembley's pitch. A player could learn how to sweep cross-field passes in that arcing space simply by sending a ball from the front door of the travel agents on one side (its window advertising Vase Weekends in London for £99) to the tavern, Dr M'Gonigles Emporium, on the other. The scene was sedate. Very ordinary. Very English. We told ourselves to make the most of it. Every weather forecast for Sunday mid-morning showed an angry patch of rain with Stockton's name prominently on it.

In the night there were thunderstorms right across the North, the spindly webs of lightning generated like something from a mad professor's laboratory. But when the day rose with great slices of sunlight over the Tees, I dismissed the meteorologists as being too pessimistic. I was wrong. Half an hour before kick-off, and with the most unsettling punctuality, the blue sky quickly got smothered in wide bands of mottled cloud, which you knew hadn't dragged good news with them.

Nearly all those who watch football have at some time played it on a Sunday. The very least of us know what it's like to arrive with last night's beer on our breath and still swilling inside us. We've turned up without our full kit and minus our full team. We've got changed in bare-boarded huts or on the back seat of someone's car. We've questioned the referee's ability to see further than the myopic Mr Magoo. We've cussed, cursed and quarrelled at our manager's lack of expertise after being dropped to the bench. We've played beside 'ringers', soon forgetting which name we were supposed to call them to perpetuate the ruse. At half time we've watched some of our team mates slope off for a fag ostensibly in secret, their location given away as smoke curled as though puffing from the funnel of a steam train. At full time we've gone home, our knees covered in cracked mud, because the showers didn't work or there were no showers in the first place. Most of all we've played on surfaces so disgracefully bad that you wouldn't even want to grow cabbages on them.

I don't think I've seen a worse pitch than the one Hardwick call home. The club hire it from the local council. It costs them £200 per season. Hardwick is two and a half miles north-west of Stockton, its population a smidgen below 7,000 according to the last census. The social club, out of which the team originally grew in the mid-1960s, offers quiz nights and snooker, bingo, dancing and live music. The team play closer to the town. Their pitch is the first in a row at the end of Talbot Street. It is called Tilery 1. This tongue of recreation ground borders long grass and an incongruous bandstand at one end and a shallow bank, swathed in nettles and dandelions, at the other. Beyond the bank was a stream in which someone had abandoned a supermarket trolley. It was sinking slowly and nose down into the dirty water. In a copse next to a grassless corner of the pitch there were discarded plastic bottles, a heap of cardboard and a bright orange carrier bag with assorted rubbish spilling out of it. Behind one of the goals were beer cans, more cardboard and even a car tyre.

I arrived early, watching a group of the players on the furthest pitch wrestle with the nets as though the nylon was not only alive but also had tentacles. I saw one of them nip off for a discreet pee beside a tree. There are no dressing rooms on site. The teams get changed in a school opposite modern terraced housing, each with a square of fenced off garden, before walking 700 yards across a car park and along the bend of the narrow road.

Spring is usually full of the scent of newly mown grass. Not in this part of Stockton, it isn't. We all know councils are under severe budgetary restraints in our apparently never-ending age of austerity. But I looked at Hardwick's pitch and could only conclude one of three things: a) The council's mower had been sold to fund other services: b) the mower was irreparably broken: c) the tank on the mower had run out of diesel and so had the money in petty cash, which meant no one could fill it up again. For surely the council wasn't too bone-lazy or just too incompetent to maintain a half-decent surface for those who had paid to play on it? The grass didn't look as though it had been cut for three weeks. Or possibly even a month. There were two fairy rings on it. In the odd patch, where little or no grass grew at all, the bare rough soil was spiked with old stud marks. There was also the occasional imprint of wheel tracks, made by some unidentifiable vehicle. The surface is so shoddy that Hardwick can't play FA Sunday Cup ties on it, decamping instead to Stockton Town.

There is a Glen Baxter cartoon in which a centre forward, wearing a 1950s-style hooped shirt and matching socks, steams along a tufted pitch and towards goal, the ball at his feet and under good control. Unbeknown to him, what hovers above his head, without casting a shadow, is an enormous boot. The size of it suggests the owner has just climbed down from a beanstalk. He has to be taller than a telegraph poll and broader than a farmer's barn. He's not only about to deny his poor victim the chance to score, but also to crush him plate-flat in the process. The caption beneath the cartoon is *'I seemed to have given United's big number five the slip'*. Baxter captures the image most of us would summon when asked to think of Sunday football. Brute strength battering silken skill and nearly every tackle flavoured with a little vinegar. When I strolled across Hardwick's pitch, I assumed I'd see that sort of stereotypical park game. The ball would spend much more time in the air than on the floor. The challenges would be like monster trucks colliding. But both Hardwick and Norton George and Dragon were undeterred. The rain came early and left late, but didn't make the tricky surface easier by softening or calming it down. The bounce was regularly unpredictable. It was as though the ball was square and, like dice tossed across a casino table, no one could be quite sure in which direction it would travel after landing. Always, and very admirably, each of them still tried to build attacks through pass-ing. The only long hoicks came from goal-kicks.

Those at the top of the professional game, managers and players alike, aren't always conscious that their behaviour filters to the bottom of it. You rarely hear about the best of it – the player who scissor kicks and scores in imitation of Ronaldo – or even the benign, such as the hack performer shelling out £300 for a pair of boots because he thinks they, like Dorothy's ruby slippers, will carry him magically to another dimension.

You do hear about the worst of it, however, because the unsavoury always attracts a headline. Most are about the harassment, physical and verbal, of referees. Only two years ago the *Daily Telegraph* carried out an investigation in which the findings were grisly. The newspaper reported that one referee was reduced to tears through bullying. Another received a death threat on social media. A third was warned that he faced a fist-fight afterwards. A fourth, in charge of a youth match, had his car blocked in. A fifth, also during a youth match, was confronted on the pitch by a snarling parent. If those few lines don't shiver coldly down your spine, the next surely will. 'Many referees,' added the *Telegraph*, 'do not report abuse, either out of fear or because they have lost faith in the ability of the county FAs to punish offenders quickly.' Eight months later the newspaper wrote that an 'estimated 7,000' refs quit the game each year.

Neither Hardwick nor Norton George and Dragon resorted to stupid assaults to claim possession. And the referee was only questioned, not intimidated. Apart from the occasional expletive, he was respectfully allowed to get on with making decisions. Spitting, the plague of modern sport, was also absolutely minimal.

From the start Hardwick, playing into the whipped up wind, were in control, making openings without accepting them. As a boy, during those Saturdays when I couldn't afford to go to a League match, I'd set off for the local recreation ground and watch the village team. I liked to stand beside a goalkeeper's left hand post. Often I'd have a conversation with him. There was a crowd of 70,000-plus in Berlin's Olympic Stadium for Germany versus Brazil. More than 50,000 were at the Etihad for the Manchester derby. The number of people I saw on the touchline at Tilery 1, excluding coaches and substitutes, totalled fifteen, plus three dogs which were walked briefly past the far end of the field. I was consequently a conspicuous figure, easily identified as a stranger despite the big black coat and a flat cap which I had supposed would make me anonymous. Norton George and Dragon's 'keeper saw me taking notes. He asked whether I was scouting on behalf of Gym United. We exchanged chit-chat about the weather, the pitch, Hardwick's achievement this season, which players I ought to watch particularly and his own team's form. His name was Lewis McDonald. He turned out to be the Man of the Match. Of the seventeen of his saves that I counted, at least nine of them thwarted goals, the odds heavily favouring the striker when he made them.

In the weeks since Stockton won their Vase semi-final, Andy Westwood has tried to protect the players for Wembley. 'You don't want anyone turning an ankle and missing out,' he said. The problem, he explained, is 'that everyone wants to play. They're on the phone asking to be picked'. Against Norton George and Dragon, he'd chosen Sonni Coleman but made Jamie Owens a sub. Owens came on, beating McDonald from close range, about a quarter of an hour from the end. McDonald, who still managed to get something on to the shot, reproached himself far too harshly after the effort beat his low dive. He thumped the ground with the flat of his hand, the ball still stuck in the corner of his sagging net.

I saw the goal from the grass bank, which provided a slightly elevated view of the pitch. Sometimes great contentment appears when there is no discernible reason for it. Despite the rain, which kept on coming, I had become so absorbed in the match, speculating on whether Hardwick would ever score, that I was disappointed when the referee later said there were only ten minutes to go. The ball went into the stream three times. It twice ended up on the pitch next door. This is Sunday football; I wish I could have joined in.

Home and Away is an epistolary trade of observation and polemic between writers Karl Ove Knausgaard and Fredrik Ekelund. These are shared during the 2014 World Cup in Brazil. Near the end of the book Knausgaard tells his friend how a photographer arrived to illustrate extracts prior to publication. The photographer brought a ball and took him to a nearby pitch. Knausgaard was asked to put it on the penalty spot and then shoot. 'The ball,' he said, 'flew towards the corner, hit the underside of the crossbar and went in . . . No goalkeeper in the world would have saved it.' Knausgaard, middle-aged and not having kicked a ball for two years, had been 'nervous' and also worried about making 'a total prat' of himself. In not doing so, he acknowledged his outrageous good fortune.

Self-deception is the most human thing. So, of course, I had hubristically believed I could take without demur every plum opening that the lads of Hardwick squandered. But I was not as lucky as Knausgaard. As I retrieved the ball from where I stood and then attempted to send it back in a triumphant demonstration of footballing genius, my foot got caught slightly in a rutted part of the field. I lost balance and the swinging kick sliced off my instep. I almost toppled over, becoming in that instant another pathetic old geezer with delusions. Youth and beauty are not accomplishments, but I ought to have made more of them, which in this specific regard should have meant playing on a Sunday until my legs fell off. I didn't, and I regret it now. I wasn't any good, but that isn't remotely the point. For there is something about the camaraderie you find in the small world of a dressing room that you can never replicate elsewhere. It stays with you too.

This was evident on Tilery 1 and again afterwards when the two teams went to the George and Dragon. They ate curry together. They drank the odd pint. They watched Arsenal v West Ham on Sky Sports.

I sat next to Westwood. He glanced up at the big screen, envious of the pitch at the Emirates, which was still baize-smooth and still intensely green after nearly nine months of the season. Somewhat wistfully, he asked me: 'Can you imagine playing on that?'

Bramall Lane isn't the Emirates, but it is very conducive to an expansive, passing side such as Hardwick Social. The game is only five minutes old. You see enough to know nonetheless that Gym United are likely to spend most of what's to come occupying their own half. In the match programme their player-manager Matt Morton reflected the rounds that had brought them here – 'long coach trips, overnight stays, a mud bath pitch (and) snow'. Hardwick are familiar to him. He watched last year's final and went to check on them again in this year's semi (old foes New Salamis were beaten at neutral Alfreton Town). He thinks 'spirit' has got Gym here.

Formed as recently as 2010, enabling friends to become a crack side, Gym have surpassed even Hardwick in the accumulation of Championships – seven on the belt so far. There is still no disguising the difference between them. One team is making all the smooth advances. The other team is resisting them. The finishing line must already seem an awfully long way off for Gym. Morton is a central defender. Without him, and his partner Nathan Clarke, Suffolk against Teesside could become a mismatch. As early as the tenth minute Clarke is called on to produce a snap tackle to stop James Ward. His and Morton's workload does not get lighter after that.

Sometimes Hardwick attempt to be too precise and too certain, wanting to do more with the ball than is practicable or necessary. Moves that start promisingly get tangled up in over-elaborate passing, allowing the Morton–Clarke combination to interrupt them. Prominent from the start are Jamie Owens and Sonni Coleman. The width Chris Stockton provides on the left also means Morton is drawn out to confront him or Clarke finds himself called on to head away crosses. Gym have only the lean and rangy Andrew Wood up front. He is more alone than Romelu Lukaku during that infamous first half at the Etihad two weeks ago. With Gym's counter attacks no more than brief squalls, seldom amounting to much, Wood has to do a lot of running and even more leaping to reach what are punched clearances rather than up-field passes towards him. He is rarely facing Hardwick's goal when the ball reaches his feet.

Were someone compiling statistics, Hardwick's possession rate would be about 65 per cent. No one examining the figures without also looking at the match would be able to work out why a goal hasn't come. What's missing is the final, killer ball. This makes Gym's goalkeeper Duncan McNally hop about in his 6-yard box in expectation of it. At the other end Michael Arthur is waiting for anyone to give him something to do. His most strenuous tasks so far have been trapping back-passes with his left boot.

On those rare holidays from defending, each excursion taking them to the fringe of Hardwick's area but seldom inside it, Gym do get free kicks. One is from 25 yards. The other is 4 yards further out. However dominant Hardwick have been, there is always the doubt, lurking in even the most confident minds, that a goal could be conceded through happenstance, a series of events that only ill-fortune can explain afterwards. A shot bobbling off someone's knee, shoulder or backside. A hasty hack away that goes into your own net. A cross which two players leave, each expecting the other to deal with it. Nothing like that happens. Gym don't pressurise Hardwick at all.

At half time, against Norton George and Dragon, Westwood gathered his team together in a semi-circle on the pitch. I heard him say: 'Stick at it and stay together. Keep passing the ball. A goal will come. You're better than them.' At half time here, also goalless, he can plagiarise himself, repeating those same instructions word for word in the knowledge that he'd be telling the truth.

I liked Sunday football, long before I ever kicked a ball in it, because of Charles Buchan's *Football Monthly*. Rather like Charles Buchan himself, the magazine is all but forgotten except by those who once read it. Buchan was a Victorian-born Londoner, an imposingly tall and elegant centre forward who won the League title and lost an FA Cup Final with Sunderland only a year before the guns of the Great War began to boom. After it, joining Arsenal, he devised the WM formation with his manager Herbert Chapman, a tactical shape revolutionary and resoundingly successful well after Buchan retired and swapped the dressing room for the press box. *Football Monthly* appeared in 1951. A friend of my father's owned a stack of them, which he'd put both into and on top of a wardrobe until his wife demanded that he winnow them down. A cardboard box, containing about four dozen of these magazines, found its way to me. There was a sheen to each cover, but it couldn't be described as glossy, and some of the thick pages had become musty. The early colourisation was primitive, and it gave every face an unnatural appearance. A portrait could be so heavily retouched with ink that it seemed as though the player had smeared rouge on his lips, like a drag queen, or wore more kohl black eyeliner than a 1920s flapper. The grass was often a shocking green. The ball glowed so fiercely orange that you imagined it could be seen from space.

The magazine was full of faces I didn't recognise and names I didn't know, making them remote to me. But I remember turning a page of one of them and finding a photograph so wondrous that I questioned there and then the very veracity of it, unable to believe what I saw really did exist somewhere. The sweeping aerial shot showed a vast spread of football pitches; so many, in fact, that both the cameraman's lens and the parameters of a page were unable to frame them all in a single shot. The outer limits were chopped off, hidden and mysterious. The pitches filled the top and bottom and both sides of this seraphic picture, stretching, I was sure, to a vanishing point, which could be only miles and miles distant. The touchlines and goal-lines, the penalty boxes and centre circles were a vividly brilliant white. The pitches were also jammed closely together – there was barely a yard of grass between them – and none of the goals had nets. I imagined the minor chaos caused as the ball from one game trespassed regularly on to another. Of course, you couldn't actually spot a ball anywhere, but only guess, like placing your X in that once popular newspaper competition, the rough location of it from the position of the players who, though no bigger than pencil dots, were seen unmistakably in swarming pursuit.

Until then I knew nothing of Hackney Marshes. I wasn't aware that on any given Sunday during the season more than 120 matches could be played there simultaneously. The Marshes hardly seemed to be the most decorous of places. It was flat, bleakly bare and windswept. There was apparently nothing – no tree, no hedge, no building or wall – to break the horizon if you were standing on any corner of it. None of that mattered. I convinced myself that one part of the world must be made entirely of football pitches.

Earlier this season I went there for the first time. It was a misty midweek, the grass cold and glistening with moisture. The original photograph I saw had been taken sometime during the Marshes' zenith in the 1950s or 1960s. More than thirty pitches have been lost since then, a dozen gone most recently to create a car park for the 2012 Olympics. I wandered about, peering through fog-cum-smog. A group of men in windcheaters, dogs at their feet, were clustered in front of the café supping tea from paper cups. A pair of jackdaws sat together on a rusted crossbar, as cosy as a courting couple on a park bench. Flocks upon flocks of seagulls had taken residence in the middle distance, refusing to budge. There were a couple of matches being played. I watched them for ten or so minutes and headed off to Ruckholt Road Bridge. From there the gleaming white top of the London Stadium and the skeletal loops of Anish Kapoor's Orbit tower rule the landscape. I looked behind me, back across the Marshes, and felt a little underwhelmed at the sight of it. The pitches were messy and scarred. The hedges were ragged. Low blocks of flats looked greyly unappealing. The rattling growl of lorries and buses dinned against my ears. The smell of exhaust was overpoweringly unpleasant.

There is a recognised psychological state called Paris Syndrome, which sounds like a leg-pull even after you learn the definition of it. A complicated malady, it explains the tourist's disappointment when the French capital fails to live up to preposterously idealised expectations. Discovering the place isn't absolutely perfect can apparently plunge some visitors into depression. I can't go that far, but the Marshes were a bit of a let down. Like those who expect Paris to be as entrancing as it is in all those movies, I had expected the Marshes to captivate me the way that old photograph first did. But the character I thought I would find wasn't there. I went around mentally picking fault instead. I had hoped for too much.

Hardwick Social and Talbot Road's Tilery 1 – despite that woefully unkempt grass, despite that rubbish strewn around it, despite the miserable weather that day – seemed much more like the spiritual home of muddy boots and the grassroots.

The second half replicates the pattern of the first. Hardwick Social get close and then closer still to a breakthrough. Gym simply attempt to cling on, banking again on something rare or spontaneous changing the flow of the match in their favour. The longer it goes on, however, the more a goal for them will count as the contraband of pirate treasure. Their attacks are about false starts and disappointments; Andrew Wood is cut off on the halfway line, lonelier than ever. Hardwick's box, never mind their goal, is a target Gym are struggling to find. When one raid does produce a quarter-chance – Michael Arthur is crouched at his near post to narrow the angle – the ball ends up almost in the top tier of the Bramall Lane Stand.

Gym aren't attractive to watch, but you appreciate the effort and application being shown collectively for them. Their clean sheet is being preserved behind the fortress wall of Matt Morton and Nathan Clarke, each of whom has a sharp eye for what is in front of them, and also the goalkeeping of Duncan McNally. A full hour still separates us from a penalty shoot-out, but we are already contemplating the possibility of it, which is a compliment to Gym's superb stubbornness. In one superlative example Morton saves them. You'd have to watch at least two dozen games to see a tackle as polished as the one he pulls off, pushing the ball to safety inside his own area. Chris Stockton, thinking he is through against McNally, finds Morton appearing on his shoulder and then sliding in toughly with the clearance. The challenge is brave because it had to be, but Morton calibrated his tackle to the half-inch. Even Hardwick's fans, once their anguish is expressed and over, applaud the fine skill and the audacity of it.

You feel one factor will be Gym's undoing. The sun, which has burnt away the clouds at last, is splashed across most of the pitch. The wind has dropped a little too. Keeping Hardwick out is increasingly becoming hot as well as weary work. All that fetching, carrying and protecting the ball in their own half doesn't only sap energy, it gnaws at the nerves too. This is a long, wide pitch and Hardwick are using every square foot of it to stretch Gym, who are shedding a lot of sweat and covering a lot of hard miles. In the last fifteen minutes, you see the consequences of that. Some of Gym's side start to clutch the back of their legs and begin to pant. Their faces are either crimson with effort or have about as much colour in them as a glass of milk. The openings mount up for Hardwick. There is an overhead kick from Ward. There is a back post header from Jamie Owens and two quick-fire shots from him that get heroically charged down. A third, a few minutes later, seems bound for the bottom right hand corner before McNally turns it away; Owens can't believe how the 'keeper got to it. As late as the ninetieth minute Nathan Mulligan shoots from 20 yards. The ball clears the bar by less than a foot.

Andy Westwood is not the kind of manager who will burst a lung hollering from his technical area. It isn't his style. He is more analytical than animated. You don't see him flinging his arms frantically about much either. As the whistle sounds for full time, he folds them tight against his chest, stares about the field and then walks slowly towards his team. He is calm and undemonstrative, which is precisely what the favourites need to see from their manager.

One of the crossings on the River Tees is the Infinity Bridge, a sleek-smart bowstring construction in which two arches form a continuous curve. It is shaped into one half of the most recognisable of scientific symbols. On sunny days the bridge's reflection in the water makes the symbol whole. In the summer, preparing for the season to come, Hardwick's players ran up and down the steps of the bridge, each determined to be fitter than a butcher's dog. Often opportunity is dressed up as hard work, which is what puts a lot of people off going for it. But, as Westwood told me after their match against Norton George and Dragon, 'the lads are fanatical about fitness'. In the lull before extra time begins, this becomes very obvious. Hardwick's team is mostly standing up as Westwood speaks to them. Gym United's is mostly lying down.

You know there can only be one winner.

Extra time's second half is almost ten minutes old, the stalemate still unbroken, when Andy Westwood brings off Chris Stockton, who has run everywhere all the time, and replaces him with Joe Posthill, a twenty-year-old making only his twelfth appearance of the season. With almost his first touch, Posthill sends the ball into the same slot where countless centres have gone before. Matt Morton and Nathan Clarke have swallowed up and spat out others exactly like this one or Duncan McNally has come assertively to claim them instead. So fatigue is possibly to blame for the confusion now. McNally can't take the ball, which escapes from his fingers. Steven Roberts pokes a boot at the rebound. From close range the ball strikes Charlie Robinson on the leg, looping up and away from him and towards his own goal. Below the bar – while McNally is on his knees and Clarke is on his backside – Stewart Walker is like a stage-contortionist, trying toraise his right leg high enough and work his body sideways and into the right position to hook the deflection away. If this had been an average Sunday on Tilery 1, there'd have been no referee's assistant to raise his flag and tell us the ball is over the line before Walker gets to it. Indeed, some assistants in the professional game wait timorously for the referee to look at them before daring to make a decision alone. Here the flag goes up in a billowing flash of yellow and without hesitation. Westwood registers it and races along the touchline, celebrating as he goes. Several hundred Hardwick fans make enough of a racket to shake the Infinity Bridge. Gym collapse. In that instant we begin to refer to their challenge for the Cup in the past tense. There is no way back. The goal, for which Robinson is blameless, sucks away whatever grains of confidence and stamina are left. Cramp and the slump of exhaustion claim many of them now.

One blow leads to another. Only four minutes later Morton puts Clarke under pressure with a slack, cross-field pass. Nathan Mulligan gets hold of it, draws McNally and squares for Sonni Coleman. When faced with an open goal, and plenty of time in which to accept it, Len Shackleton, also from the North East, always wanted to dribble the ball to the goal-line, get down on his hands and knees and then head it in. Coleman could almost do this. Instead he pushes his shot into the gaping net. He goes on a curving run, ripping off his shirt and wheeling it around his head the way soldiers of the Middle Ages wielded the flanged mace into battle.

There have been happy moments in the match for Gym, but no happy ending. Even pouring their heart all over the pitch hasn't been enough to better Hardwick, who have been punishing company. The Shah's trophy, which Westwood handed to the courier less than eight weeks ago, is about to be returned to him, freshly polished and tied up in the FA's ribbons.

It's usually easier to be precise about the end of something rather than the start. The start can be hazy and indecisive – full of half-steps or sideways shuffles, decisions nearly taken or the incremental piling up of different circumstances. We lose our bearings in trying to identify one from the other, so in most cases that definitive moment – the real beginning of a thing – can't quite be pinned down. But Hardwick Social can trace back their recent success to source, which is Andy Westwood's decision to take over from his father.

Shortly before the trophy presentation, which will take place on a stage the FA assemble for them, I watch Westwood come to the front row of the stand, where his fiancée and two children are sitting. I asked him a week ago how many hours he spent per week on Hardwick's behalf. He tried to calculate them and then gave up. The future Mrs Westwood, he said, was 'very understanding' about his commitment even though she wasn't a rabid football fan.

Westwood was still a player when his father died and saw himself as such. He became manager to 'keep the club going' in his memory and also for the sake of his pals, who were in the team. He had to learn how to drop some of them from the side on occasions, but still retained their friendship. There is always something to do: checking on players, answering texts and emails, following the progress of other teams, always planning for the next match. Often he even finds himself acting as agony-uncle. Players will share problems about jobs, relationships, life. 'We're a family,' he says of Hardwick. He then adds the short explanation that binds them together, making this match and all the others worthwhile. 'We love football – every one of us'.

This is just as well. Hardwick have another game on Tuesday night.

29 April 2018: Gym United v Hardwick Social
Gym United 0 Hardwick Social 2 (AET)

Gym United: McNally, Bond, Morton, Clarke, White (Walker 106), Bailey, Bolton (Robinson 76), Brame, Melanson, Call (Proctor 73), Wood.
Subs not used: Viner, Thurrold

Hardwick Social: Arthur, Carter, Risbrough, Roberts (Mulligan 110), Bishop, Coulthard, Mulligan, Ward, Coleman, Owens (Garbutt 95), Stockton (Posthill 107).
Subs not used: Petijean, Hannah

SCORERS
Hardwick Social: Robinson 109 (og) Coleman 114

BOOKED
None

Referee: K. Johnson
Attendance: 422

THE KINGS OF THE CAR PARK

6 May: Asda, Manchester Road, Bolton

Already, though kick-off is more than three hours away, the sun is so hot that no cloud would dare interfere with it. There isn't even a faint drag of breeze to draw the early heat from the day. Often, at this time of year, there is so much rain that we stop believing in the possibility of summer, but this is going to be an afternoon for deckchairs on the cut lawn, charcoal barbecues and cold beers. The car park at Asda, within strolling distance of Bolton's town centre, is slowly beginning to fill. Sunday's baroquely outdated trading laws mean the supermarket can't actually sell anything until 11a.m., but is able to slide open the front doors half an hour beforehand. Customers can pull things off the shelves and then queue to pay for them as soon as the clock strikes.

But I haven't come to shop. I have come to walk about and look around.

This Asda, like every other, wouldn't win an architectural prize for artistic innovation or aesthetic niceties. It is flat-roofed. The façade is ghost-white panelling or sheet glass, slightly tinted. The retail park on which it counts as the major attraction is dully prosaic. There is a dry cleaner's, a craft superstore, a rival – but much more modest – food 'emporium', a sandwich takeaway, a fitness centre. You don't linger, but come and go as quickly as possible. Across the busy, two-lane Manchester Road is The King William IV, a pub that has had no beer for almost two decades. Only the signage of its old self remains, clinging to the building as though no one is prepared to accept the finality of closure. Nearby are rows of terraced housing. Some slope uphill, and the small slates on the roof of each home catch the sun, shining at you like pocket mirrors.

It is said that anything can look half-beautiful in the right light. I am no longer entirely convinced of that. You'd struggle to prettify this scene without a lot of tarting up first. But the spot as it is today – mundane and unglamorous – isn't the point. What it was yesterday is all that counts.

The Premier League still has another week to run, but Manchester City will collect their trophy at tea-time, barely 13 miles away. The FA Cup Final is a fortnight from now, but again and so predictably throws together two of the mighty top six when the competition really needs a scrap between underdogs to stir some romance into the occasion. The World Cup is almost upon us too, the odds on England's reshaped side cut to 20-1. But every story requires a full stop and this is the only logical place to put that dot on to the page. Wherever I have gone, however circuitously, has always been leading here. The end has taken me back to the beginning, which is appropriate.

Unlikely as it seems, this is where L. S. Lowry came in his long black coat and his black trilby. This is what inspired his painting *Going to the Match*. This was once Burnden Park, the artist's blessed plot. If you didn't know this in advance, you would barely realise it now. There isn't much to alert keen football tourists to that fact or to draw them further in. Near the entrance to Asda, fixed to the wall, you hardly notice the gold-plate plaque that commemorates the thirty-three people who died in a crush at the Railway End of the ground in 1946. High above the tills are square black and white photographs, which stretch back to the late 19th century. You have to severely crick your neck to see them properly. Here is the Bolton team of the 1880s. The waxed moustaches worn by a few of the players are impressively luxuriant. Here are the trio of FA Cup wins that made the 1920s roar for the club. Here, thirty years on, is a fourth Cup success at Wembley in 1958. These photos, just a token and an unimaginative nod to the past, are grandly branded 'The History of Bolton Wanderers'. If this is history, it is brief and incompletely told. It is the equivalent of sticking up a dozen facsimiles of Lowry's work and then claiming each of them represents everything you'll ever need to know about his long life. The gallery at Asda also offers, albeit unsatisfactorily, glimpses of

Burnden Park as it used to be. None adequately conveys even what I, who came only rarely, remember of the sight and the scale of the ground.

New experiences provoke old memories. I first saw a match at Burnden Park near the end of the 1970s; Lowry had only recently died, aged eighty-eight. It was drizzling and I followed a bloom of black umbrellas from the railway station. The floodlight pylons, colossally taller than the covered stands, were ablaze like the beam of a lighthouse. The windows of that now defunct pub, affectionately known locally as 'The King Bill,' were ablaze too, a mellow yellow. The Railway End still existed then. Not long afterwards I came back and saw the club's own photographs, hung in black wooden frames along the narrow corridors around the board room. The finest of them, Burnden Park at its best, was taken in 1952, pre-dating even *Going to the Match*. The photographer displays a genius for evocation. A train chuffs along the line that once ran above the Railway End. The train has gone a little way past the goalposts, bringing both impact and balance to the composition. From the black funnel white steam streams in fat clouds across the sky. The engine and the trail of that steam, instead of the players and the heaving terrace, is where the eye travels first, moving from left to right.

I only ever saw Burnden Park in the dark, which is why working out the angle from which Lowry chose to capture it proved difficult. I also didn't recognise the stands in front of me from his painting. I put this down merely to time and tide. Art is the result of the character and the quirks of whoever produces it. And artists can get away with tweaking or wholly adjusting the landscape – leaving something out, reducing something else in size that would otherwise be a blot on the picture. I didn't realise until much later that Lowry had been more concerned with capturing 'atmosphere' than depicting the ground faithfully. 'If I had shown things as they were it would not have looked like a vision,' he'd said.

Today, taking in the retail park, I can plot across it the longitude and latitude of where things used to be. Even former kings can be found in car parks, so it doesn't sound absolutely ridiculous to admit that I saw the tarmac and concrete as a spread of grass. I could be standing in the same place where Frank Worthington nutmegged a stricken defender; the same place where Sam Allardyce scooped an attacker over the perimeter wall with a tackle typical of 1970s subtlety; the same place – near the penalty spot perhaps – where Nat Lofthouse climbed to head in so powerfully that the goalkeeper didn't see the ball but heard only the swishing sound it made against the net. I dwelt for a while on Lofthouse. When I met him, and we spoke about Lowry, he was in his early sixties, a still sturdy man in good physical shape. He could have bundled me over the line with a nudge of his right shoulder.

Bolton said goodbye to Burnden Park in 1997. Their final game, a 4–1 win over Charlton, was immaterial to promotion because the League One Championship already belonged to them. The trophy was picked up and paraded that night, a send-off sentimentally perfect. When the match was over, the last ball kicked, fans liberated mementoes of whatever was at hand and could be carried away. As the decades roll by, and the generations die out, fewer and fewer will remember Burnden Park. But planks of seating, like pieces of driftwood, or part of the stands, slices of turf and other rescued bits and pieces will remain of it, heirlooms to be inherited.

And, of course, there will always be *Going to the Match*.

Emphasising that football was a passionate part of his hinterland, Lowry painted other scenes of it. A couple of them show a game from behind one of the goals, the ball airborne. (Possibly Lowry chose that location because he couldn't let go of his own boyhood heroics between the posts.) Another is seen distantly and from above, the crowd standing dozens deep on the touchline. The mass of people resembles a dark mount around a picture. Another still focuses solely and close-up on the spectators; the players aren't there at all. You wouldn't refuse any of them as a present to put above the mantle – each is trademark Lowry, after all – but none surpasses *Going to the Match*.

We never know what we will regret not seeing until fairly late in our lives when, looking back, we apportion proper worth and value to our experiences. We don't normally agonise over what happened before we were born either. We accept that what we missed wasn't our fault, which makes mourning it irrational. But if some physicist does eventually invent H. G. Wells's Time Machine, I'd buy a ticket for the early 1950s to see what Lowry saw at Burnden Park. I wish I'd been there, holding the oils and the brushes for him. Lowry may or may not have taken the odd slither of Maine Road or Turf Moor and added them to the ground's portrait. I don't mind and it doesn't matter. He achieved that 'atmosphere' and the ardour for football, which he sought. It pours out of the canvas.

If you try hard enough, you can still feel it while standing in Asda's car park. With imagination, the painting will rise up in front of you. I still see it when the Macron Stadium, Bolton's home for the past twenty years, looms out of the landscape twenty minutes later.

I bought a seat in advance for Bolton Wanderers v Nottingham Forest. I almost didn't turn up to use it. I was reluctant to let that match get in the way of L. S. Lowry's. I was even more reluctant to allow the gabled architecture of the Macron to impinge on 'his' plain and simple Burnden Park. But Bolton, facing relegation, need to win and must hope that the two clubs immediately above them, Burton Albion and Barnsley, don't do likewise.

It is ironic that Burnden Park became a retail park and that the Macron sits alongside one too. There is even an Asda here. The Bolton fans meander around it, subdued through apprehension. The only shouting comes from a town crier in tricorn hat and embroidered regalia. He is ringing his bell. The temperature is in the early seventies and so, I'd guess, is he. He is grey-bearded and red-faced and looks as though he might be about to melt in his heavy suit, leaving nothing behind but a heap of hot woollen clothes.

Expediency rather than wanderlust brought Wanderers here. The Macron is out of town, beside the M61 and green shallow hills. You see its elevated struts, spread above the ground's roof like a spider's web, well in advance of reaching it.

I didn't expect much from the match. The high stakes engendered only low expectations. The first half, nervy and goalless, fulfilled them. Forest missed three classic chances. One of them was directly in front of goal and 6 yards out. Bolton did nothing but smack the base of a post. The news, which wasn't good, came in from Pride Park, where Barnsley were facing Derby, and Deepdale, where Burton were pitted against Preston. The Bolton fans groused and grew bitter or stewed in their silence. The Forest fans, hemmed into the top tier of the South Stand, were quieter still.

During that FA Cup tie against Arsenal at the City Ground, I'd heard what I still regard as the club's signature song. It is based on 'Mull of Kintyre', appropriated almost as soon as Wings released it three and half months into Forest's League Championship season. The lyrics, bespoke to them and sung without the accompaniment of bagpipes or pipe drums, put the City Ground where the west coast peninsula should be, and then tell of the mist that rolls in from the Trent rather than off the Atlantic, which is exactly what used to happen when the stand behind the goal was a modest shed with a corrugated roof and the fog, congealing like a London pea-souper, would occasionally force the postponement of matches or their abandonment mid-way through. The Trent End is not a melodiously sweet choral choir and the song is not a euphony either, but hearing it dragged me back in one blinding flash of floodlit memories to Forest's great team of that era. Football songs release the bathroom vocalist in all of us too inhibited to go solo in public. There is no better example of it than the YouTube clip of Hibernian supporters singing 'Sunshine on Leith' at the Scottish Cup Final of 2016. Only search for it if you want to be grabbed emotionally by the gut. Even two verses will leave you reaching for a hankie. The rendition is as tender as a lullaby and every expression in it is imbued with the love of supporting that club at that moment.

The genesis of adopting the likes of 'Sunshine on Leith' or of amending 'Mull of Kintyre', as well as the genealogy of how each tune took hold, can be contested things, like paternity. But who cares who sang, way back, the opening note of 'You'll Never Walk Alone' on The Kop at Anfield? Or when those pretty bubbles first began floating high into the East London air at West Ham? What matters is only the way in which these songs capture community togetherness, which is what football provides and revives. And because each is passed on like folklore – fathers teaching sons what their own fathers taught them – the music becomes layered and meaningful.

I had hoped to hear a burst of 'Mull of Kintyre' to enliven the drabness of the game. This never came, but in the end we didn't need it.

*   *   *

The Booker Prize winning novelist Julian Barnes is Leicester-born and committed for life to the club of his home city. He is 'a Fox' and 'entirely monogamous about it', he says. In the year Claudio Ranieri took Leicester to the title, Barnes, as pleased and as bewildered as everyone else, wrote about fandom. 'As the run in approached, my behaviour began to show the nerves my team seemed immune to . . . I knew how much I really, really wanted Leicester to win.' Fandom, he concluded, 'routinely consists of a swirling mix of stupid love (and) howling despair.' Barnes is right, but rarely do the emotions he described bump up against one another within a minute and a half.

Strange things occur on the last day of the season. None, though, is stranger than here. In the sixty-seventh minute Bolton take the lead with a shot that seems to slice fortunately off the outside of a boot. For three, dizzy minutes more the Macron thinks of itself as a safe haven from the drop. Then Forest equalise. It is a long-range shot that bounces in front of the goalkeeper, eludes his slow flop of a dive and pokes into the far corner of the net. With eleven minutes to go, as though things for Bolton could hardly be darker, Forest score again. A volley, well struck but hardly a missile, finds the gap between four defenders and also the three feet of space between the 'keeper and the post.

Those who think Bolton's chances of survival have shrunk to nothing begin to get up and go. This is either from disillusionment or because not being there when the trap door swings open will allow them to pretend it hasn't happened at all until the League Two fixtures for 2018–19 are published next month.

The dead rise slowly at first.

Bolton go deep into the Forest half. It is clear that, even while ahead, Forest could break, and so you wait for the snap. The first crack is heard with only three minutes left. That hoariest trick of all – the long ball – renders Forest indecisive as it falls, spinning out of the sun, and can't be scrambled away. A weak shot takes a deflection and dribbles in. Bolton are level. Those fans who had left most recently, but are still on the stairwells, find themselves wrong-footed. Enticed by screaming that can only mean one thing, they make a U-turn. Heads reappear at the top of the steps. Even then you suppose coming back is a sucker's errand; Bolton surely can't score again because Forest surely can't be caught twice in the odd few minutes that remained.

A club's fortunes will always climb and sink and climb and sink again. Seldom does this occur so spectacularly. There's another long ball. There's more flinching from Forest. There's a cross from the byeline. There's a header, buried inside the far post. The scorer is Aaron Wilbraham. He is thirty-eight. He's had a journeyman's sort of career, but not an unsuccessful one. Beginning in the same year that Burden Park closed down, it has taken him to ten different clubs. This is only his second goal for Bolton, their rescue assured because of it. Barnsley and Burton are heartsick instead of them.

Dust gathers quickly on seasons past because the following one is always just over the nearest hill. But the finale to this game, rousing and so overwhelming, will be remembered, not only in August, when Bolton return again, but long afterwards. The boys who were here will one day recall the match as old men, but still talk about it in a young voice. The match programme will be saved. So will the ticket stub, the team sheet, a photo or two, a press cutting.

To their credit, Bolton annually hold a service of 'Remembrance and Thanksgiving' to commemorate their past, including Burden Park. The next is in early June. I look at the advertisement for it in today's match programme and wonder whether L. S. Lowry would want to immortalise the Macron Stadium in paint. Probably not. As attractive as it is – much better than most – the ground would be too modern for a Victorian such as him. But would Lowry want to paint the fans who, intoxicated by this result, took over the pitch? Yes, absolutely. It's astonishing how many plump-cheeked, portly men can suddenly run at a goodly speed, belly wobbling, when the mood takes them and the incentive is there. The pitch was soon covered in them. A club never loves you the way you love it. It is too big for that. But there are times, especially when months of anguish are redeemed by late glory, when it seems you and it are indivisible from one another. It was like that for Bolton and their fans. You heard it from their lips. You saw it in their eyes.

You always have to pay particular attention to the extremities in those Lowry's paintings featuring crowds. There are usually a couple of figures who stand out at the edges, slightly away from the mainstream or loitering among an isolated group. Lowry urges you to look at these individuals, who have been picked out and planted there deliberately to represent the multitude. Were Lowry living and painting at this hour, preserving the celebrations, I know which scene would serve that purpose today.

At first I didn't see them. I was trying to take everything in panoramically and so missed the young boy and his father who had come to a stop in the penalty area. The boy was blonde and he wore a replica shirt with a number 7 sewn on to the back of it. I assumed the shirt was a birthday present. I also assumed the number could be his age. A few yards away the father, kneeling in front of him, was about to snatch a photograph. Other Bolton fans, generously respectful of the moment, made curved runs around both of them, giving the father the space he needed to complete the shot. Father and son then chased one another towards the centre-circle, where I quickly lost sight of them. I thought afterwards about how that prized photo would look in the family album. The father had deliberately framed his son in the goalposts that Bolton had just been attacking. The goalposts were a fixed point that attached the boy specifically to this date and to this match and also authenticated the photo of him there.

And so I remembered Liverpool . . .

Michael Kirkham is a kind of L. S. Lowry with a camera instead of a brush. He's Liverpudlian, rather than Mancunian, but he and the painter have things in common. Like Lowry, Kirkham roams obscure streets and explores the nooks and niches that are usually familiar only to the locals. These places exist down back-roads, through alleys, around corners or at the bottom of cul-de-sacs. No guide books record them. No tourist buses take you there. Also like Lowry, he feels duty-bound to record what fascinates him before it is washed away, pulled up, knocked down or built over. He's attempting, as Lowry did, to hold on to what he knows will disappear, possibly very soon. His hope is to grab an image of it before that happens, passing on the present so someone else can appreciate it in the future. Unlike Lowry, however, his work doesn't have people in them; for people would only get in the way and obstruct the view.

For the past three and a half years Kirkham has been grafting on an unpaid project called Urban Goals. He began wandering about the areas he knew well in Liverpool, and then migrated to others around the country that he hardly knew, if at all. He's been taking photographs of goalposts. The great, majestic photos of football are nearly always about movement – the action in something or the reaction to it. A shot filling the net. A defender charging into a striker or tussling with him for a high ball. A manager's or a player's expression, the emotion so pronounced that only the skimpiest of captions is required to explain it.

Kirkham's pictures are still life in a landscape. You'll find goals in deserted roads, chalked or painted on to walls, the red brick pockmarked and crumbling. You'll find some rusty posts on scrub land, where the grass has either been worn away to brown dirt or become thickly overgrown like Hardwick Social's pitch on Tilery 1. You'll find others in front of blocks of flats or drab tenements that were built during that phase of uncouth, brutalist design in the 1950s and 1960s. Some goals, net-less of course, exist among buildings that are ruins, half demolished. The rubble has been left to decay before clearing it up begins. Urban Goals sounds a curiously quixotic endeavour, but Kirkham is creating something that is moving, beautiful and very worthwhile.

The afternoon before I met him I strolled through Liverpool to look at the Mersey. When I got to it, the water was as muddy-brown as the Mississippi. The day was dark, even shortly past noon, and flakes of snow the size of a baby's fist fell rapidly. The flakes blew into my face and refused to melt in the cold. They stuck in layers to my black coat and to my flat cap. I stared at myself in the doorway of the Tate; I looked like a crystal chandelier.

But the following morning was brilliantly blue. The two of us set off from near St Luke's, Liverpool's bombed-out church (weeks later I thought of it again when I stood in the Kaiser-Wilhelm Gedächtniskirche in Berlin) and then headed towards Toxteth and Sefton Park. We walked wide roads that had lovely over-hanging trees on them and past high-windowed Georgian homes. Kirkham spoke about how he grew up here. About how he turned to photography in early adulthood (he is thirty-nine). About how he'd done an assortment of jobs beforehand, including roofing. We also talked about his love of Liverpool as a city and of Liverpool as a football club. About his ambition to turn Urban Goals into an exhibition and, eventually, into a book too. And about how, now the idea has received a little publicity, he regularly receives emails from friends and strangers alerting him to goals scattered far and wide. Before setting off to find them he tries to locate others close by on Google Street Maps, maximising his return from train and bus fares on a shoestring budget. 'Sometimes,' he says, 'I'll get there and discover that what I'm looking for has just been painted over. Or I'll be told the building was demolished a few weeks before.' He adds philosophically: 'I'm chasing these things down against time.'

We stopped off at Jermyn Street. A goal was neatly painted, white on red, on the side of a house that is supposed to have once belonged to a naval captain in the 19th century. 'Anyone anywhere in the world will recognise what a goal is if it's painted on to a wall. You don't have to tell them what it is,' said Kirkham, articulating the way in which football impacts even on the lives who of those don't follow it.

On Threlfall Street, a minuscule cul-de-sac running parallel to a former school, Kirkham pointed out a car repair shop, the faint outline of a goal on its green-blue wooden door. The paint had blistered badly in the sun. There are three other goals in this small space. As a boy, Robbie Fowler kicked a ball about here. We agreed that English Heritage should put up a red plaque to commemorate that.

The pricking spire of St Bede's Church and the tower of the Anglican Cathedral are the backdrop to Loudon Grove. Here the goals are scrawled in beige paint on a slatted fence and on a wall that face one another. Between them is an oblong of land about 20-odd yards long and 10 yards wide. Terraced housing, four storeys high, overlooks it.

The bar for football movies isn't high – think of *Escape to Victory*, for pity's sake – but *The Miracle of Bern* clears it by a country mile, achieving a height too competitive for the opposition. The film uses Germany's World Cup win of 1954 to portray a human drama. A father, an emaciated prisoner from the Russian front, finally returns home. His family don't recognise him and he's unaware his wife has given him a second son, born shortly after his military service began.

The son is football mad, but he and the father, who was once a decent amateur, can't bond even over the game. In a short stand-out scene the father walks alone on to the wasteland where his son often plays. There are two small goals, each lopsidedly out of shape, and a ball that is as ragged as a cauliflower. The father wears a dark brown double-breasted suit, stiff shoes and a floppy-brimmed trilby. He begins playing keepy-uppy, flicking the ball from foot to knee to shoulder. You see in his pinched features the sheer, simple release of doing something that is ordinary and fulfilling. He is summoning a pleasant past in which he can also take refuge. He finally bicycle-kicks a shot between the posts, the ball bouncing once before the line and once after it. From then on you know for sure the estrangement between father and son is over. The glue of reconciliation will be football. Anyone who has ever gone to a match with their father will look at it and think of him. And anyone who hasn't will think of him also, wishing dearly he had taken them to a game just once.

This bit of Loudon Grove reminded me of the makeshift pitch in *The Miracle of Bern*. The ground was charred black near the halfway spot, the ashy evidence of a bonfire still traceable. A white plastic chair, one leg broken, and an assortment of carrier bags littered the grass. This is nonetheless someone's Wembley. Or Anfield. Or Goodison Park. Countless cup finals, internationals or Merseyside derbies have been fought here. You can turn it into anything you want. At the end of this month Kirkland's team, Liverpool, go to Kiev to face the holders, Real Madrid, in the final of the Champions League. No doubt that game will be replayed here as well; and those in it will hear that baroque Uefa adaptation of Handel's 'Zadok the Priest' as each goal flies in.

More than any other sport football mirrors our times socially, culturally and economically. Today, who and what counts as 'working class' is hazy in a way that it certainly wasn't when I grew up. But Kirkham's photos also remind you of a different era, not so terribly long ago. When football was played regularly in the street. When men employed in manual labour left behind, for ninety blissful minutes, hardscrabble lives. When women, if not a rarity at matches, were scarce inside grounds to say the least. There was a foolish snobbery about football then. Some thought it was beneath them, a 'crude game' for 'common people'. That attitude hasn't been prevalent since the early 1990s, but Kirkham's photos show the difference between the soul of the modern game and the soul of the old one. They are social history. They are also art. And they tell a story for anyone who has enough imagination to see it and enough emotional rapport with the game to know how much it matters.

At the Macron Stadium, Bolton's fans, still in a slightly dazed state, trail away in the mid-afternoon sunshine, not quite sure what to do with their weekends for the next two and a half months. Their secular faith, like ours, will be fed by the arrival and departure of players, the manager's optimism, the promise of the opening week's fixtures and their own high hopes and unrealisable expectations, which always accompany the fresh start of each new season. Until then the fortunes or misfortunes of England in Russia will sustain us.

The match we've just seen, as though it had been deliberately staged that way, gave us more than we could ever have expected. In that soap opera finish, greeted as though everyone in Bolton was celebrating a birthday, we saw how fandom can leave you with a lump in the throat and why people, otherwise rational, have every reason to become compulsively passionate about it. We also saw why, increasingly, we identify the success of towns and cities – as they identify themselves – through the club that represents them.

It isn't easy being a fan, which is why we can be so contradictory. We'll criticise a player for leaving our club, accusing him of disloyalty, but welcome a defector from someplace else with an embrace and without a qualm. We'll venerate a manager, as if he's worthy of canonisation, until he loses half a dozen games. Then we'll hound him out. We'll excuse the sneaky little acts of gamesmanship our own team employs while condemning everyone else's as wicked cheating.

It doesn't stop there.

We complain that we have to pay so much for tickets so players can earn so much in wages, but we demand nonetheless that our chairman buys big. We know that the lives and livelihoods of the worshipped (the player) and the worshipper (us), once not so far apart, are hugely separate now. We pander willingly to it nonetheless, buying the merchandise and perpetuating the starry glamour. We're aware the game can be over-hyped, but succumb to it all the same. We understand this too. Football, caught often in internecine politics, has a bad habit of dealing with unpalatable things by either fudging them or by pretending they don't exist in the first place. We appreciate there is corruption – both great and small – because the top level is there to make a buck or two. And we're perfectly aware that those who run the game will nearly always place the need of the product ahead of the need of the consumer; they know more than enough of us will simply fall into line.

No, football isn't perfect. But what is?

We return to it, week after week, because it helps some of us to enjoy life more and others to endure it better. Because it is a common language among strangers, even with rival allegiances. Because we can't wait to see another blazing goal, another blinding save, another match like the one today. Because we can't stop thinking about it.

My father, beginning with spring, would go through the meteorological seasons only because he could then add what he'd call 'the Fifth'. It was football, ever present.

I leave Bolton remembering that and hearing him say it, knowing the statement to be even truer now than when he originally came up with it. I am thinking of Newcastle in last August's first game, which seems half a lifetime ago . . . of Davide Zappacosta's screamer against Qarabag (no, he didn't mean to shoot) . . . of modest Nethermoor Park and Guiseley, glumly relegated . . . of sublime Mo Salah and also the statue of Sir Stanley Matthews in the gloaming at Stoke . . . of a Kevin De Bruyne pass . . . of Paul Pogba in that Manchester derby we'll recollect till breathing our last breaths . . . of that Beatles song played to no one but me in the deserted Scottish Football Museum . . . of Wembley, finely dressed, on League Cup Final day . . . of Andy Westwood, the lads of Hardwick Social and the Shah's small pot of silver . . . and, lastly, of grey Salford on the summer solstice and L. S. Lowry's love letter in oil paint that hangs in his own gallery.

You're supposed to have taught yourself something by the end of any great journey. I have taught myself that harking back is harmless, but the higher purpose of nostalgia is surely to show us something. What it shows me is that football, which has had such a long claim on my attention and my affections, is better now than it's ever been. Emphatically so, in fact. It is quicker and slicker, and more attractively skilful and tactically smarter. We're actually in a bit of a Golden Age – though we're in danger of realising that only retrospectively.

I've also learnt that what doesn't change – and never will – is the visceral experience you get from football, a level of happiness that seems unreasonable sometimes. The fan, who fell for football irrevocably and at first sight, understands this intuitively and deeply. There's no need for further elaboration because football is something you feel and something you need, like water. It is a game of and for the heart.

Lowry knew that. He tells us so every time we look at *Going to the Match*.

6 May 2018: Bolton Wanderers v Nottingham Forest
Bolton Wanderers 3 Nottingham Forest 2

Bolton: Alnwick (Howard 45), Little, Wheater, Beevers, Robinson, Pratley (La Fondre 59), Henry, Ameobi, Vela, Morais (Noone 77), Wilbraham.
Subs not used: Taylor, Karacan, Buckley, Burke

Forest: Kapino, Darikwa, Hobbs, Fox, Osborn, Bridcutt, (Vellios 76), Colback, Watson (Guedioura 76), Lolley, Brereton, Tomlin (Cash 61).
Subs not used: Lichaj, Mancienne, Bouchalakis, Smith

SCORERS

Bolton: La Fondre 67, Wheater 87, Wilbraham 88
Forest: Osborn 70, Colback 79

BOOKED

Bolton: Robinson, Pratley, Wilbraham
Forest: Darikwa, Fox, Bridcutt, Lolley

Referee: S. Duncan
Attendance: 18,289

WHAT HAPPENED NEXT

What Happened Next? Well, you already know and won't forget it, which makes the question a little superfluous. Somewhere in *Going to the Match*, I make the point that life constantly has a habit of turning out in wild ways we don't expect and so can't foresee. Those four and a bit weeks of the 2018 World Cup is undeniably proof of that. We never saw coming what we got; damn fools us.

When, not long before the finals kicked off, Harry Kane put on his best poker face and insisted that England were going East determined to 'win' the thing, we responded with derision. We assumed, as captain, Kane was obliged to pretend for appearance's sake; he was being preposterously aspirational. We didn't imagine he sincerely meant all he said – or that he intended us to take him seriously too. England as potential World Cup winners? Well, Kane would say that, wouldn't he? A few other long shots seemed much more plausible then. World peace at last, perhaps. Finding extra-terrestrial life on other planets – or extra-terrestrial life finding us on ours. The invention of some nifty home-gadget allowing you to spin straw into gold.

We were sceptical at best and sorely mocking at worst because England had hardly inspired hope, let alone expectation, in the build up to the tournament. We had experienced before so many crashes, dismal failures and let downs that we were bracing ourselves for another. Even as the World Cup progressed successfully, the soberly hard-headed among us still kept one foot solidly on the floor. Only in the latter stages did our mood really shift. Perhaps we could be all-conquering after all.

Human nature dictates that we don't usually over-analyse when our lives go well. We worry doing so will tempt Fate, causing it to go badly again. But, during the build-up to the semi-final, I gave in to temptation. I re-read the reports and the reaction to the England-Slovenia match at Wembley, which had secured our qualification for Russia early last October.

No, I hadn't misremembered. It truly was *that* awful – yawningly dull, dispiriting, devoid almost entirely of merit. Paper planes did fly. Wembley, hardly full in the first place, did empty quickly at the end, leaving the England players to applaud empty seats. The politest descriptions of England's performance on that miserably rotten night was 'lacklustre' and 'mediocre'. Other criticisms had sharper edges: among these were 'hopeless', 'useless', 'dire' and 'inept' – etcetera, etcetera. The dictionary was almost exhausted of insults. Afterwards the team was labelled 'The Unconvincables'. A headline went so far as to ask: 'Why has a nation fallen out of love with England?' The response on social media was far bloodier. You got a choice education in how many expletives can fit into 140 characters without losing the thread or the sense of a sentence.

I could go on . . .

One former England international (ok, it was Phil Neville) reckoned England were 'a million miles away from winning the World Cup'. At that stage, his estimation of our chances sounded like a miscalculation only insofar as the mileage he mentioned seemed a little conservative. A bookmaker even cheekily offered fans the chance to 'watch paint dry' rather than another England match. The paint, seen actually drying, was streamed live from its Facebook page.

If a week is a long time in politics, then nine months – in effect a whole league season – is an epoch in football.

Only five of the team that started against Slovenia also started in the Luzhniki Stadium against Croatia. Six of the 12 substitutes at Wembley didn't go with the squad to Russia. Jordan Pickford and Harry Maguire, establishing themselves as national treasures in only a few matches, didn't make their England debuts until later in the autumn.

In the build-up to the quarter final against Columbia, the BBC showed a brief excerpt from the recently released biographical documentary about Sir Bobby Robson: *More than a Manager*. His widow, Elsie, held a piece of white, A5 paper on which her husband had written eleven principles of good management. These included:

Be passionate
Be open minded – a good listener
Set good examples
Understand individuals
Be trustworthy

As Lady Elsie read out each of them, I thought what Sir Bobby had left us was a patently decent blueprint for life as well for the game he loved and which loved him in return. That, of course, was the mark of the man.

The BBC used the piece of film to illustrate how much Gareth Southgate's outlook mirrored Sir Bobby's. We owe a debt to Southgate. Those of us who already own a wardrobe full of waistcoats are especially grateful to him. For once, we're ahead of the fashion curve. More significant than sartorial style is Southgate's demeanour. There was no arrogance in him or about him. There was no grand-standing swagger either. You never got the idea that Southgate thought himself to be above his team or superior to the supporters following them. Quite the opposite.

People often reach a turning point – but still refuse to turn because it is safer, more convenient and less contentious to hold the same course, maintaining the line of least resistance. With hindsight, I see the game against Slovenia as a hinge moment for England. Southgate surely recognised it as such too and began then to reshape and rethink for Russia. You still needed balls the size of pawn shop brass to do it as he did, pinning your belief in the young.

It may not be sensible to hold your breath over this, but I'd hope that a few managers – their preening self-obsession almost on a par with Narcissus' – might try to tone it down a bit this season after witnessing Southgate's modest and undemonstrative approach in the technical area and at every press conference (no, you're right, we're probably asking too much on that score).

Truth to be told, and however churlish it seems to linger on this, you have to admit that England's passage to the semi final (wins over Panama, Tunisia, Columbia and Sweden) was about scaling a craggy outcrop rather Annapurna's south-face. It was as though a series of magic coincidences had weaved themselves together to make our half of the draw deliberately more comfortable. We took meaning from that synchronicity while it was occurring, as though destiny was lending us a hand.

Our run of good luck ran out against Croatia; extra time was a half-hour too far for us. We also search still for that midfielder who is capable of delivering the ball with a nip of creative flair. The consolation – a major one – is that we out-shone so many others during an outstanding World Cup.

Russia became an unlikely beauty spot for football. The tournament was 32 days of wonder, the drama spilling out of it. One great match always seemed to produce a greater match still. We saw some extraordinarily fabulous goals. Players, when faced with a ball that spun towards them like a whipped top, merely struck it first-time from distance between the angle of post and bar. Easy, really. We saw extraordinarily fabulous saves as well; goalkeepers reacting with reflex leaps and dives, beating down what seemed impossible to reach, never mind stop. The quality of the passing wasn't bad either . . .

In the last paragraphs of *Going to the Match* I mention a Golden Age that we risk acknowledging only retrospectively. Russia just may have awoken us to it. In fact, the World Cup – in ways big and small – summoned back so much of the previous season for me and crystallised it too.

Firstly, there were the personnel: De Bruyne and Hazard, Kane and Alli, Kompany and Willian and Kante *et al*. The Premier League provided almost 45 per cent of players who appeared in the semi-finals. I especially followed the progress of Paul Pogba. I thought always about the abuse he got at the Ethiad. There he was – only 99 days later – a World Cup winner with France. The goal he got in their 4–2 win over Croatia in the final was striking. More striking still was his decision not to dye his hair at all.

Secondly, there was the role of television. Not only did it showcase the matches superbly – every angle microscopically covered, every goal seen a dozen different ways, every action and reaction captured, replayed, analysed. It also reminded us of something very significant. Football will go on banking the cash, becoming expedentially richer from the money subscription TV tips into it, but terrestrial channels ought never to be starved of live games. The audience for the game widens when everyone can see it; otherwise you're playing only to the converted who are already well enough off to fork out a thousand quid a year to stay that way. (I don't know what it was like where you live, but I saw an enormous rise in the number of park kick-abouts.)

Thirdly, there was VAR, which is already changing the game and is about to change it further. The case in its favour is closed now; Russia did that.

Fourthly – and most importantly – the World Cup proved again that football is the globe's common language. And as for the way it unifies disparate people ... You saw this in the flags and the bunting, the street-parties and the sprayed beer, the crowds gathered in front of screens in public places and also the conversations in pubs and super-markets, on street corners and over the garden fence. For a while we forgot about everything else other than the next game. We were happy.

Apart from the obvious moments, I'll always remember the eccentric optimism of that chap from Leeds who got *England 2018 World Cup Winners* tattooed across his stomach during the group stage. We thought then he'd had a touch too much of the sun, the summer already so hot that it initially revived memories of 1976 rather than 1966. He had a 'premonition', he said, during half-time against Panama. If the tattoo was done, England would bring back the trophy.

He's been left with a unique souvenir of a memorable World Cup, which for us was the story of a beautifully heroic near miss. During it you'd have heard the phrase 'Football's Coming Home' so often that you probably sang it in your sleep. I can only say this:

Coming Home? It's never been away.

Newcastle v Tottenham

Against all expectations, and primarily because of the management of Rafa Benítez, **Newcastle** finished tenth in the Premier League. They got no further than the fourth round of the FA Cup, losing 3–0 to Chelsea, and lost in the second round of the League Cup to Nottingham Forest – at home. Jonjo Shelvey revealed he was seeing a psychologist to 'work on the mental side of things'. In December he was sent off again against Everton. Mike Ashley withdrew from negotiations to sell the club in mid-January.

There was no trophy for **Tottenham**. They came third in the league and lost the FA Cup semi-final to Manchester United – their eighth successive defeat at that stage of the competition. Harry Kane scored thirty goals in the League. Dele Alli claimed nine. At the season's end, Kane signed a new six-year contract and Mauricio Pochettino agreed a five-year deal.

Guiseley Town v Hartlepool United

Guiseley, despite going full-time, won only seven matches and finished bottom of the National League. Adam Lockwood was sacked two days after the game. His replacement, Paul Cox, was sacked in mid-February. The club appointed Sean St Ledger, the former Republic of Ireland international, as interim boss. A fourth manager was appointed for the 2018–19 season. James Ferguson stood down as chairman in April. The playing staff is part-time again and, near the end of the season, it was announced that Nethermore Park would remain the team's home.

Hartlepool, who finished fourteenth, parted company with Craig Harrison. He spent only eight months in charge. He was replaced by Matthew Bates, who became Manager of the Month for March after a run of five games unbeaten, the basis of survival. In December, the club was put up for sale and narrowly avoided the slide into administration. The new owner is ex Darlington chairman Raj Singh. Scott Loach, the goalkeeper, was named both the Supporters' Player of the Year and the Players' Player of the Year.

Chelsea v Qarabag

Chelsea reached the last sixteen, where Barcelona beat them comfortably. They finished outside the top four, thus failing to qualify for the Champions League, but won the FA Cup against Manchester United. Their season was dogged by almost constant speculation about the future of manager Antonio Conte. He was sacked in July. Plans to rebuild Stamford Bridge were suspended.

Qarabag retained their Azerbaijan League title, but got knocked out in the quarter-finals of the Cup. Despite finishing bottom in their Champions League group, they had the consolation of twice drawing with Atlético Madrid. Gurban Gurbanov remains in charge.

Davide Zappacosta admitted he was trying to cross the ball rather than score.

Burnley v Huddersfield Town

Burnley did more than cling on to their Premier League place. They were one of the teams of the season, qualifying for the Europa League after finishing seventh, a performance which brought acclaim for their boss, Sean Dyche. Chris Wood was their top scorer with eleven goals.

Huddersfield avoided relegation, drawing at both Manchester City and Chelsea to finish sixteenth. David Wagner was rewarded with a new, three-year contract amid speculation that other teams were chasing him.

Leicester City v West Bromwich Albion

Craig Shakespeare left **Leicester** that week after only four months in charge. A month and a half later he went to Everton as first team coach. Leicester appointed Claude Puel, who took them to ninth place. Jamie Vardy scored twenty goals.

Tony Pulis lasted only a month more at **West Brom**. When the sack came, the team was a point above the relegation zone and without a win in ten games. He went to Middlesbrough, losing in the Championship play-off semi-finals.

Alan Pardew took over at the Hawthorns, but left in April when the team were all but relegated. Darren Moore, as caretaker, performed miraculously before the drop was confirmed. Boaz Myhill made no further Premier League appearances.

The latest battle for Premier League rights, starting in 2019, saw Sky pay £3.57b – a discount of 14 per cent on its present deal – for four packages of games (128 matches per season) and BT pay around £900m for one package (52 games per season). In June Amazon handed over an undisclosed sum to show twenty Premier League matches from 2019. A fan wanting to watch every live game screened from 2019 to 1920 will pay about £1,000 per season.

Manchester City v Bristol City

Manchester City finished second to Chelsea in the WSL – six places above **Bristol City** –and also lost to them in the semi-final of the WFA Cup. Izzy Christiansen left the Ethiad to join Lyon in the summer. Their Champions League challenge ended in the semi-finals too – beaten by Lyon, the eventual trophy-winners. In the 2018–19 season, West Ham and Brighton will join the WSL and Manchester United, newly created, will appear in the Championship. During the season the new England manager, Phil Neville, complained to the FA after his team had to fly to America for a tournament in economy class. The FA have since 'reviewed' flight arrangements.

Stoke City v Liverpool

Stoke manager Mark Hughes was sacked on the night his side lost to League Two Coventry in the third round of the FA Cup. Stoke, under new boss Paul Lambert, went on to be relegated. Hughes moved on to manage one of his former clubs, Southampton, who avoided the drop. He got a new three-year contract because of it.

Liverpool finished fourth and reached the final of the Champions League, beaten by Real Madrid. Mo Salah became the PFA Player of the Year and the Football Writers' Player of the Year after scoring thirty-two goals in thirty-six games. It was a new Premier League record. Goalkeeper Simon Mignolet lost his place to Loris Karius, guilty of two mistakes in the Champions League Final (though concussion was subsequently cited as a mitigating factor for each of them).

Celtic v Hamilton Academical

To their League Cup triumph, **Celtic** predictably added the Championship, forcing Aberdeen into second spot and Rangers into third, and also the Scottish Cup. They lost to Zenit St Petersborg 3–1 on aggregate in the last thirty-two of the Europa League. **Hamilton** finished tenth in the SPL.

Nottingham Forest v Arsenal

Nottingham Forest appointed Aitor Karanka as manager barely before the dust had settled on their FA Cup win, but got knocked out in the next round – beaten by fellow Championship side, Hull – and finished only seventeenth in the table.

Arsenal. See Carabao Cup Final.

Wolverhampton Wanderers v Sheffield United

Wolves won the Championship with ninety-nine points – nine better than Cardiff. Diogo Jota finished as top scorer with sixteen goals. Benik Afobe, who hit six goals in 16 appearances, completed his £10m move from Bournemouth on 1 June. On 12 June he signed a six-month loan deal at Stoke. The deal contained an 'obligation to purchase him for an undisclosed fee'.

Sheffield United missed out on the plays. They finished sixth.

Manchester City v Arsenal

Manchester City: See Manchester derby.

In May Arsène Wenger left **Arsenal** after twenty-two years, 1,228 games and ten trophies. His win ratio was over 57 per cent. He failed only in not winning a European trophy. He spoke graciously of a passionate love for Arsenal that was present in 'every cell in my body'. He thanked the supporters for 'being such an important part of my life'.

Fleetwood Town v Plymouth Argyle

The fear of relegation was soon shed at **Fleetwood Town**. They finished on fifty-seven points – ten away from the drop. John Sheridan left at the end of the season. As early as mid-April, Fleetwood announced that Joey Barton would be their new manager. Sheridan was in charge for thirteen games, winning five of them. Nathan Pond also said his farewells to the club. He moved to Salford City.

Three points separated **Plymouth** from a play-off spot.

Germany v Brazil

Joachim Löw agreed a new contract, tying him to his job until 2022, before Germany went to Russia. There, the champions lost their first group game to Mexico, and later failed to qualify for the latter stages of the tournament for the first time since 1938. Brazil, who for a while looked so promising, lost in the quarter finals to Belgium.

Manchester City v Manchester United

Manchester City won the title with five games to spare – a Premier League record. They accumulated 100 points (another record) with thirty-two wins (a third record), overwhelmed second placed **Manchester United** by nineteen points (a fourth record), scored 106 goals (a fifth record) and had a goal difference of +76 (a sixth record). The others were: Most away wins (16). Most consecutive wins (18). Highest average possession (71 per cent). Most passes (28,242). A week after winning at the Etihad, United lost to the bottom club, West Brom, at Old Trafford, handing City the title. United's last chance to win a trophy evaporated in the FA Cup Final, losing 2–1 to Chelsea.

Gym United v Hardwick Social

Gym had the consolation of winning both the Bury and District Sunday League and the Knight's Lowe Knock Out Division One Cup. **Hardwick** retained their league title in the Stockton and District League by a margin of six points. It was their sixth title in a row and their eighth in nine years. Thirteen of their team figured in the FA Vase Final, which Stockton Town lost 1–0, to Thatcham. At the end season Hardwick decided to 'retire' as a team, resting on their achievement as double FA Sunday Cup winners.

AUTHOR'S NOTE AND ACKNOWLEDGEMENTS

The end of any book is about crossing i's and dotting t's (yes, surreally, think of it that way round) and taking commas out and then putting them back in again. I went through the process for *Going to the Match* on the weekend that Wembley staged three Cup finals. I looked up long enough from my desk to watch all of them.

The FA Cup Final, between Chelsea and Manchester United, scarcely energised the neutrals, thus confirming the common sense of my decision not to trek southwards to see it. In the FA Vase Final Stockton Town – a.k.a Hardwick Social – lost narrowly to Thatcham. Especially near the end, as the minutes ran away from them, I kicked every ball with the lads of Hardwick, a club for whom I felt such an instant affinity. Wanting them to win meant defeat was hard to take.

The FA Trophy pitted Bromley against Brackley Town.

I rooted not so much for Bromley as for my friend Dave Roberts. Dave is Bromley's Boswell. He is the author of *The Bromley Boys*, which details how a boyhood infatuation became a lifetime commitment and, more recently, of *Home and Away*, his shadowing of their first season in the National League.

It under-plays Dave's passion for Bromley more than just a bit to describe him as 'a supporter'. He is passionately devout. Few love a team the way Dave loves Bromley. Read the pinned tweet on his Twitter page:

'Woke up this morning and decided not to go to Barrow v Bromley. It's a four-hour journey. It's freezing. I've got a cold. I can't afford it and the game isn't exactly crucial. So how come I'm now on a train heading to Barrow?'

We know the answer to that question, and so does he.

Dave and I live in the same village. We get together about once a fortnight for lunch. We sift through the perfect nonsense and serial absurdities of the world before the conversation switches to the dominant topic, which is always one aspect or another of football and footballers. Sometimes, indulging in harmless whimsy, we speculate about what it would be like to kick a ball about again ourselves, each of us realising the ridiculousness of that even as we talk about it.

For more than half a century Dave had longed to watch Bromley at Wembley and to see them win there. The late 1960s side to which he lost his heart was so abjectly bad that wins came only very occasionally and every goal was rare enough to produce a moment of ecstatic surprise. Things improved from there, but producers of silver polish have seldom had Bromley as a customer.

I desperately hoped Dave would be rewarded for the bitter task of his fandom for them. Prospects, it has to be said, were set fair. Bromley's hour in the sun seemed, in the build-up, predetermined, actually. The draw had been benevolent towards them throughout the competition. The fiercer beasts of the National League had fallen reasonably quickly. And Brackley were a rung lower on the League ladder. Dave was still cagey. It was as though he feared that being even tentatively optimistic about the result would put a hex on everything.

He bought a seat in an executive box. He wore his replica shirt. He was interviewed shortly before kick-off on *BT Sport*. From my horizontal position on the sofa, I confidently waited for the foregone conclusion.

Nudging in front fairly early in the first half, Bromley couldn't extend their lead but held on to it despite a few squeaks, the odd lucky bobble, the occasional gasp and blow of relief. With a minute to go, tempting Fate, I sent Dave a text: 'Hope they let you receive the trophy,' I said.

With twenty-one seconds left, Brackley equalised.

I prayed Dave wouldn't blame my presumptuousness for the goal and thought nonetheless that Bromley would go on to roll Brackley over, reducing my stupidity to something he'd rib me about later on.

Then extra time came and went again in a slow, weary drag. What came next was the dread of the penalty shoot-out.

Bromley went ahead from the off, after Brackley missed weakly, and had soon successfully tucked away kicks two and three as well. I thought about sending Dave another text to make up for the previous one. Nothing could possibly go wrong for them now.

At this point you may sense that a 'but' is looming . . . well, here it is. But their fourth penalty cleared the bar like a rugby conversion. Their fifth smacked against the goalkeeper's left hand post.

Bromley were down, out, beaten 5–4.

I sent Dave another text. 'Speechless,' I wrote, which is hardly something that someone making a living from words ought ever to admit.

I thought about him turning away from Wembley and his solemn train ride home. I thought of him reliving the game before he slept that night and again as soon as he awoke next morning. I also thought that the saddest words really are 'What Might Have Been' because the mind is forever wandering up and down old roads, looking again for that turning you could/should have taken. Knowing how much Bromley are a part of his life meant I also knew, for certain, the inconsolable emptiness he would feel.

Our next lunch?

I will leave the account of it blank because the experience is Dave's story to tell, and he will do so in his own book.

I have dedicated *Going to the Match* to fans, particularly those who follow modest clubs with only a modest chance of ever winning a trophy. Dave, I think, embodies them. I *almost* want Bromley to go back to Wembley and win for him as much as I want Newcastle to go to Wembley and win for me. Until that happens, I thank him for his help with *Going to the Match*.

Every work is a collaboration. You rely a lot on the help/advice/ support of friends and strangers alike. So plaudits must also go to:

My agent, the ever patient Grainne Fox, for her gentle cajoling and also her good humour. Like the best football scout, she has a great eye and great sense for what will work and what won't. Based in New York, she is also first rate when it comes to recommending those television programmes that the Americans see well before we do.

My editor, Roddy Bloomfield – a gentleman with courtly manners and a sharp mind and more stories than the 1001 that belong to the *Arabian Nights*. I can pay him no higher compliment than this: I wish I'd known him an age ago. His colleagues at Hodder, Fiona Rose and Miren Lopategui, have also proved invaluable. I especially owe a debt to the brilliant Phil Shaw, who saves authors like me from themselves.

I'd like to thank James Ferguson for talking to me about Guiseley and Jim (you never did give me your surname) at the Scottish Football Museum for his kindness on that wettest of days in Glasgow. Toby Jones and Tony Cannon were incredibly helpful in discussing their adoration of Plymouth Argyle and John Lloyd deserves credit for putting me in touch with both them. Michael Kirkham generously gave up so much of his time to walk me around the streets of Liverpool. I wholeheartedly recommend his website Urban Goals, which can be found at: https://urbangoals.tumblr.com

Whenever I approach someone for information and/or an interview, I go through the necessary rigmarole of explaining a little of who I am . . . what I am doing . . . and why I want to do it. I can weigh up quickly those people who will be a delight to deal with. Even on the telephone, as the two of us first got into conversational pleasantries, I knew Andy Westwood was a very decent bloke. So it proved. We talked about football long after the chapter I wrote was finished.

Andy was interesting and unfailingly helpful. That help extended far beyond supplying information about Hardwick Social. He kindly rescued my wife Mandy's handbag after she left it in the George and Dragon pub. She realised it was missing only when we walked through our front door (thanks also to Libby, landlady of the pub, for returning it safely and promptly by post).

As you'll figure out from that piece of information, I didn't always go to games alone. The 'I' in the main text of *Going to the Match* is done purely for the reader's convenience. Mandy came to many of the games. Thankfully, she brought the car with her.

Robert Louis Stevenson said that it's sometimes better to travel hopefully than to arrive. Believe me, the arrival – specifically, walking into the ground of whichever town or city the fixture list took me – was never a problem. The travel to that town or city proved to be a far different matter. I grimace whenever I hear Sir Richard Branson lordly declare that he'll soon be ferrying tourists out into space and towards Mars. Good luck to all who sail in that particular ship.

As I write this, Virgin Trains is about to disappear from the East Coast line, which is just as well. For me, Sir Richard's inter-planetary ambitions sat incongruously beside it. Before planning to take passengers the 33.9 million miles from Earth to Mars, I always thought the old boy should really have tried a wee bit harder to get some us the 194 miles from Leeds to London's King's Cross without disruption and delay. A word of warning for those tempted to buy a ticket for the stars. If you have to clear Doncaster and Stevenage en route to the Red Planet, then the 'We apologise for any inconvenience caused' message will have worn itself to a thin croak before you hit the mesosphere. And don't for pity's sake get me started on Northern or Transpennine Express. The donkey that once carried Stevenson across the French mountains may not have been faster, but was surely a more reliable mode of transport than either of them.

Mandy fortunately reduces the number of rail journeys I have to make. I am indebted to her motoring skills because I've never been competent enough to pass a driving test. In fact, I ought to confess that Mrs H puts up with a lot – but mostly she puts up with me, which is a heavyweight load of Sisyphean proportions. Driving is the least of it. I tell people that couldn't find a pair of matching socks without her. They think I am joking . . .

In truth she finds the books I never can – even when one of them is sitting on the shelf right in front of me. She infallibly relocates what I regularly lose – glasses, papers, pens and even myself on occasions. She crosses i's and dots the t's of my entire life.

I know I'm very lucky. I also know you're probably asking yourself what she gets out of the deal.

I'm afraid you'll have to ask her. I really haven't a clue.

PHOTOGRAPHIC ACKNOWLEDGEMENTS

The author and publisher would like to thank the following for their permission to use photographs:

The Estate of L.S. Lowry. All Rights Reserved, DACS 2108, Alex Livesey/Stringer/Getty Images, George Wood, Darren Walsh/Contributor/Getty Images, Hulton Archive/Stringer/Getty Images, Ian MacNicol/Stringer/Getty Images, Movie Poster Image Art/Contributor/Getty Images, Shaun Brooks/Contributor/Getty Images, Richard Heathcote/Staff/Getty Images, Bob Thomas/Popperfoto/Contributor/Getty Images, Tom Flathers/Contributor/Getty Images, Douglas Miller/Stringer/Getty Images, Richard Heathcote/Staff/Getty Images, Andrew Powell/Contributor/Getty Images, Shaun Botterill/Staff/Getty Images, Steve Feeney/Contributor/Getty Images, Getty Images/Staff, Manchester City FC/Contributor/Getty Images, GLYN KIRK/Contributor/Getty Images, Rob Newell – CameraSport/Contributor/Getty Images, Stuart Franklin/Staff/Getty Images, Popperfoto/Contributor/Getty Images, Kevin Button/Contributor/Getty Images, PAUL ELLIS/Staff/Getty Images, Simon Stacpoole/Offside/Contributor/Getty Images, Mark Fletcher, Bentley Archive/Popperfoto/Contributor/Getty Images, Michael Kirkham

SELECTED SOURCES

Books

Arlott, J: *Soccer: The Great Ones* (Pelham, 1968)

Balague, G: *Pep Guardiola, Another Way of Winning* (Orion, 2012)

Barclay, P: *The Life and Times of Herbert Chapman: The Story of One of Football's Most Influential Figures* (Weidenfeld, 2014)

Bellos, A: *Futebol, The Brazilian Way of Life* (Bloomsbury, 2002)

Black, P: *The Mirror in the Corner: People's Television* (Hutchinson, 1972)

Bower, T: *Broken Dreams* (Simon and Schuster, 2003)

Butler, B: *One Hundred Seasons of League Football* (Queen Anne Press, 1998)

The Official History of the Football Association (Queen Anne Press, 1993)

The Giant Killers (Pelham, 1982)

Calvin, M (ed): *Life's A Pitch, The Passions of the Press Box* (IntegR8 Books, 2012)

Living on the Volcano; The Secrets of Surviving as a Football Manager (Century, 2015)

Campomar, A: *Golazo! A History of Latin American Football* (Quercus, 2014)

Conn, D: *Richer than God: Manchester City, Modern Football and Growing Up* (Quercus, 2012)

The Beautiful Game? Searching for the Soul of Football (Yellow Jersey, 2005)

Cox, M: *The Mixer: The Story of Premier League Tactics, from Route One to False Nines* (Harper Collins, 2017) [indent second line]

Davies, H: *Boots, Balls and Haircuts: An Illustrated History of Football from Then 'til Now* (Octopus, 2003

The Bumper Book of Football (Quercus, 2007)

Downing, D: *The Best of Enemies England v Germany* (Bloomsbury, 2000)

Durarte, F: *Shocking Brazil: Six Games That Shook the World Cup* (Arena, 2014)

Fabian, A. H. and Green, G: *Association Football*, Four Volumes (Caxton 1960)

Frewin, L: *The Saturday Men* (Macdonald, 1967)

Gallacher, K: *Jock Stein, The Authorised Biography* (Stanley Paul, 1988)

Glanville, B: *The Sunday Times History of the World Cup* (Times Newspapers, 1973) (and subsequent editions of The History of the World Cup)

The Footballer's Companion (Eyre and Spottiswoode, 1962)

Soccer: A Panorama (Eyre and Spottiswoode, 1969)

England Managers: The Toughest Job in Football (Headline, 2007)

People in Sport (Secker, 1967)

For Club and Country: The Best of the Guardian's Footballing Obituaries (Guardian Books, 2008)

Glendenning, R: *Just a Word in Your Ear* (Stanley Paul, 1953)

Goldblatt, D: *Futebol Nation: A Footballing History of Brazil* (Penguin, 2014)

The Ball is Round: A Global History of Soccer (Riverhead, 2006)

Gray, D: *Saturday 3pm: 50 Eternal Delights of Modern Football* (Bloomsbury, 2016)

Green, G: *Great Moments in Sport: Soccer* (Pelham, 1972)

The Official History of the FA Cup (The Naldrett Press, 1949)

Soccer in the Fifties (Ian Allan, 1974)

Soccer, The World Game: A Popular History (SBC, 1954)

Gullit, R: *How to Watch Football* (Viking, 2016)

Hall, W. and Parkinson, M: *Football Report* (Pelham, 1973)

Hamilton, D: *Provided You Don't Kiss Me* (Fourth Estate, 2007)

The Footballer Who Could Fly: Living in My Father's Black and White World (Random House, 2012)

Immortal: The Approved Biography of George Best (Random House, 2013)

Hardaker, A: *Hardaker of the League* (Pelham, 1977)

Harding, J: *For the Good of the Game: The Official History of the Professional Footballers' Association* (Robson, 1991)

Hattenstone, S: *The Best of Times: What Became of the Heroes of '66?* (Guardian Books, 2006)

Herd, M (ed): *The Guardian Book of Football: Fifty Years of Classic Reporting* (Guardian Books, 2008)

Hill, J: *The Jimmy Hill Story* (Hodder & Stoughton, 1998)

Hoby, A: *One Crowded Hour* (Museum Press, 1954)

Holmes, B: *Caesars, Saviours and Suckers: The Good, Bad and Ugly of Football's Foreign Owners* (BH, 2016)

Honigstein, R: *Englischer Fussball* (Yellow Jersey, 2009)

Das Reboot: How German Football Reinvented Itself and Conquered the World (Yellow Jersey, 2015)

Hopcraft, A: *The Football Man: People and Passions in Soccer* (Collins, 1968)

Hughes, R. and Francis, T: *Trevor Francis: Anatomy of a £1 million Player* (World's Work, 1980)

Hugman, B. J: *Rothmans Football League Players' Records: The Complete A–Z 1946–1981* (Rothmans, 1981)

Hurrey, A: *Football Clichés* (Headline, 2014)

Inglis, S: *The Football Grounds of Great Britain* (Collins, 1983, 1987 and 1996)

The Best of Charles Buchan's Football Monthly (English Heritage, 2006)

James, B: *Journey to Wembley: A Football Odyssey from Tividale to Wembley* (Marshall Cavendish, 1977)

England v Scotland (Pelham, 1969)

James, C: *On Television: Criticism from the Observer 1972–1982* (Picador, 1983)

Joannou, P. and Candlish, A: *Pioneers of the North: The Origins and Development of Football in North-east England & Tyneside* (Breedon, 2009)

Knausgaard, K. O. and Ekelund, F: *Home and Away Writing the Beautiful Game* (Harvill, 2016)

Ledbrooke, A. and Turner, E: *Soccer From the Press Box* (Nicholas Kaye, 1950)

Macdonald, R and Batty, E: *Scientific Soccer in the Seventies* (Pelham, 1971)

Maradona, D. A. and Arcucci, D: *Touched by God* (Constable, 2016)

Marquis, M: *Sir Alf Ramsey: Anatomy of a Football Manager* (Arthur Baker, 1970)

McColl, G: *Scotland in the World Cup Finals* (Andre Deutsch, 1998)

England:The Alf Ramsey Years (Andre Deutsch, 1998)

'78: How a Nation Lost the World Cup (Headline, 2006)

McIlvanney, H: *On Football* (Mainstream, 1995, 1996, 1999, 2002)

McIlvanney, H and Hopcraft, A: *World Cup '70*, (Eyre and Spottiswoode, 1970)

Meisl, W: *Soccer Revolution* (Phoenix House, 1955)

Miller, D: *Stanley Matthews, The Authorized Biography* (Pavilion, 1989)

Moore, B: *The Final Score: The Autobiography of the Voice of Football* (Hodder & Stoughton,1999)

Moran, J: *Armchair Nation, An Intimate History of Britain In Front of the TV* (Profile, 2013)

Morris, D: *The Soccer Tribe* (Jonathan Cape, 1981

Motson, J: *Match of the Day: The Complete Record Since 1964* (BBC, 1992)

Second to None: Great Teams of Post War Soccer (Pelham, 1972)

Moynihan, J: *The Soccer Syndrome: From the Primeval Forties* (Simon and Schuster, 1966)

Football Fever (Quartet, 1974)

Soccer: Reflections on a Changing Game (Sports Pages, 1989)

Park Football (Pelham, 1970)

Mulchrone, V: *The Best of Vincent Mulchrone* (Daily Mail, 1978)

Northcroft, J: *Fearless: The Amazing Underdog Story of Leicester City* (Headline, 2016)

Oltermann, P: *Keeping Up with the Germans: A History of Anglo-German Encounters* (Faber, 2012)

Pawson, T: *Observer on Soccer* (Unwin, 1989)

100 Years of the FA Cup: The Official Centenary History (Heinemann, 1972)

Pelé: *The Autobiography* (Simon and Schuster, 2006)

Preece, I. and Cheeseman, D: *The Heyday of the Football Annual* (Constable, 2015)

Priestley, J. B: *English Journey* (Heinemann, 1934)

Ramsden, J: *Don't Mention the War : The British and the Germans since 1890* (Little Brown, 2006)

Reng, R: *Matchdays: The Hidden Story of the Bundesliga* (Simon and Schuster, 2015)

Richards, T (ed): *Soccer and Philosophy: Beautiful Thoughts on the Beautiful Game* (Open Court, 2010)

Ridley, I: *There's a Golden Sky: How Twenty Years of the Premier League Have Changed Football Forever* (Bloomsbury, 2011)

Schneider, P: *The Wall Jumper* (Penguin, 1982)

Berlin Now: The Rise of the City and the Fall of the Wall (Penguin 2014)

Seddon, P: *Football Talk: The Language and Folklore of the World's Greatest Game* (Robson, 2004)

Sharpe, I: *The Football League Jubilee Book* (Stanley Paul, 1963)

Soccer Top Ten (Stanley Paul, 1962)

40 Years in Football (The Anchor Press, 1952)

Shaw, P: *The Book of Football Quotations* (ninth edition) (Ebury, 2014)

Shears, W. S: *This England: A Book of the Shires and Counties* (The Right Book Club, 1938)

Smith, M: *Match of the Day; 40th Anniversary* (BBC, 2004)

Steen, R: *Floodlights and Touchlines: A History of Spectator Sport* (Bloomsbury, 2014)

Steen, R, Novick, J, Richards, H: *The Cambridge Companion to Football* (Cambridge University Press, 2013)

Taylor, D: *I Believe in Miracles:The Remarkable Story of Brian Clough* (Headline, 2015)

Taylor, R. and Ward, A: *Kicking and Screaming: An Oral History of Football in England* (Robson, 1995)

Tennant, J: Football: *The Golden Age* (Cassell, 2001)

Toussaint, J-P: *Football* (Fitzcarraldo Editions, 2016)

Turnbull, J, Satterlee, T, Raab, A: *The Global Game: Writers on Soccer,* (University of Nebraska Press, 2008)

Ward, A. and Williams, J: *Football Nation: Sixty Years of the Beautiful Game* (Bloomsbury, 2009)

Wilson, J: *Inverting the Pyramid: The History of Football Tactics* (Orion, 2008 and 2013)

The Anatomy of England: A History in Ten Matches (Orion, 2010)

Winter, H: *Fifty Years of Hurt: The Story of England Football and Why We Never Stop Believing* (Bantam, 2016)

Wolstenholme, K: *Book of World Soccer* (DM, 1962)

Book of World Soccer (WDL, 1968)

Wright, B: *The World's My Football Pitch,* (Stanley Paul, 1953)

One Hundred Caps and All That (Robert Hale, 1962)

Young, P: *Football Book Facts and Fancies* (Dennis Dobson, 1947)

No Author Identified: *The Rules of Association Football, 1863* (Bodleian Library, 2006)

The FA Book for Boys (Heinemann, 1966)

The FA Book for Boys (Heinemann, 1969)

Private Eye's Book of Boobs (Andre Deutsch, 1973)

DVD/Video

Boys from Brazil: The Official History of the Brazilian World Cup Team, 1930–1980 (BBC, 1986)

Champions of Europe: The Official Story of the World's Greatest Club Football Competition (Uefa, 2005)

The FA Cup Finals (Pathé, undated)

Goal! Official Film of the 1966 World Cup (private collection)

Matthews: The Original Number 7, (Spectrum, 2017)

The Miracle of Bern, (Soda Pictures, 2005)

Shankly: Nature's Fire (Thunderbird, 2017)

INDEX